The Big Walks

CHALLENGING MOUNTAIN WALKS AND
SCRAMBLES IN THE BRITISH ISLES

THE BIG WALKS

Compiled by
Ken Wilson and Richard Gilbert

with editorial assistance
from Mike Pearson

maps by Don Sargeant

Diadem Books · London

Also by Ken Wilson

The Black Cliff
(with Jack Soper and Peter Crew)

Hard Rock

Classic Rock

The Games Climbers Play

Also by Richard Gilbert

Memorable Munros

Hill Walking in Scotland

Young Explorers

Published in 1980 by Diadem Books Limited, London
Second impression February 1981

All trade enquiries to:
Cordee, 249 Knighton Church Road, Leicester

Copyright © 1980 by Richard Gilbert

British Library Cataloguing in Publication Data

Wilson, Ken, b. 1941   Gilbert, Richard, b. 1937
    The big walks
    1. Great Britain — Description and travel —
    1971 — Guide-books
    2. Mountaineering — Great Britain
    3. Walking — Great Britain
    I. Title
    796.5'22   DA632
    ISBN 0-906371-60-0

Frontispiece: On the Skye Ridge, heading
south from Bruach na Frithe. *Photo: Gordon Gadsby*

Colour separations by
Colourcraftsmen, Witham, Essex

Production by
Chambers Green Limited, Tunbridge Wells, Kent

Printed in Great Britain by
Fakenham Press, Norfolk

Contents

Note: All uncredited chapters written by Richard Gilbert

Preface

When Ken Wilson and I decided to join forces in compiling this book, we spent a great deal of time defining our objectives. For a start, *The Big Walks* had to appeal not only to experienced walkers, but also to their less experienced brethren in search of new horizons. In addition, we felt that it should probably be of value to the rock-specialist who was interested in occasional energetic days in the hills, and certainly to the armchair mountaineer reliving his past experiences. Above all we were determined to provide a mouth-watering collection of the very best mountain walks to be found in the British Isles.

As the mountain-walking expert of the team, it was my task to decide which walks to include, and my choice was governed by several factors, not least of which was a strong personal element. As a result, most of my own favourites are included, together with those of some of my friends and acquaintances. I was also influenced by Ken's argument that any book of mountain walks should include some of our great classics. Finally, I tried to give the walks an adequate geographical spread, so as to cover most areas of high and moorland country in Britain, as well as adding a selection from the fine mountain ranges of Ireland. But *The Big Walks* is not merely designed to act as a stimulant to those with an interest in the hills. It is also a practical guide to fifty-five long walks. Each essay contains enough information for the walker to follow the suggested route on the map and to plan his day.

Of course a total of only fifty-five walks leaves many gaps, and I apologize for this. Mountaineers are notoriously subjective in their likes and dislikes, and I am sure that my selection will give rise to discussion. But I am satisfied that the walks form a cast-iron framework for the aspirant hill walker and I defy even the strongest walker to be disappointed by the challenge that many of them offer: a severe test of stamina and self-sufficiency over rugged hill country.

There are single mountain objectives, long mountain traverses, moorland crossings, valley walks and rock scrambles. There are classic walks, popular walks and hidden walks. How many of the thousands who slog through the Lairig Ghru in the Cairngorms know of the delightful alternative pass of Glen Tilt? Who but H. H. Symonds would think of traversing the Lake District 'the wrong way', from Shap to Ravenglass? How many walkers have stood on the pointed summit of Sgurr na Ciche in remote Knoydart? There should be enough variety here to satisfy everyone.

Whilst poring over maps during the compilation of the book I was constantly reminded of how lucky we are to have so much wild mountain country on our doorstep: a lifetime of endeavour could never cover it all.

Many of the essayists in *Hard Rock* struck a note of tension, even hysteria, in their writing, and we can imagine the racing mind, the coursing adrenalin and the bulging muscles — the *raison d'être* of the hard rock climber. In *Classic Rock,* on the other hand, as Ken Wilson observed in his preface, the writing is more restrained, reflecting the relaxed nature of the (easier) climbing. The pressure is off, there is time to savour the position, the exposure and the texture of the rock. Aesthetic appeal is there, perhaps filling the gap left by the reduced challenge of the climb.

But where does this leave the mountain walker? What satisfaction does he obtain from his long and arduous mountain traverses? I believe that answer is to be found in *The Big Walks.* The walks display a marked diversity of character, but the essays are linked by a common theme — enthusiasm. In particular, contributors like Tom Price and Showell Styles, who have spent their lives amongst the hills of Lakeland and North Wales, show an irresistible love for their mountains which comes out strongly in their writing. No mountaineer reading these essays or looking at these photographs should be able to resist reaching for his boots and planning his next venture into the hills.

Hill walkers, in my experience, thrive on challenge and many of them like to undertake a long-term project, such as the Munros, Round Britain, the Pennine Way or some other long distance footpath. The accomplishment of such a target is immensely gratifying. I well remember the overpowering feelings of anticipation, amounting almost to illness, as I neared my final Munro and the completion of a journey first embarked upon ten years before. Phil Cooper, in his account of the Black Mountains walk, describes similar feelings experienced when he attained his last 2,000ft. peak in England and Wales. Such a project provides motivation — enough to get you out of your sleeping bag on a freezing cold or wet morning to puff and pant your way up into the mountains. Once the initial effort has been made the rewards are there for the taking. I hope that *The Big Walks* will prove similarly motivating. The photographs alone should stir the most dormant mountaineer into action.

The last ten years have seen an almost exponential rise in the number of walkers seeking a real challenge in the mountains. Membership of the exclusive Bob Graham Club and the Hundred Mile Club of the Long Distance Walkers' Association is ever growing. The Karrimor Two-Day Mountain Marathon attracts over 2,000 entries a year, and events such as the Fellsman's Hike, the Lakeland Three Thousanders Walk and the Yorkshire Three Peaks Race are heavily over-subscribed. Moreover hill walking can provide a challenge that even the hardest of climbers can find irresistible. In March, 1960, I was one of a student party staying in the CIC Hut under Ben Nevis. Sharing our cramped quarters were Robin Smith, Jimmy Marshall and Dougal Haston. On a day of lowering cloud and swirling snow-flurries, when even the Terrible Trio could not climb on the face, Robin Smith strode out alone to return in the early hours having traversed the entire Mamore range. I would not care to guess what motivated him, or gave him those huge reserves of energy, but the satisfaction was unmistakable as he burst into the hut scattering snow, his face split in a broad grin.

Many walkers will agree with Harold Drasdo when he recommends that the Rhinogs walk should be done alone. Solitude is no deprivation to the hill walker. Alone one may become a harmless egotist, choosing one's own route and one's own pace, and responding to the mountains without the influence and suggestion of others. But rich experiences need to be shared and only on certain walks would I choose to be alone. The Rhinogs would probably be one of them, although I have not done it in its entirety. The little-known Rois Bheinn ridge in Moidart is another that comes to mind. On walks like these you can guarantee solitude; they are magnificent but unfashionable excursions, and the masses get syphoned off to the more glamorous Snowdonia, Cader Idris and Glencoe.

One word of warning: many of the walks, particularly those in Scotland, are exceptionally long and arduous and there may be no easy escape routes. There are many subtle hazards involved and, mindful of the risks likely to be encountered by the inexperienced, I have discussed these in detail in a special appendix. I do urge anyone whose experience of the hills is limited to consult this section before setting out on any of the walks.

The routes described in this book do not necessarily follow rights of way, but I have rarely been apprehended in the hills and you should be free to wander at will. In Scotland, there is no law of trespass and, provided you observe the Country Code, you may walk anywhere in the mountains. Certain areas may be restricted in the stalking season (9th August to 20th October) and during the grouse shooting season (12th August to 9th December). Always check locally before venturing into the hills during these periods; the Estate Factors will tell you which hills are being worked on which days. The letting of sporting rights may well be the principal source of income from many of the large Highland estates and the landowners' wishes must be respected. If you have to climb a deer fence be sure to do so at one of the massive corner posts, otherwise the wires can be damaged. These fences are vital to protect young trees from the ravages of deer.

A note on the grades and times given in the summaries: grades of mountain walks have never been universally accepted, as they are for rock climbs and alpine routes; there are too many variables. I have attempted to grade the walks in simple language. Comments refer to good weather conditions in summer, unless otherwise stated. The times given are average for a strong and fit party, and they do not include stops. If you are in any doubt on this point you can easily compare your own times over well known walks with those given in *The Big Walks*. I have also added an appendix listing the best methods of shortening the described routes into less challenging expeditions. The same section includes notes on a number of other worthwhile walks.

Several of the walks involve sections of quite tricky rock scrambling and one, the Round of Coire Lagan, has proper rock pitches. Experienced rock climbers will have little difficulty with the scrambling sections, and most able bodied hill walkers shouldn't be troubled in optimum conditions. It is worth remembering that adverse conditions can change a normally straightforward scramble into a serious undertaking. Less confident climbers are advised to carry a rope for use whenever difficult sections are encountered, taking proper belays and precautions.

I have decided to omit the accents on the Gaelic place-names because there is little agreement as to their precise application, even in guidebooks and on O.S. maps. I can only offer apologies to Gaelic scholars if this omission offends them. Likewise the spelling of many names varies, and in general I have kept to that used on the current O.S. maps, even though this throws up some unexpected versions, such as 'Meagaidh' and 'Stob Binnein'.

Each of the walks is fully illustrated. We have been lucky to secure the co-operation of many fine photographers, and it was decided from the outset that the inclusion of a large number of colour illustrations would give the book extra impact and meaning. Of course this has had an affect on the price, but I am sure you will agree that the results achieved fully justify the expense. Ken Wilson has devoted many hours of meditation to the choice of photographs and their presentation. The intention has been to link the pictures intimately with the text, to provide the reader with a strong visual impression of the environment as he progresses through each chapter.

As with the other books in the series, we hope that *The Big Walks* will serve not only as a gateway to many days of happiness and satisfaction, but also as a lasting record of adventurous past, enabling the reader to rekindle memories of stimulating days among our fine mountains.

RICHARD GILBERT
Crayke, York 1980

Acknowledgements

We could not have produced this book without the assistance of a large number of people: photographers, walking companions and specialists in particular regions, knowledgeable and responsive to the mountains' appeal.

It is not an easy task to write an article which must contain enough information for the walk to be followed and yet still convey a feeling of atmosphere and personal enthusiasm. A glance through some of the chapters contributed by our eighteen guest authors will reveal how skilfully they have matched up to the task. Less obvious are the vicissitudes often experienced by photographers in searching for the ideal view. We are particularly indebted to David Higgs, Gordon Gadsby, Donald Bennet and Irvine Butterfield for the special efforts they have made to secure photographs to illustrate specific sections of the book. Butterfield's journey through the Fisherfield Forest, resulting in the fine picture used on the jacket, displayed a keenness well beyond the call of duty, for which we were both suitably grateful.

Many other photographers have been good enough to scour their collections on our behalf. We have been entrusted with hundreds of valuable colour slides and negatives, without complaint; when we ruthlessly thinned the pictures down to a short-list, returning, with little explanation, fine pictures that for countless detailed reasons didn't quite fit our brief, the decision was accepted without grudge. The reputations of many of the photographers are well known, but we have been greatly encouraged by the discovery of fine work from hitherto little-known experts. In this regard the photographs of Ken Andrew and Gordon Gadsby displayed such high quality and scope that we have used many of their pictures in the book. Finally, the black-and-white illustrations of the late Robert Adam formed a valuable backbone for all the Scottish chapters.

The following is a list of everyone who has helped in the production of *The Big Walks* — both photographers and authors. We offer our sincere apologies in advance to anyone we may inadvertently have overlooked. Robert Adam collection, John Allen, Bruce Atkins, Peter Baker, Donald Bennet, Geoffrey Berry, Robert Brotherton, Irvine Butterfield, Malcolm Boyes, John Cleare, Richard Carter, R. J. Clow, Phil Cooper, Len Copley, Sandy Cousins, Willie Cunningham, John Dewar, Tom Dodd, Harold Drasdo, Donal Enwright, Garry Farrell, Derek Forss, Jo Fuller, Gordon Gadsby, Leonard and Marjorie Gayton, Oliver Gilbert, Basil Goodfellow collection, Bill Gregor, Alf Gregory, Shelagh Gregory, David Higgs, Phil Ideson, Alan Kimber, E. Hector Kyme, Terence Leigh, Joss Lynam, W. S. Matthews, Neil Mather, A. D. S. Macpherson, C. Douglas Milner, Tom Parker, Richard Pearce, Jim Perrin, Walter Poucher, Tom Price, Roger Putnam, Denis Rankin, Roger Redfern, Alan Robson, Sean Rothery, Kenneth Scowen, Ernest Shepherd, Gerard Simpson, Simon Stewart, Showell Styles, Maurice and Marion Teal, Walt Unsworth, Bertrand Unne, Adam Watson, Tom Weir, Viv Wilson, John and Patricia Woolverton, John Woodhouse, Peter Wild, Geoffrey Wright.

KEN WILSON & RICHARD GILBERT

1   Foinaven and Arkle

Walk   Foinaven and Arkle.
Maps   O.S. 1:50,000 Sheet 9
Start from Gualin House (ref. 305565).
Finish at Laxford Bridge (ref. 237468).
Grading   A fine walk of intermediate standard over
two of Sutherland's most spectacular peaks. Mixed
terrain including narrow quartzite ridges.
Time   10 hours.
Distance   20 miles.
Escape Routes   From the bealach between Arkle
and Foinaven a good path leads S.W. to Loch Stack.
From several places on the main ridge of Foinaven a
way may be found down the screes to the E. to reach
Strath Dionard.
Telephones   Gualin House; Rhiconich; Laxford
Bridge; Achfary.
Transport   Railway Station at Lairg. Daily bus
service from Lairg to Durness passes through Laxford
Bridge and Rhiconich.
Accommodation   Hotels at Scourie, Rhiconich and
Durness. Bed and Breakfast in Durness.
Youth Hostels at Durness and Tongue.
Guidebooks   S.M.T. Guide *The Northern
Highlands; The Scottish Peaks* by W. A. Poucher
(Constable).

The visitor to North-west Scotland cannot fail to be impressed by the highly complex geological structure of the mountains. There is constant interplay between grey Lewisian gneiss, the oldest rock in Britain, fully 1,500 million years old, Torridonian sandstone laid down 800 million years ago, and the more recent white Cambrian quartzite.

Devotees of the 'Big Walks' will meet Torridonian sandstone on Liathach and Suilven, and quartzite on Beinn Eighe. Further north, earth movements have thrust layers of Lewisian gneiss over the quartzite to produce Ben More Assynt, and we need to venture to the Reay Forest of northern Sutherland before the correct order is again restored.

The peaks of Torridon, An Teallach, Coigach and Assynt inspire the north-bound traveller, but few cross the Kylesku Ferry to see Foinaven and Arkle, after which there is nothing but flat bog to the northern limit of Britain at Cape Wrath.

The layman associates the names Foinaven and Arkle with the brilliant racehorses owned by the Duchess of Westminster, but these thoroughbreds were christened after the two equally magnificent peaks in the Reay Forest. The two peaks dominate the far north-west, rising high above the scarred bedrock of gneiss. Foinaven throws down excessively steep scree slopes from a fine ridge which connects with Arkle by a low bealach.

North-west Sutherland suffers its own weather, and forecasts are unreliable. Frontal troughs which pass north of Britain very often just clip the hills of the Reay Forest, and in four visits I have never escaped a drenching.

Four miles along the desolate A838 road north of Rhiconich stands the isolated Gualin House, and this feature makes as good a starting point for the walk as any. Weave your way through the myriad of shallow lochans and make for the bealach between Cnoc a'Mhadaidh and Ceann Garbh. There is no path and the going is terrible across the undrained moor, where the coarse purple moor grass grows at its thickest and the sphagnum is deepest.

As you gain height the terrain eases, and you can plan your route ahead through the bluffs of rock and boulder fields which make up the eastern ridge of Ceann Garbh. Looking to the west, you enjoy a watery landscape with lochans filling every trough and fold. The sea, too, penetrates far inland with the long fingers of Lochs Inchard and Laxford. A unique scene, unrivalled in Britain.

A change in the rock to crumbling quartzite marks the summit of Ceann Garbh and the end of your climb. The main ridge of Foinaven now stretches away south and the highest peak, Ganu Mor (2,980ft.), can be seen clearly only half a mile away, at the end of a superb ridge which sweeps round with mathematical precision forming a perfect parabola.

On a still summer's day a climber sitting on the summit of Ganu Mor can hear the constant shifting of the quartzite screes — an eerie sound.

The main ridge of shattered quartzite blocks continues south from Ganu Mor over the subsidiary top of A'Cheir Gorm. A sharp secondary ridge branches off north-east, but you must continue south-east to the bealach of Cadha na Beucaich, bypassing a huge rock pinnacle on the west side. Now follow the cliffs eastwards and make for the summit of Creag Dionard at 2,554ft.

As you descend southwards from Creag

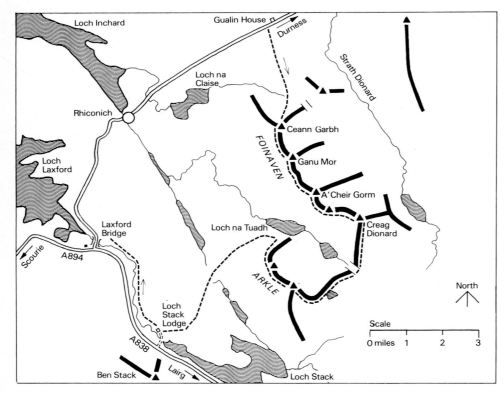

Dionard, keep the cliffs overlooking Loch an Uaine on your right. The bealach under Arkle is only 1,200ft. above sea level, and it is a relief to find areas of moss and grass to cushion your feet, in place of the sharp and bruising quartzite blocks. On the bealach itself there is a lochan and a path leading down to Lone and Achfary, which can be used as an escape route if necessary.

The broad eastern flanks of Arkle hold several other lochans, and the ground is characterized by areas of grey quartzite and countless mounds and hummocks not shown on the map.

The south summit of Arkle at 2,486ft. is marked by a large stone heap. Descend quite steeply northwards along the obvious ridge which narrows dramatically in one place to a razor edge. Some of the massive stone blocks across which you walk are split down the centre, leaving deep fissures resembling the limestone pavements of the Yorkshire Dales. Just before the northern top, at 2,580ft., the boulders give way to a deep carpet of moss, and the fat and well constructed cairn is unmistakable.

The summit ridge of Arkle now bends round to the north-east, but after another half

Above: The grey quartzite screes of Arkle rise above Loch Stack in northern Sutherland. This peak is connected to its higher neighbour, Foinaven, by a fine ridge which gives views over the western seaboard to Cape Wrath at the northern tip of Britain. *Photo: John Woolverton*

Above: Looking back to the summit ridge of Foinaven from the bealach under Arkle. The walker reaches this point after traversing the skyline ridge from left to right. *Photo: Ken Andrew*

mile you must leave it to make a steep and bone-shattering descent down the quartz screes in a northerly direction towards Loch na Tuadh. This is the only foolproof way off the northern ridge of Arkle and, although it looks terrifyingly steep, it is quite safe and simple, and after 1,000ft. the angle relents and you reach tussocky grass.

From the east end of Loch na Tuadh a narrow track is followed for four miles to Loch Stack Lodge on the Laxford Bridge – Lairg road. Don't think you can take a more direct line to Loch Stack Lodge, for the ground is very difficult, with bogs, streams and countless lochans filling the dips and hollows of the underlying gneiss. The stalkers' track is well constructed and takes a sensible but tortuous route to the grey shooting lodge overlooking

the Laxford river and Loch Stack. Arkle looks most impressive from this (west) side, particularly after rain when the sun sparkles on the wet quartzite scree slopes and cliffs below the summit ridge. Arkle makes maximum use of its mere 2,580ft.

From Loch Stack Lodge to the end of the walk at Laxford Bridge is only three miles and if you are weary you may prefer to take the road. But by far the most picturesque route is to follow the path on the east bank of the river. The Laxford is a superb salmon river whose name is of Viking origin, for the Norse *Lax fjord* means salmon fjord. In season you can watch the salmon at rest lying head to tail in the clear pools or flashing like silver as they leap the rapids.

2 Suilven

Anyone who drives along the A835 between Ullapool and the Kylesku Ferry will be captivated by the remarkable mountain scenery of Assynt. The base rock is of ancient Lewisian gneiss, which acts as a plinth for the spectacular peaks of Torridonian sandstone that rise quite separate from each other as great monoliths of rock, many of them capped by white Cambrian quartzite.

Cul Mor, Stac Polly, Canisp and Quinag rise impressively from the barren moor, but the queen of them all is Suilven. Viewed from the main road Suilven appears as a long, serrated, whale-back ridge, but from the fishing village of Lochinver it is dramatic. The west end of the Suilven ridge rears over the village and completely dominates the view inland; this western summit is called Caisteal Liath, the Grey Castle. There is no other mountain in Scotland that makes more of its modest height, for it is only 2,399ft.

Suilven is remote and difficult of access from any direction. The impervious gneiss holds many shallow lochs which interconnect and guard the steep flanks of the mountain.

The usual way of ascent is either from Glencanisp Lodge on the west side or from Inverkirkaig on the south. Both these routes climb up steep gullies to a low bealach on the summit ridge of Suilven. The route I recommend traverses the mountain from east to west, starting from Ledmore at the junction of the A835 and A837 and finishing at Lochinver. You should arrange transport back to your starting point in the evening, because the bus service is very infrequent.

From Ledmore Junction, walk north along the main road for half a mile, then cross the river Ledbeg by a bridge near some farm buildings. Strike up the open hillside towards a low hill, Cnoc an Leathaid Bhig, passing a small fir plantation on the way. Once over this initial rise you have an uninterrupted view of the eastern pinnacle of Suilven, still five miles away. The going is quite good, although there is no trace of a path. I walked this way to Suilven one clear and intensely cold March day when the bogs were frozen solid and the small Loch a'Chroisg, which is passed on the way, was covered in thick and smooth ice. Stones could be skimmed hundreds of metres across its surface, accompanied by a high-pitched, resonant, zinging noise.

Beyond the loch the mass of Meall na Braclaich (1,100ft.) can be bypassed on the north side and, although the ground becomes rockier, very little height is gained or lost until the steep slopes of the eastern pinnacle of Suilven are reached.

The ascent to the ridge is a simple scramble up a succession of ledges, and you soon gain the summit of Meall Beag, the eastern end of the Suilven ridge. Ahead of you lie two other summits, Meall Mheadhonach (2,300ft.) and Caisteal Liath (2,399ft.), but as you walk westwards along the ridge you come first to a curious cleft, caused by a fault in the sandstone strata, which can easily be stepped across, and then to an abrupt drop where cliffs fall away precipitously for 100ft. The way down to the bealach below involves an airy scramble down the north side of the ridge, followed by a traverse westwards to gain easier ground and hence the bealach. This section is dramatic, but not really difficult. Thereafter the ridge is a delightful walk, and you will notice the ordinary routes coming up steep gullies to the north and south of the bealach under the main peak of Caisteal Liath.

The summit of Suilven is mainly grassy, with a few scattered quartzite boulders, and the ground falls away precipitously on three sides. It is a magnificent view-point for the mountains of Assynt, Coigach and An

Walk Suilven.
Maps O.S. 1:50,000 Sheet 15
Start from Ledbeg (ref. 243133).
Finish at Lochinver (ref. 093225).
Grading A moderate walk over remote country. Some easy scrambling on the summit ridge.
Time 8 hours.
Distance 16 miles.
Escape Routes None. The easiest way down from the summit ridge of Suilven is north from the bealach under Caisteal Liath.
Telephones Lochinver; Inverkirkaig; Inchnadamph; A.A. Box at Ledmore Junction; Elphin.
Transport Daily bus service, Sutherland Transport, from Lochinver to Lairg (rail head) via Ledmore Junction.
Accommodation Hotels at Lochinver and Inchnadamph. Youth Hostel at Achmelvich, 3 miles north of Lochinver.
Guidebooks S.M.T. Guide *The Northern Highlands; The Scottish Peaks* by W. A. Poucher (Constable).

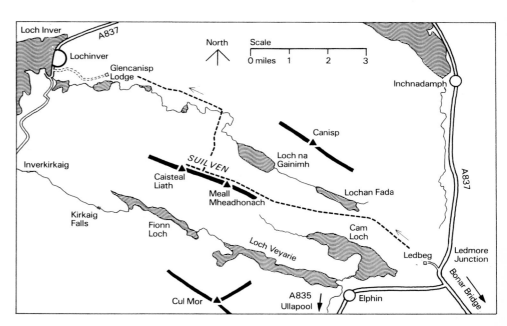

Teallach and, of course, for the western sea-board. Every islet and creek can be seen, from the Summer Isles in the mouth of Loch Broom to the Point of Stoer and Handa Island in the far north-west. On a windy day you can see the lines of white foam and can almost hear the breakers on the rocks. Like the Cuillins of Skye and Rhum it provides a perfect combination of sea and mountain scenery.

Retrace your footsteps to the bealach under Caisteal Liath and descend the steep and rather loose gully which runs down the north side. Make for the west end of Loch na Gainimh; you can see this loch as you descend the gully, which enables you to plan the best way through the myriad of tiny lochans that must be negotiated. A good path is met on the north side of Loch na Gainimh which leads west, past the ruined croft of Suileag to

Glencanisp Lodge, a distance of four and a half miles.

Glencanisp Lodge is a beautifully maintained house in the best Scottish tradition. It is surrounded by a luxuriant growth of shrubs and rhododendrons and it looks over Loch Druim Suardalain to the amazing Caisteal Liath of Suilven. The path skirts the lodge on the north side, before joining a narrow motor road which leads through the heather, gorse and wild raspberry canes to the white fish port of Lochinver and tea at the Culag Hotel.

3   The Fannichs

Walk   The Fannichs.
Maps   O.S. 1:50,000 Sheets 19 and 20.
Start from Loch Glascarnoch (ref. 278742).
Finish at Braemore Junction (ref. 209777).
Grading   A long walk with considerable up and down work but mainly good going underfoot.
Time   12 hours.
Distance   26 miles.
Escape Routes   From Sgurr Mor descend N.E. to the bealach under Beinn Liath Mhor and make for the Mhadaidh Glen and the A835 road. From Sgurr nan Clach Geala descend easy slopes to the E. end of Loch a'Bhraoin.
Telephones   Braemore Junction; Aultguish Inn at W. end of Loch Glascarnoch.
Transport   Railway Station at Garve 13 miles. Twice daily bus service (Inverness–Ullapool) passes starting and finishing point. Infrequent service Braemore–Dundonnell.
Accommodation   Aultguish Inn. Dundonnell Hotel. Hotels, Bed and Breakfasts and Youth Hostel in Ullapool 15 miles.
Guidebooks   S.M.T. Guide *The Northern Highlands*.

The Fannich Forest is a compact group of mountains, containing nine separate Munros, lying south of Braemore on the Garve – Ullapool Road. The mountains are mainly rounded and grassy although the highest peak, Sgurr Mor (3,637ft.), rises to a beautifully sharp and pointed summit, which is easily seen when looking back east from Loch Broom side. The Fannich range provides excellent walking country, for the Forestry Commission bull-dozers have not yet made inroads into these mountains, and the open slopes are not yet covered with conifers.

The hills are well situated to provide views out to the western seaboard, and from Sgurr Mor I have seen the mountains of Harris way beyond the Summer Isles at the mouth of Loch Broom. They provide good views, too, of the spectacular peaks of the Coigach and Assynt areas, as well as the much nearer Beinn Dearg Forest. To the west, An Teallach dominates the view, and to the south rise the Torridon giants of Slioch, Beinn Eighe and Liathach.

The entire range, except for two outlying peaks, can be traversed in a single day, starting from the main A835 road at the west end of Loch Glascarnoch and finishing on the A832 Braemore – Dundonnell Road, three miles south of Braemore Junction.

Loch Glascarnoch is dammed at the eastern end, and in summer, when the level is low, the exposed shore makes a sorry spectacle. The loch provides water for the huge Loch Luichart

hydro-electric scheme to the south. At the western end of Loch Glascarnoch the main road crosses the sizeable Torrain Duibh burn by a bridge, and a concrete runnel feeds water into the burn at this point. This is where you should leave the road and walk up the western side of the burn. The path soon peters out and the going is terrible, with deep heather, peat hags, hidden boulders and hummocky moraines. After two miles, which seem much longer, strike up the heathery slopes of Meallan Buidhe. The route takes a line between the two small lochs named Loch Gorm and Loch nan Eun. From Meallan Buidhe you will be able to see the bealach between An Coileachan and Meall Gorm, at a height of 2,500ft. Take the steep slopes to the left of the bealach, which lead you to the summit of An Coileachan. The going becomes easier the higher you go, until at about 2,100ft. you finally leave the heather and peat hags behind. Now you have won your first summit, at 3,015ft., the rest of the day is very much easier and you can look forward to a high level walk of ten miles to A'Chailleach, your last peak of the day.

Descend An Coileachan in a north-westerly direction until you reach the bealach, and then continue in the same direction to Meall Gorm (3,109ft.). The mountainside is bouldery and you pass a subsidiary summit with a small cairn, and later a small shelter built of stones. The slopes on the east side of Meall Gorm fall away quite steeply in broken cliffs to a succession of lochans. As you continue towards the spire of Sgurr Mor, two miles away, two more lochans appear below. The ridge is covered in moss and flat stones and makes for fast walking, but the final slopes of Sgurr Mor are steep. There is no difficulty, however, and you will soon reach the large and well constructed cairn on the summit.

Across Coire Mhoir to the west you will see, under Sgurr nan Clach Geala, a triangular shaped face of bare rock split by deep gullies. This is the largest rock face in the Fannichs and rock climbers have recently recognized its

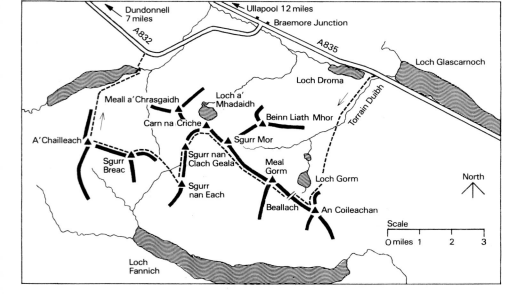

Top right: Setting out from Meall Gorm towards Sgurr Mor. *Photo: Irvine Butterfield*

Bottom right: Sgurr nan Clach Geala from Sgurr Mor. This is the only peak in the Fannichs which can boast a significant cliff of interest to the climber. *Photo: Ken Andrew*

Top: The view west from Sgurr Breac towards A' Chailleach (left) and beyond to the more distant Sgurr Ban (centre). The final part of the Fannichs traverse descends the transverse ridge in the middle distance. *Photo: John Allen*

Above: Cornices near the summit of Sgurr Mor. *Photo: Tom Weir*

potential.

Now descend steeply in a north-westerly direction to the small summit of Carn na Criche, and then swing round 90° to ascend the north-east ridge of Sgurr nan Clach Geala. This is another fine mountain in the heart of the Fannich range, the Gaelic name meaning 'Crag of the White Stones'. Continue due south to a bealach and then climb the modest hill of Sgurr nan Each, which just rates Munro status at 3,026ft. Your final two summits lie to the west across a deep glen and you should descend from the summit of Sgurr nan Each in a north-westerly direction, traversing the grassy slopes to make the watershed under the craggy eastern ridge of Sgurr Breac at 1,900ft.

Find a way up through the rock outcrops to the ridge; if you keep bearing left you will avoid the difficulties, and climb up to the flat top of Sgurr Breac (3,240ft.). It is now an easy walk across the broad ridge to A'Chailleach. I once walked across this high open ridge on a freezing November's day, when a fierce wind drove silver rain in sheets across the mountains. I was soon encased in ice and, with my legs rapidly becoming numb and the ground treacherous, I beat a hasty retreat to lower ground.

The north ridge of A'Chailleach leads down to Loch a'Bhraoin, through stands of very old and decaying Caledonian pine trees. You will meet a path above the loch side which you should follow to the east end of the loch, where the outflowing river is bridged. Continue on the path to the boathouse where you meet the Land-Rover track leading in three-quarters of a mile to the main road, three miles south of Braemore Junction.

4 An Teallach

by Tom Weir

Nowadays we are all very sophisticated. No more mountain mysteries remain. Oh! for the days of 1893, when Scottish Mountaineering Club members were heading for An Teallach to investigate the vague tradition of an unclimbed mountain chain above the village of Dundonnell in Wester Ross.

The man who gave his name to the 'Munros' was there, with aneroid and prismatic compass, to investigate and climb the unknown peaks which had been described by Thomas Pennant, over 120 years earlier, as 'horrible and awful with summits broken, sharp and serrated and springing into all terrific forms!' Added to the allure was the Ordnance Survey map of the time, which showed nothing of this in its shading or contours.

However, Pennant was confirming what an important traveller and geologist had found when he climbed to 3,000ft. and saw ahead of him '. . . a rocky ridge serrated into peaks', which he likened to the Arran granite formation, yet An Teallach was of sandstone.

Imagine the joy of the pioneer SMC party when the true nature of the mountain was spectacularly divulged: '. . . the glorious hills themselves, suddenly bursting through the storm clouds that had enveloped them all day, stood out black, snow slashed, and jagged against a setting sun'.

Just forty-five years later, following a spring day of turbulent storm, I beheld An Teallach for the first time, when the wind dropped and a bulging peak heaved itself above the pink tinged clouds. My youthful pencil-written diary records the unforgettable sight of:

'Sunset over the pinnacles of An Teallach, with a foreground of silhouetted pines and cloud lanes of different colours on Loch Droma as foreground'.

There is a time in the life of every hill man when ardour for mountains is keener than at any other time. That period was still with me, and was intensified by being alone, with a tent and a bicycle. I had been reading of the exploration of An Teallach in an old SMC journal. Now I was to savour it for myself.

I had never met anyone who had climbed An Teallach, so I identified with Munro as I cycled from my camp on the summit of the Destitution Road to Dundonnell. The ascent

from sea level at Dundonnell to the frost-shattered quartzite summit of Glas Mheall Mor at 3,217ft. offered little hint of what lay ahead, since the route followed a very ordinary hill ridge.

No route-finding problems to the next peak blocking my view of the way ahead, the highest summit, Bidein a' Ghlas Thuill (3,484ft.). From there I could grasp the truth of what Pennant saw, in a sudden narrowing of the mountain to pinnacled crest, buttressed in plunging walls of bristling rock, tier upon tier of pinkish Torridonian sandstone. My own peak had an offshoot eastward, the spur of Glas Meall Liath dividing two deep corries round which the main peaks gracefully curve.

I could hardly wait to get on to Sgurr Fiona (3,473ft.), where the exciting moving begins up the sharp point of Lord Berkeley's Seat, which actually tilts over the plunging face, although the easy approach involves no more than a staircase of steps to its top. In traversing the set of four pinnacles which is Corrag Bhuidhe, I realized how true were the observations of the pioneers that An Teallach, like the other mountains where Torridonian sandstone is exposed, '. . . should suit all who like rocky ridges without difficulties'.

But this did not lessen the joy of being there on a day that held everything for which I yearned, including diamond-hard visibility in all directions. On every side were peaks and glens which, hitherto, I had only read about: the fabled monoliths of Coigach and Sutherland, Stac Polly, Cul Beg and Cul Mor, Suilven and, southward beneath my feet, Loch na Sheallag and the roadless wilderness extending over A'Mhaighdean to Slioch and Loch Maree.

But Munro had specified one difficult bit on the ridge from the top known as Corrag Bhuidhe Buttress, half a mile on from the pinnacles. In the 1970s this became known as the 'Bad Step' because of two fatalities. I doubt if it is as difficult, but it need not be climbed, unless you keep to the ridge crest. To avoid it, merely traverse west in a descending movement and rejoin the ridge further on.

All that remained now was Stob Cadha Gobhlach (3,145ft.) and Sail Liath (3,129ft.), given fine character by rock towers and a fine view of the whole precipitous corrie cradling a loch at its foot. And, leading down to it, I could

Walk   An Teallach.
Maps   O.S. 1:50,000 Sheet 19
Start and finish at Dundonnell Hotel (ref. 089880).
Grading   A high and rugged mountain traverse. Some Difficult rock climbing is involved if all the rock pinnacles are traversed but the Difficult pitches may be avoided.
Time   9-10 hours.
Distance   12 miles.
Escape Routes   South down Cadha Ghoblach between Corrag Bhuidhe and Sail Liath. From Sail Liath N.E. towards Coire a'Ghuibhsachain, thence to the Dundonnell road by the Garbh Allt. A straightforward descent to Loch Toll an Lochain down boulder slopes between Bidein a' Ghlas Thuill and Sgurr Fiona. Emergency shelter at Shenavall bothy.
Telephones   Dundonnell.
Transport   Railway to Garve. The Inverness–Ullapool bus connects with a Monday and Saturday service from Braemore Junction to Dundonnell.
Accommodation   Hotel and Bed and Breakfast in Dundonnell. Climbing Hut, The Smiddy, Dundonnell, J.M.C.S. Edinburgh Section.
Guidebooks   S.M.T. Guide *The Northern Highlands; The Scottish Peaks* by W. A. Poucher (Constable).

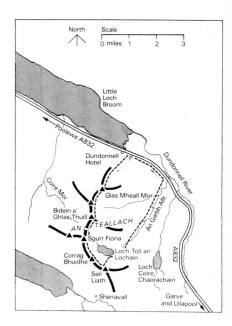

Right: The stupendous peaks of An Teallach towering above Loch Toll an Lochain. The route described in the essay traverses the skyline from right to left, first crossing Sgurr Fiona, then over the sharp monolith of Lord Berkeley's Seat, and thence across the pinnacles of Corrag Bhuidhe. From the pinnacles the route drops down to Corrag Bhuidhe's South Buttress (the pointed peak in the photo) with its infamous 'Bad Step'. *Photo: Tom Weir*

Above: Another view of the Corrag Bhuidhe pinnacles and Lord Berkeley's Seat, from the slopes of Sgurr Fiona. *Photo: Irvine Butterfield*

see a snow gully which I judged would take me swiftly and easily down. It did.

There, among the litter of giant blocks, looking up from the corrie floor to the sandstone serrations 1,700ft. over my head, I could hardly believe that I had been up there, so savage was the scene. Even the gully I had come down looked like a vertical snow couloir, now that it was in shadow, with only its rim shining like the rim of a sugar bowl, edged by sandstone, bright pink in the gilded light.

I was thinking of all I had seen up there that day, the changing surprise of the twisting ridge which the modern guidebook describes as '. . . a stiff day's expedition, and in winter one

which requires no small amount of mountaineering experience'. Add to that the constant delight of having the western seaboard stretching north and south, out to the Cuillin of Skye, as a final touch of pure magic.

Just to be in the great hollow of this corrie of rock and loch completed the fulfilment of the tops, and I savoured every step of the way down, where the burn foams through rivers of boulders deposited by the outwash of the glacier which debouched here, leaving erratic blocks and ice-scraped rock slabs to mark its passage. Five miles to go to get back to my bike and I was hungry. I didn't realize my tiredness until it came to pushing my way uphill for most of the journey to the bliss of the tent, and

the meal I soon cooked up.

I have been back to An Teallach many times since then and at all seasons of year. I can claim to know it as a very moody mountain, so savage one day of March gale and flying spindrift that we dared not venture on the narrow ridge. Then, another March day when the play of moving mist swallowed and disgorged pinnacles and buttresses, making sheer magic of the traverse; when one moment we would see into the dark abyss of the corrie, then next a huge fang of rock would spiral suddenly out of the enshrouding vapour. Between times there would be glimpses of the Summer Isles, green pastures on the sunlit sea.

Another memory, in the severe winter of

1963, is of verglas everywhere on the slabs, and bunches of icicles hanging transparent in the sun. The traverse called for guile, but even so we managed to edge down the direct descent of Corrag Bhuidhe Buttress. Equally exciting was the time we climbed the vertical ice-pitches of Hayfork Gully on an unrelenting day when even the ordinary descent of Coir' a' Ghlas Thuill demanded extreme care on the wind-polished snow-ice.

Yes, An Teallach ranks with the best in Britain for everything that spells magic in mountaineering. The mountain is too big ever to be known intimately and there is a lonely bothy in Strath na Sheallag, called Shenavall, to add to its lasting joy.

Above: The isolated majesty of the An Teallach massif is well seen in this fine photo from the Fannichs. The described route traverses the mountains from right to left, before descending into the shadowy left-hand corrie and heading back to Dundonnell on the extreme right. *Photo: John Allen*

Top left: The pinnacles of Corrag Bhuidhe and Sgurr Fiona seen from Bidein a'Ghlas Thuill (3,484ft.), An Teallach's principal summit. *Photo: Phil Ideson*

Bottom left: An Teallach's weathered sandstone castellations, seen to good effect in this picture of the lower pinnacle of Corrag Bhuidhe. *Photo: Gordon Gadsby*

Overleaf: Traversing Corrag Bhuide *Photo: Gordon Gadsby*

5   Across the Great Wilderness: Dundonnell to Poolewe

I discovered this magnificent walk when, following a resurvey, the extremely remote mountain of Ruadh Stac Mor was elevated to Munro status. Having completed the ascent of all other Munros a few years previously, I was determined to bag Ruadh Stac Mor at the first opportunity. This opportunity arose on the evening of May 31, 1975, when a glorious spring day gave every prospect of a fine and clear night. Ruadh Stac Mor is equidistant from Poolewe, Kinlochewe and Dundonnell so I decided to walk through the mountains from Dundonnell to Poolewe.

It was a clear cold evening as I set out at 10.00 p.m. along the Achneigie track from Dundonnell House. For the first mile the track passes through mixed woodland of pine, birch and alder, and the leaves, just out, were a delicate shade of green. The gorse and broom were in full flower and there were bluebells under the trees. A cuckoo was singing. The gullies and folds of An Teallach were picked out in relief by the last rays of the sun and I did not worry too much about the bank of grey cloud building up in the north.

I spent a few minutes memorizing the map and some important bearings, because I had not brought a torch and I knew it did not become light until 3.30 a.m. The first star appeared at 11.00 p.m., but it never became

completely dark.

The track is easy to follow. After a mile it crosses the burn and climbs up open stony hillsides to the watershed, before gradually zig-zagging down to Strath na Sheallag. When the path starts to descend steeply you can cut straight down the slopes to the lonely cottage of Achneigie. From there to Shenavall bothy it is only one and a half miles along the Strath.

As I walked towards Shenavall in the near darkness, I caught a whiff of wood smoke and realized the bothy must be in use. I found there a man and a boy sitting in front of a good fire and I joined them for a few minutes and ate some sandwiches.

Shenavall is dominated by the beautiful peak of Beinn Dearg Mhor rising to 2,974ft. across the Strath. Its pinnacles and knife-edged ridges surrounding the grand east-facing corrie rival even those of An Teallach.

The Sheallag river was very low and I was able to cross it dryshod (there is no bridge), but the next half-mile across the wet bog to Larachantivore was hideous, as I could not see well enough to pick out the dry parts. Grey patches of ground looking like stone would turn out to be liquid mud, leaving me cursing with a boot full of ooze. I was disappointed to find the suspension bridge above Larachantivore cottage damaged and almost useless.

Walk Across the Great Wilderness: Dundonnell to Poolewe.
Maps O.S. 1:50,000 Sheet 19
Start from Corrie Hallie (ref. 113852).
Finish at Poolewe (ref. 857808).
Grading An exceptionally long and arduous walk across a remote and mountainous wilderness.
Time 12 hours.
Distance 29 miles.
Escape Routes None. Shelter may be obtained at the open bothy at Shenavall and, in emergency, at Carnmore.
Telephones Dundonnell; Poolewe.
Transport The Inverness–Ullapool bus connects with a Monday and Saturday service from Braemore Junction to Dundonnell. In the summer a bus runs from Dundonnell to Poolewe and back on Thursdays. Inverness–Poolewe service on Tuesdays and Fridays throughout the year.
Accommodation Dundonnell Hotel. Hotels and Guest Houses at Poolewe. Youth Hostels at Aultbea and Carn Dearg. Climbing Hut, The Smiddy, Dundonnell, J.M.C.S. Edinburgh Section.
Guidebooks S.M.T. Guide *The Northern Highlands.*

Left: The traveller from Dundonnell to Poolewe cannot fail to be impressed by the superb little peak of Beinn Dearg Mhor, which rises above the lonely bothy of Shenavall in the Strath na Sheallag. The peak, with its dramatic north-facing corrie, ringed with sandstone buttresses, is often mistaken for its loftier neighbour, An Teallach. *Photo: E. A. Shepherd*

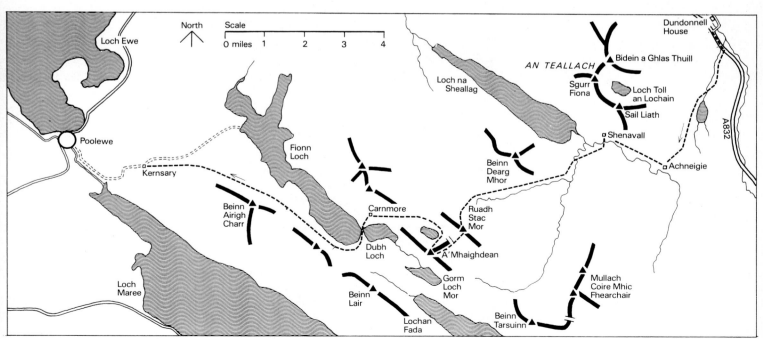

The centre planks were missing and the cables were not held together, calling for a performance of the splits over mid-stream. With a heavy pack and the river in flood the crossing would have been highly unpleasant.

The path now proceeds due south up Glen na Muice, but a mile after Larachantivore it turns right and ascends more steeply into Glen na Muice Beag. The turning-off point is just before the conspicuous north-facing cliff called Junction Buttress.

I was unlucky enough to miss this path and I blundered my way through the heather and rocks up into Glen na Muice Beag before I found it again. The sky was now overcast, and it was snowing, and it was a great relief to be on the Carnmore path which is well constructed and was easy to follow in the bad light.

At 2.30 a.m., I reached the small loch named Lochan Feith Mhic'illean, at the watershed. This was one of my reference points and I turned off on a bearing of 170° up the slopes of Ruadh Stac Mor. From the map this mountain looks to be easy-angled and uninteresting; however, it is a fine sharp rocky peak and is ringed with broken cliffs. The snow was something of a problem, for it was settling above 1,500ft. and was two inches deep already. It was difficult negotiating the rocks and boulders, for they were horribly slippery and I could imagine the consequences of a broken leg. I had no ice-axe or gloves, and my face

and clothing were iced-up and frozen. Although this mountain was a new Final Munro for me, I did not linger for a moment at the cairn. I was ill-equipped for such a mountain in what amounted to winter conditions.

At 4.0 a.m., I reached the bealach under A' Mhaighdean, after a tedious and tricky descent down steep rocks from Ruadh Stac Mor. Dawn had arrived but it was still snowing hard. I ate an early breakfast of peanuts and felt much better.

From the bealach between Ruadh Stac Mor and A' Mhaighdean the ascent to the latter is easy. There were sizeable patches of old snow on this, the north, side and I kicked my way up to keep warm, arriving at the small summit cairn above the precipitous face at 5.0 a.m.

The summit of A' Mhaighdean is a wonderful view-point for this wild and complex area. Straight down below is the small Gorm Loch and beyond stretches Lochan Fada, with Slioch rising behind. Ahead is the line of cliffs of Beinn Lair and to the east the Dubh Loch nestles under dark cliffs, while the Fionn Loch stretches away north-west for six miles. Smaller lochs each in their rock basins abound.

I had intended to descend the rocky north-west ridge, but in the unexpectedly severe conditions I decided against it and went down to the east end of Fuar Loch Mor instead. I felt very unsure of myself without an axe and I took the steep snowy slopes very gingerly, whereas with an axe for security I would have romped down.

From the west end of Fuar Loch Mor a short descent leads you past the tiny Fuar Loch Beag, and below you can see the Dubh Loch. The Carnmore path is met again on the north side of the Dubh Loch.

I reached the Dubh Loch at 6.45 a.m. and soon passed the remote farm of Carnmore which is supplied by boat from across the Fionn Loch. The clouds were dispersing and I had some sunshine for the long walk out to Poolewe. The track is poor and non-existent in places, but it goes under the impressive north face of Beinn Airigh Charr, which has a large area of vertical or overhanging clean grey rock. At Loch Kernsary I was once again out of the bleak mountains and the loch was entrancing in the early morning sunshine, ringed with luxuriant growth of gorse, broom, rowan and birch. This loch and the surrounding estate were given to the young Osgood MacKenzie, who built Inverewe Gardens, by his father so the boy could pursue his own sporting interests.

I finally reached Poolewe at 10.15 a.m. after a most enjoyable night's walk. Surely this is one of the finest mountain walks in Scotland. Looking back east to the snow-covered Beinn Eighe and Beinn Lair I realised that even after 279 Munros I still had not appreciated the possibility of winter conditions on the last day of May.

Left: The remote mountain country of the Fisherfield Forest between Dundonnell and Poolewe. The primeval mystery of the area is well illustrated in this view from A'Mhaighdean, one of the most inaccessible mountains in Britain. An Teallach, with its many snow-filled couloirs, can be seen in the distance behind the shadowy profile of Beinn Dearg Mhor. The prominent shoulder on the right is a spur of Ruadh Stac Mor. *Photo: Tom Weir.*

6 Liathach

by Sandy Cousins

Each person gets his own thing from a hill and Liathach is for me one of the special hills. It offers me a fine variety of pleasure, ranging from a summer walk through to an exciting winter ridge-traverse.

I have camped in the old pine woods of Glen Torridon under the towering buttresses of the south face. I have surveyed the pinnacles and teeth of the summit ridge from across Loch Coulin, the classic view. I have sat by the Scottish Mountaineering Club's Ling Hut beside Lochan an Iasgair, under the east summit of Liathach, while a salmon leapt from the water, showering blue, purple and silver in the low sunlight. But my favourite haunt is Coire Mhic Nobuil which runs under the northern precipices of Liathach. Like all Highland burns the Abhainn Coire Mhic Nobuil gives a variety of scenery, from deep gorges and waterfalls to clear sun-warmed pools for a welcome bathe, and of course the sweet-tasting soft water. Casting a fly (try a black pennel) on some of the lochans has provided me with trout for tea.

Somewhere out there on the moor I once slept out. It was a perfect calm night and, lying in the heather, I listened to a natural symphony. Trout rising, myriads of insects, a fox barking, drumming of snipe as they dived, the liquid notes of the gliding curlew and the uneasy coughs of hinds who could scent but not see me. This is great wandering country, where there is always a boulder howff or shelter of some kind for the walker without a tent. There was talk of building a bothy behind Liathach but the National Trust for Scotland, who manage the area, wisely left well alone.

A preliminary walk through Coire Mhic Nobuil will show you the five north-facing corries of Liathach. In early or late sunlight the buttresses and gullies will be picked out sharply and you can see where access up or down is feasible.

The complete traverse of Liathach is best made from east to west, for you will then be walking down into Glen Torridon in the evening. That special soft Highland evening light — laden with the scents of the day, bog myrtle, heather, pines — will fill the glen and the sun will be dazzling as it glitters off the waters of Loch Torridon. What a great gift is human emotion.

Park the car at the entrance to Coire Dubh

Mor, which divides the massifs of Liathach and Beinn Eighe. The easternmost summit of Liathach, Stuc a'Choire Dhuibh Bhig, throws down broken cliffs and slabs of rock on all sides, but the purist can ascend by a very steep gully scramble from the Coire Dubh Mor path.

An easier and much pleasanter ascent is from the Glen Torridon road, one mile west of the Coire Dubh Mor car-park. An indistinct path leads up into the upper corrie from whence a route can easily be found, skirting the outcrops, to reach the main ridge just west of Stuc a'Choire Dhuibh Bhig.

The red sandstone buttresses give way to quartzite rubble on the main ridge and the walking is easy, although rough, while the views are exceptional. In summer your eyes are kept busy with the close-up interest of the sparkling rock and the tiny alpine plants peering from fertile cracks. The surrounding peaks are as grand in character as their names are music to the ear: Beinn Eighe, Baosbheinn, Beinn an Eoin, Beinn Alligin and Beinn Dearg. Distant in the west the Cuillin skyline calls.

Soon after passing the main summit of Spidean a'Choire Leith (3,456ft.) comes the scramble along the Am Fasarinen pinnacle ridge. The razor-sharp sandstone crest overlooks the plunging cliffs of Coire na Caime, but the faint-hearted can bypass this section by means of a narrow path on the south side. In winter conditions, though, the pinnacles may have to be taken direct.

Beyond the Am Fasarinen pinnacles, the ridge broadens and the pyramidal summit of Mullach an Rathain blocks the view west. This summit throws out a jagged ridge, containing

Walk   Liathach.
Maps   O.S. 1:50,000 Sheet 25; O.S. 1:25,000 Outdoor Leisure Map — The Cuillin and Torridon Hills. Start from Glen Torridon Car Park (ref. 958568). Finish at Torridon House (ref. 869576).
Grading   A high mountain traverse which can become serious in bad conditions. A rope should be carried.
Time   7 hours.
Distance   9 miles.
Escape Routes   N. down scree slopes beyond the Fasarinen Pinnacles into Coire na Caime. S. down Coire Leith between Spidean a' Choire Leith and Bidein Toll a' Mhuic. S. down the Slugach scree slopes ¼ mile W. of Mullach an Rathain.
Telephones   Kinlochewe and Torridon.
Transport   A daily bus service runs through Glen Torridon from Kinlochewe to Torridon. A Kinlochewe–Inverness service runs on Tuesdays and Fridays.
Accommodation   Ling Hut, Glen Torridon (S.M.C.). Hotels at Kinlochewe and Torridon. Youth Hostel at Torridon.
Guidebooks   S.M.T. Guide *The Northern Highlands; The Scottish Peaks* by W. A. Poucher (Constable); *Undiscovered Scotland* by W. H. Murray (Diadem, 1979) has a colourful account of a winter ascent of the Northern Pinnacles of Liathach.

Left: The mighty buttresses of Liathach reflected in the waters of Loch Clair in Glen Torridon.
Photo: Walter Poucher

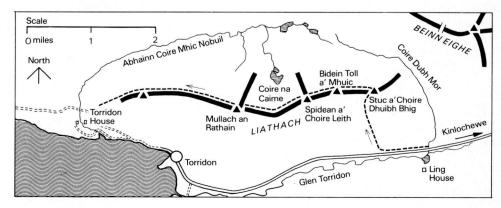

Above: A view from the summit of Liathach (Spidean a'Choire Leith) towards Beinn Eighe in the east. *Photo: Roger Redfern*

Top right: Looking west along the summit ridge of Liathach to Mullach an Rathain. The walker is about to tackle the exposed pinnacles of Am Fasarinen, which can be avoided, if considered too difficult, by a traverse path on the south side (behind the pinnacles in this view). *Photo: John Allen*

the Northern Pinnacles, towards upper Coire Mhic Nobuil. The Northern Pinnacle ridge is spectacular but dreadfully shattered and loose, and it is best left to an experienced party in winter conditions when the rocks are cemented by ice.

Proceeding westwards from Mullach an Rathain, easy gullies lead down to Coire Mhic Nobuil on the north side and to the Slugach scree-run on the south. The latter provides a rapid and simple way to Torridon village. The

west end of the ridge, above Torridon House, is an easy grass slope and on a platform is to be found a small pool, a fine place to strip off and lie in the sun-warmed water.

In winter, Liathach can change completely. The fast moving weather can replace the blue and white Alpine conditions with a raging world of tearing wind and drift. Spending a wild day on Liathach can be enjoyable, as the world shrinks to arm's length, the wind sings and roars around the crags and you add

another day to your experience.

One good winter day towards Easter, I had a ridge walk over Liathach on hard snow in brilliant sunshine. On the south side it was summer, green and warm, yet the north side was silent and hard. Winter gripped the blue-iced gullies between the Pinnacles, and the snow slopes, grey and cold in the shade, swept out to the unbroken sunshine on the frozen Loch Coire na Caime. The Northern Pinnacles, festooned in ice, were more stable than in summer.

I shall be back again to Liathach, one of the great hill walks of Scotland. Perhaps I envy now those who will go for the first time down the little road from Kinlochewe into one of Scotland's deepest glens, 3,000ft. in one unbroken sweep. The experience will enrich their lives and, I hope, engender love and concern for our beautiful country.

Above: Liathach seen from the north-west, from the 'Horns' of Beinn Alligin. Mullach an Rathain is in the centre of the picture, with Spidean a'Choire Leith on the left. The walk described in the essay traverses the mountain from left to right, starting and finishing in Glen Torridon which is on the far side of the massif. *Photo: Ken Andrew*

Overleaf: A view of Liathach's main summit, Spidean a'Choire Leith (3,456ft.), from the east, near the start of the traverse. Glen Torridon is on the left and Coire Mhic Nobuil is on the right. *Photo: Roger Redfern*

7   Beinn Eighe, a Torridonian Giant

Walk   The Traverse of Beinn Eighe.
Maps   O.S. 1:50,000 Sheet 25; O.S. 1:25,000 Outdoor Leisure Map – The Cuillin and Torridon Hills. Start from Glen Torridon (ref. 958568). Finish at Kinlochewe Hotel (ref. 028620).
Grading   A long and high mountain traverse involving some easy rock scrambling. A rope should be carried.
Time   8-9 hours.
Distance   13 miles.
Escape Routes   The steep quartzite screes can be descended to the Torridon road from many places on the main ridge.
Telephones   Kinlochewe and Torridon.
Transport   A daily bus service runs through Glen Torridon from Kinlochewe to Torridon. A Kinlochewe–Inverness bus service runs on Tuesdays and Fridays.
Accommodation   Ling Hut Glen Torridon (S.M.C.). Hotels at Kinlochewe and Torridon. Youth Hostel at Torridon.
Guidebooks   S.M.T. Guide *The Northern Highlands*; *The Scottish Peaks* by W.A. Poucher (Constable).

Glen Torridon stretches for eleven miles from Kinlochewe to Loch Torridon and the scenery rivals even Glencoe for grandeur. The two giant monoliths, Liathach and Beinn Eighe, rise steeply on the west side of the glen, each boasting a long and sharp ridge. Liathach is terraced with walls of old sandstone which soar upwards in ledges and buttresses, while Beinn Eighe is clothed in white quartzite screes, which give the appearance of snow when the sun glances off them. The mountains of Torridon remind me of Ruskin's lines:

'These great cathedrals of the earth,
with their gates of rock, pavements
of cloud, choirs of stream and stone,
altars of snow, and vaults of purple
traversed by the continual stars.'

From the road Liathach looks to be the more impressive of the two, since the sheer sides of the mountain, coupled with its summit pinnacles, make it like a battleship. From the west, however, it is Beinn Eighe which wins the day, for the western end of the mountain contains one of Scotland's most stupendous corries, Coire Mhic Fhearchair. The summit ridge of Beinn Eighe is as narrow and airy as Liathach's, as well as being longer, and for these reasons I have chosen it for inclusion in this book. The complete traverse of the mountain is a major undertaking and in winter conditions a dawn start is necessary and it is essential to carry a rope.

The entire eastern half of Beinn Eighe is a

National Nature Reserve, but access is permitted except on certain days in the stalking season. The Information Centre at Kinlochewe provides details of the access and you should be able to buy a leaflet listing the wide variety of fauna to be seen, if you are lucky, in the Reserve.

Start the walk from the car park at the mouth of Coire Dubh Mor which divides the mountain massifs of Liathach and Beinn Eighe. A path which passes a ruined cottage near the road leads up the glen, keeping to the west side of the corrie burn. The path climbs up to 1,200ft., before passing under the steep eastern

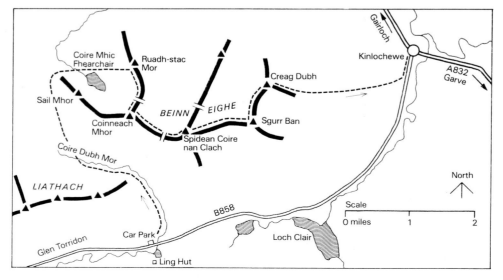

slopes of Liathach, where it flattens out and crosses the burn. The path then divides and you should take the right-hand branch, which is cairned and makes a rising traverse across the very rough shoulder of Sail Mhor. The left-hand branch goes down Coire Mhic Nobuil on the north side of Liathach.

As you work round to the north side of Sail Mhor you pass under towering buttresses of red sandstone and then quite suddenly you are in Coire Mhic Fhearchair, confronted by one of the most dramatic sights in all Scotland. A dark lochan spills out over the lip of the corrie in a cascade of waterfalls, while above the lochan

rise three giant buttresses of white quartzite standing on a plinth of sandstone. The cliffs are fully 1,300ft. high and provide excellent rock climbing on clean and sound quartzite. The left-hand (easternmost) buttress gives the easiest climb at about 'Difficult' standard.

The view looking west out of the corrie mouth is equally delightful, but in complete contrast to the triple buttresses. The hills of the Flowerdale Forest rise abruptly from the flat boggy floor, Beinn an Eoin and Baosbheinn being particularly prominent.

Ruadh-stac Mor, at 3,309ft. the highest of the Beinn Eighe peaks, lies on the east side of

Above: The magnificent whale-back spurs of Beinn Eighe enclose the celebrated hollow of Coire Mhic Fhearchair, with its three great buttresses (seen emerging above the intervening ridge of Sail Mhor). From this viewpoint, looking east from Beinn Dearg, Beinn Eighe's summit, Ruadh-stac Mor (3,309ft.), can be seen as a slight rise on the top of the left-hand spur. *Photo: Ken Andrew*

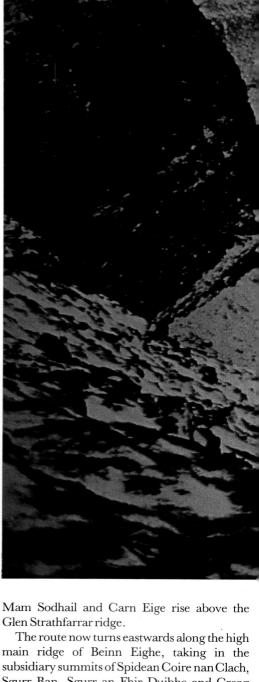

Top: The last main top of the Beinn Eighe chain: the cliffs of Sgurr an Fhir Duibhe from Sgurr Ban. *Photo: Donald Bennet*

Bottom: The three great buttresses of Coire Mhic Fhearchair. *Photo: Walter Poucher*

Coire Mhic Fhearchair and it is an easy but exasperating 1,500ft. climb up the scree slopes to the summit cairn. The ridge is now followed south to Coinneach Mhor which is a better view-point than Ruadh-stac Mor. The sharp summits and the pinnacles on the north ridge of Liathach stand out across Glen Dubh Mor, and further west, Beinn Alligin, with its characteristic gash in the summit ridge, and Beinn Dearg complete the quartet of Torridon giants. To the north-west the serrated ridge of An Teallach is clearly seen, while to the south,

Mam Sodhail and Carn Eige rise above the Glen Strathfarrar ridge.

The route now turns eastwards along the high main ridge of Beinn Eighe, taking in the subsidiary summits of Spidean Coire nan Clach, Sgurr Ban, Sgurr an Fhir Duibhe and Creag Dubh. Nowhere does the ridge fall below 2,700ft., although the going is slow with the need to pick your way carefully over the jumble of quartzite blocks. The Ordnance Survey trig point is on Spidean Coire nan Clach, where subsidiary ridges go off to the

north and south. The southern slopes are of steep scree, but to the north broken cliffs fall away to high corries. The actual ridge is often extremely narrow and a sense of exposure is always present, particularly on the section beyond Sgurr Ban. After a steep descent for 400ft. to a bealach, the ridge climbs up to Sgurr an Fhir Duibhe, which has a series of rock pinnacles or teeth. These pinnacles are known as the Black Men and their negotiation requires care; there is no easy way round.

When the Black Men of Sgurr an Fhir Duibhe are behind you, the ridge broadens and becomes mossy. You pass over a subsidiary summit before descending slightly to Creag Dubh which marks the end of the Beinn Eighe ridge. Here the ridge divides and you should take the right-hand, eastern, branch. For 1,500ft. the descent is extremely tiresome as you pick your way down the boulder strewn slopes, but when you reach the Allt a' Chuirn burn the hillsides are firm and peaty. A path on the north side of the burn leads to the road, less than a mile south of Kinlochewe.

Above: Looking down Coire Mhic Fhearchair towards Baosbheinn. The snow-covered castellations of Sail Mhor rise above the lochan, beyond the dark profile of the great buttresses on the left. *Photo: Ken Andrew*

8   Kintail: the Five Sisters Ridge

Walk Kintail: The Five Sisters Ridge.
Maps O.S. 1:50,000 Sheet 33
Start from Cluanie Inn (ref. 075117).
Finish at Sheil Bridge (ref. 935190).
Grading A moderate walk over an undulating and at times rocky ridge.
Time 9-10 hours.
Distance 14 miles.
Escape Routes The low bealach W. of Saileag provides an easy way down to Glenshiel. On the N. side of the ridge shelter may be found at Camban bothy and possibly at Glenlicht House which is owned by E.U.M.C.
Telephones Cluanie Inn; Shiel Bridge
Transport Bus services from Edinburgh to Uig, Glasgow to Portree, and Inverness to Portree, run through Glenshiel.
Accommodation Cluanie Inn. Hotels at Shiel Bridge. Youth Hostel at Ratagan.
Guidebooks S.M.T. Guide *The Western Highlands; The Scottish Peaks* by W. A. Poucher (Constable).

There are really eight major peaks lying in the Kintail Forest north of Glen Shiel and between Cluanie and the head of Loch Duich. These mountains form a high ridge running parallel to, but further west than, the equally fine South Kintail Ridge. Of these eight mountains it is the five most westerly which are universally known as the Five Sisters, and they are very conspicuous when you drive east alongside Loch Duich from Kyle of Lochalsh. They are even more prominent when viewed from the Mam Ratagan pass between Shiel Bridge and Glenelg, when every fold, gully and excrescence is highlighted by the evening sun.

The highest of the Sisters is Sgurr Fhuaran, which throws out massive grassy shoulders to the west; these slopes, 3,500ft. high, are possibly the longest in all Scotland. One of Scotland's most classic romantic views is that of Eilean Donan Castle with the Five Sisters of Kintail in the background rising above the dark waters of Loch Duich.

Starting from the Loch Duich end of the ridge, the Five Sisters are called Sgurr na Moraich, Sgurr nan Saighead, Sgurr Fhuaran, Sgurr na Carnach and Sgurr na Ciste Duibhe. Beyond Sgurr na Ciste Duibhe the ridge continues for another five miles before dropping down to Cluanie Inn, and it includes three more fine mountains: Saileag, Sgurr a' Bhealaich Dheirg and Sgurr an Fhuarail.

The complete traverse makes a long and arduous, but very rewarding, day and in order to enjoy the best of the west coast views it should be tackled from east to west.

From Cluanie Inn you must strike straight up the steep grassy slopes, well to the west of the Allt a' Chaoruinn burn. After 1,800ft., you reach a subsidiary summit at the south end of a well formed ridge, which runs off from the eastern summit of Sgurr an Fhuarail. Follow this hummocky ridge for a mile until you reach this lower eastern summit, marked 3,241ft. on the map. The true summit is half a mile away to the west and the route involves a sharp drop to an intervening bealach and a corresponding pull up to the cairn at 3,284ft. You can now enjoy the magnificent panoramic view to the north. The sharp pointed peak straight ahead is Ciste Dhubh; beyond rises the huge and complex Sgurr nan Ceathreamhnan, with the Glen Affric giants, Mam Sodhail and Carn Eige, further to the east. Due east across Glen Caorunn Mor is the high ridge separating A'Chralaig and Mullach Fraoch-choire.

Drop down 750ft. to a low bealach on the west side and ascend Sgurr a' Bhealaich Dheirg which involves a climb of nearly 900ft. The summit cairn of this mountain is poised at the end of a short subsidiary ridge, jutting out north from the main ridge. It is an airy scramble to gain the true summit but should only give difficulty in winter conditions. The main ridge now broadens out and, after Saileag (3,124ft.), you descend to the lowest point of the whole ridge at 2,400ft. Easy grassy slopes lead south to Glen Sheil from this bealach, if you should need an escape route.

With the first section of the ridge completed, you now start on the Five Sisters proper. One and a half miles of easy ridge lead to Sgurr na Ciste Duibhe (3,370ft.) and on the way you traverse Coirein nan Spainteach. This intermediate peak is quite rocky with steep slopes on the north side; between it and Sgurr na Ciste Duibhe the ridge is snake-like and boulder-strewn. Sgurr na Ciste Duibhe is an imposing mountain from the east and north, with a 500ft. face of broken cliffs.

The ridge now turns towards the north and descends 600ft. before rising again to the pointed summit of Sgurr na Carnach. For most of the day you have been able to see Sgurr Fhuaran ahead, and from every angle it looks a fine peak. It stands haughtily above its neighbours and the low bealachs on both sides give it individuality.

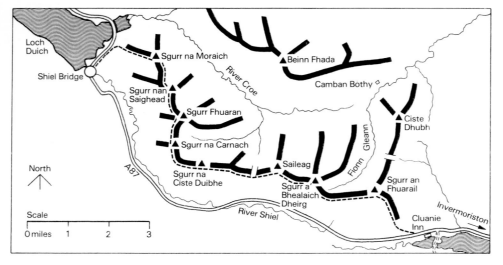

After Sgurr na Carnach the going continues to be rough, with some scrambling over slabby rocks, and it is another steep pull to the summit of Sgurr Fhuaran, where there is a large cairn. This summit has been described as one of the finest view-points in Scotland. On a clear day Skye and the Inner Hebrides look very close, and the Outer Hebrides have been seen stretching from Harris to Barra Head. On the mainland you can see peaks ranging from Assynt to Ben Alder and Ben Cruachan, while nearby, just across Glen Shiel, the Saddle dominates the view. One exceptionally still winter's day I could smell the aroma of wood smoke drifting up from the cottages in Glen Shiel, 3,500ft. below.

Although the south and west sides of Sgurr Fhuaran are grassy, the northern slopes fall away in considerable, though broken, cliffs. Descend the steep north ridge to the bealach under Sgurr nan Saighead. Keep close to the edge of the steep corrie on the right, which leads to the summit of Sgurr nan Saighead. A further small corrie lies beyond, and again you should keep to the lip before the ridge descends to the bealach under Sgurr na Moraich. This mountain, the last of the Five Sisters, is a huge flattish mass, 2,870ft. high. A rapid descent can be made down the grassy western slopes to meet the main road one mile north of Shiel Bridge.

Top: The Five Sisters of Kintail above Loch Duich. The highest peak is Sgurr Fhuaran (3,505ft.). The walk described in the essay traverses the skyline from right to left. *Photo: Robert Adam*

Bottom: The north peak of Sgurr nan Saighead (2,987ft.), the twin-peaked summit to the left of Sgurr Fhuaran in the upper photograph. *Photo: Robert Adam*

9   Glen Affric and Mam Sodhail

Walk Glen Affric and Mam Sodhail.
Maps O.S. 1:50,000 Sheets 25 and 33
Start from Loch Beinn a' Mheadhoin (ref. 215242).
Finish at Cluanie Inn (ref. 075117).
Grading An exceptionally long and arduous
mountain traverse. The few stretches of rock
scrambling can be avoided.
Time 13-14 hours.
Distance 26 miles.
Escape Routes From Bealach Coire Ghaidheil W.
of Mam Sodhail an escape may be made S. to Glen
Affric. Shelter may be obtained at the Alltbeithe Y. H.
It is left unlocked even in winter.
Telephones Cannich and Cluanie Inn.
Transport Cannich is served by a daily bus service
from Beauly where there are connections to
Inverness. The Edinburgh–Uig, Glasgow–Portree
and Inverness–Portree services pass Cluanie Inn.
Accommodation Hotel and Bed and Breakfast at
Cannich. Cluanie Inn, Youth Hostels at Ratagan,
Alltbeithe (Glen Affric) and Cannich.
Guidebooks S.M.T. Guide *The Western Highlands*.

Top right: Ascending Sgurr nan Ceathreamhnan
(3,771ft.) from the south. This fine mountain at
the head of Glen Affric forms the climax of the
described walk. The route traverses the skyline
from right to left and descends these slopes.
Photo: John Allen

Bottom right: The view north from Carn Eige
(3,877ft.), the highest mountain in Scotland
north of the Great Glen. This normally
monotonous view over rounded ridges, is
transformed by snow into one of
splendour. *Photo: Phil Cooper*

This magnificent and demanding walk takes
you across the main watershed of Scotland
from east to west, and traverses the highest
range of mountains north of the Great Glen. It
is Scotland at its most wild, remote and
beautiful.

Make sure your party is fit and competent,
and arrange to have tented accommodation or
a car at the finish, which is the Cluanie Inn in
Kintail.

From Cannich, drive west alongside Loch
Beinn a'Mheadhoin until you reach the bridge
at the entrance to Gleann nam Fiadh, two miles
short of Affric Lodge. Affric is a most spectacular glen, with stands of Scots Pine on the lower
slopes of the mountains and a roaring river
below. I have seen capercaillie in the woods.

Walk up Gleann nam Fiadh by a good path
on the right-hand side of the burn, but after a
mile and a half strike northwards up steep
grassy slopes to Toll Creagach. The going is easy,
though monotonous, and the ascent is 2,500ft.
However, once you have gained the summit of
Toll Creagach, at 3,452ft., you have ahead a
ridge walk of eleven miles which is sheer
delight. Loch Mullardoch is the long, grey loch
below in Glen Cannich, and beyond rises the
shapely peak of Sgurr na Lapaich. Loch
Mullardoch is dammed at the east end,
thereby raising the water well above its natural
level. In former times, by the loch shore, there
was a house, Benula Lodge, where accommodation could be found with the keeper, but
both the lodge and the access road to the west
end of the loch are now submerged beneath the
waters.

Descend the broad shoulder of Toll
Creagach, passing over a subsidiary rise, until
you reach the low bealach under Tom a'
Choinich. The old stalkers' path from Affric
Lodge to Benula Lodge crossed this bealach; it
was well constructed and is still easily visible.
From the bealach climb the slopes ahead,
grassy at first and then rocky, to the summit of
Tom a' Choinich. Your next mountain, Carn
Eige, is three miles away along a prominent
ridge, which in places is rocky and narrow with
crazy pinnacles or gendarmes. The rock is
green with moss and lichen and, although the
pinnacles could be taken direct, it is much
quicker to skirt them to one side. To the north,
across Loch Mullardoch, is the long high back
of An Riabhachan, while to the south you
catch glimpses of Loch Affric, sparkling far
below with stands of pine and birch on the
water's edge.

Carn Eige (3,877ft.) is the highest mountain
in the North West Highlands, but that is its
only distinction. It is well rounded on all sides
and it needs a steep corrie of high cliffs to give it
character. Beyond Carn Eige the ridge turns
south and less than a mile away, separated by
another bealach, rises the sister peak of Mam
Sodhail (3,862ft.). Mam Sodhail (or Mam
Soul) was one of the principal sighting stations
during one of the early surveys of Scotland and
the summit boasts a very large cairn, while the
ruins of a stone shelter, used by the surveyors,
lie nearby.

Mam Sodhail is indeed a magnificent view-
point, and if you are lucky to get a clear day it
is well worth ten minutes of your time to enjoy
it. There is probably no better in Scotland.
Mam Sodhail is less featureless than Carn Eige
and it throws out a long east ridge, ending after
two and a half miles in a fine mountain, Sgurr
na Lapaich, overlooking Loch Affric. The
summit ridge of Mam Sodhail contains a few
rocky outcrops and, one golden November's
day, after the first appreciable snowfall of the
winter, I saw a dark brown fox padding across
the snow to its den in the rocks. You will see
ptarmigan and possibly snow bunting on the
Mam Sodhail ridge.

You still have a long walk ahead before you
reach Cluanie, and the next major objective,
Sgurr nan Ceathreamhnan (3,771ft.), can be
seen rising high above its neighbours, five
miles away as the crow flies. From Mam
Sodhail the general direction is south-west; the
ridge is broad and undulating and for a mile
you mostly maintain your height. Don't be

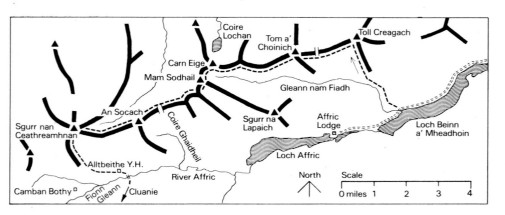

tempted to follow the ridge round the edge of Coire Coulavie, but, from the cairn on the subsidiary summit marked 3,508, descend steepish boulder strewn slopes to the Bealach Coire Ghaidheil, 1,000ft. below. You should be descending due west, not south, here.

If you are behind schedule at this point, it is easy to escape down Coire Ghaidheil to Glen Affric and thence to Cluanie. It will take you about three and a half hours to walk from the bealach to Cluanie, but of course you will miss the ascent of Sgurr nan Ceathreamhnan, by far the most attractive summit of the day.

From Bealach Coire Ghaidheil climb the ridge ahead to An Socach (3,017ft.). The name of this mountain is not marked on the one-inch map, but it is a separate Munro, your fifth of the day. The east ridge of Sgurr nan

Above: Mam Sodhail from Glen Affric. *Photo: Robert Adam*

Ceathreamhnan is reached after three more infuriating subsidiary summits, but once on the mountain proper you can enjoy the height and the ever-widening views. The cluster of wooden houses down in Glen Affric is the Alltbeithe Youth Hostel, and the huge table-like mountain to the south across Glen Gniomhaidh is Beinn Fhada. The Youth Hostel is never locked, even in winter, and it could serve as an emergency refuge if the need arose.

The twin summits of Sgurr nan Ceathreamhnan lie at each end of a narrow ridge, the east summit being the higher one. It is only 100ft. less than Carn Eige which is very conspicuous away to the east. It is cheering to realize that the long ridge is behind you and from now on you are homeward bound.

Five steep corries, bounded by five major ridges, plunge down from the summit of Sgurr nan Ceathreamhnan and, although they are not precipitous, they give the mountain grace and stature. It is essentially a mountain for the mountaineer, not the tourist — its remoteness sees to that. The only sign of civilization you are likely to see is a plume of smoke from the farm at Carnoch, five miles down the glen to the north-west. The west-facing corries drain to the Glomach River and thence via the Falls of Glomach, the highest in Britain, to Loch Alsh on the west coast.

Walk across to the west summit of Sgurr nan Ceathreamhnan and descend the grassy slopes of the south ridge to Glen Affric. It is a long and wearisome descent for tired legs, nearly 3,000ft., and you will probably elect to wade the Affric River in order to reach the Cluanie path, rather than detour threequarters of a mile to cross by the bridge at Alltbeithe. In wet weather, though, do not attempt to cross the river unless you are safeguarded by a rope, and in times of flood the crossing is quite impossible and you must use the bridge.

The path to Cluanie passes the pointed peak of Ciste Dhubh on the east side and then after crossing a bealach at 1,370ft. it descends the An Caorunn Mor. At first the path is not very distinct; take care not to confuse it with the path through the Fionn Glean to Glen Lichd. The latter passes a stone bothy at Camban, while the Cluanie path strikes due south, keeping to the left-hand side of the burn, going up. The remains of a crashed plane litter the slopes just above the Affric River.

The watershed is very boggy and the path seems unending, but three miles before Cluanie you reach a Land-Rover track which leads to the main A87 road, one mile before Cluanie Inn. I hope you reach it before closing time.

10 Seven Munros: the South Kintail Ridge

To the south of Glen Shiel, and roughly between Cluanie Inn and the Glen Shiel battle site, where the Redcoats fought the Jacobites in 1719, lies a high ridge eight miles long and containing no less than seven separate Munros. If you are interested in Munro-bagging, there is no pleasanter or more productive day in all Scotland. The walk is most enjoyable when done from east to west, for then you will get the best of the views down Loch Duich, Loch Hourn and across to Skye. Northwards lie the three great glens of Affric, Cannich and Strathfarrar, with their accompanying mighty peaks, while to the south lie the peaks around Loch Quoich, Loch Arkaig and Glenfinnan.

In summer the ridge makes an entirely delightful excursion. The going is easy and with several simple escape routes down to Glen Shiel you should have a carefree day. In winter or spring the walk is equally delightful but the condition of the snow will determine the length of your day.

From Cluanie Inn an old road crosses the western end of Loch Cluanie by a causeway and then continues south over the shoulder of Creag a' Mhaim to Loch Loyne. The road is no longer driveable but it provides an easy route to the summit of Creag a' Mhaim, your first objective of the day. Follow the old road for one and a half miles, until you come to the bridge over the Allt Giubhais burn, and then climb the broad north ridge to the summit. The first part of the ridge is flat and uninteresting and you will make good speed to Druim Shionnach, your second Munro. The two mountains to the south across the dividing glen are Spidean Mialach and Gleouraich, which have fine high corries and steep-sided ridges.

Beyond Druim Shionnach the ridge becomes narrower and more interesting. After a mile you climb to the highest point of the day, Aonach air Chrith (3,342ft.), which is the easternmost summit of a considerable mountain mass called Maol Chinn-dearg. The north face of Aonach air Chrith is precipitous and huge rock buttresses are thrown out into the amphitheatre below.

One March day after a week of snow and gales I traversed this ridge and found the snow had been driven with such force against the north side of the ridge that it had built up into a plume over 30ft. high, curled over like a

wave about to break, and overhanging the ridge proper. This fantastic plume continued for about 600ft., and it was quite unclimbable. Luckily, at this point the south side of the ridge is not too steep and we were able to traverse along under the plume. It must have been formed by powder snow blowing up the corrie, for, strangely, on the summit of Creag a' Mhaim, the snow had been blown clean off leaving bare frozen grass and rocks.

The western end of Maol Chinn-dearg is a spot height of 3,214ft. and a separate Munro. The ridge continues towards the west with few changes of direction and it undulates gently without descending to low bealachs. The next summit is Sgurr Coire na Feinne (2,958ft.) and then, half a mile further on, you collect your fifth Munro, Sgurr an Doire Leathain (3,272ft.), the summit cairn of which lies a short way off the ridge to the north.

The shapely conical peak ahead is Sgurr an Lochain, named after the tiny lochan in the high corrie below the summit. The final slopes of Sgurr an Lochain are steep on all sides. One winter's day I sat on the summit and pulled the picnic lunch out of the rucksack; it was to be a special lunch, a whole cooked chicken neatly wrapped in a polythene bag. Unfortunately the bag slipped from my frozen fingers and tobogganed gently away down the snow to Upper Glen Quoich, disappearing out of sight into the mist.

One more sharp subsidiary summit, Sgurr Beag (2,926ft.), lies ahead and then you

Walk Seven Munros: The South Kintail Ridge
Maps O.S. 1:50,000 Sheet 33
Start from Cluanie Inn (ref. 075117).
Finish at Glenshiel Battle Site (ref. 990132).
Grading In good conditions this is an exhilarating and fairly straightforward mountain traverse.
Time 7-8 hours.
Distance 13 miles.
Escape Routes Many of the bealachs on the ridge provide easy ways down to Glen Sheil.
Telephones Cluanie Inn; Shiel Bridge.
Transport The Edinburgh–Uig, Glasgow–Portree and Inverness–Portree bus services run through Glenshiel.
Accommodation Hotels at Cluanie and Shiel Bridge. Bed and Breakfast at Shiel Bridge. Youth Hostel at Ratagan.
Guidebooks S.M.T. Guide *The Western Highlands*.

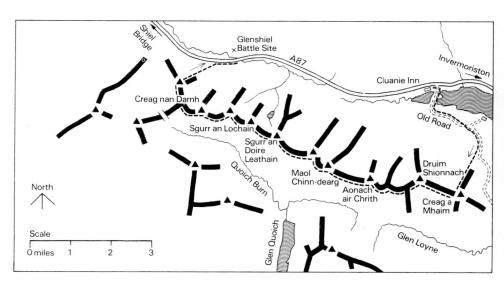

descend to the lowest bealach of the day, at 2,383ft., under your last peak, Creag nan Damh (3,012ft.). The slopes are mainly grassy and present no problem.

If you have time in hand stay on the summit of Creag nan Damh for a few minutes and admire the view. The dominating peak to the west is the Saddle, while, across Glen Shiel, Sgurr Fhuaran tops the neighbouring peaks and the Five Sisters of Kintail. The sharp pointed peak to the south is the very inaccessible Sgurr na Ciche above Loch Nevis.

Above: In crisp, clear conditions the massif of Ladhar Bheinn dominates the view to the west from Creag nan Damh on the South Kintail Ridge. The fine cornice formations that develop along the ridge are also seen to their best advantage at such times. *Photos: John Allen*

Right: Deer roam the remote Glen Loyne to the south of the South Kintail Ridge (left). *Photo: Robert Adam*

11   Ladhar Bheinn and the Rough Bounds of Knoydart

Walk   Ladhar Bheinn and the Rough Bounds of Knoydart.
Maps   O.S. 1:50,000 Sheet 33
Start from Kinlochhourn (ref. 950067).
Finish at Inverie (ref. 766001).
Grading   A long and rough walk over a remote and mountainous area. Some mild scrambling along an exposed ridge.
Time   11 hours.
Distance   22 miles.
Escape Routes   None. If time is short the ascent of Ladhar Bheinn can be missed out and the Mam Barrisdale pass descended to Inverie.
Telephones   Kinlochhourn and Inverie.
Transport   On Mondays, Wednesdays and Fridays a mini-bus service runs from Invergarry to Kinlochhourn. Inverie to Mallaig by a thrice weekly mail boat service, private hire or the Knoydart Estate boat.
Accommodation   Hotel at Tomdoun, 20 miles east of Kinlochhourn. Possible Bed and Breakfast at Inverie, otherwise Hotels and Guest Houses in Mallaig.
Guidebooks   S.M.T. Guide *The Western Highlands.*

Right: A view to the east of Ladhar Bheinn towards Barrisdale Bay and the upper end of Loch Hourn. *Photo: Ken Andrew*

When I am asked to name my favourite mountain in Scotland I answer without any hesitation, 'Ladhar Bheinn in Knoydart.' I cannot be alone in this choice because Ladhar Bheinn offers the perfect combination of grandeur and remoteness, together with the close presence of the sea. In fact the easiest way to gain access to Ladhar Bheinn is either to cross Loch Hourn from Arnisdale in the north, or to cross Loch Nevis from Mallaig in the south.

The walk I recommend, however, involves not only the ascent of Ladhar Bheinn but also a traverse on foot of the famous and aptly named Rough Bounds of Knoydart. Apart from the small settlement at Inverie on the south side of the Knoydart peninsula and a farm at Barrisdale Bay on the north, the area is uninhabited. The motor road through Glen Garry, which passes Tomdoun and Loch Quoich, ends at the coastal hamlet of Kinlochhourn.

Kinlochhourn is the start of the walk, but before you stride away into the wilderness you must check the availability and times of the infrequent ferry service across Loch Nevis from Inverie to Mallaig. There is no accommodation at Inverie and the Estate Factor does not take kindly to visitors camping on his territory, but you should be able to secure a motor boat from Mallaig or from the Inverie Estate to take you across Loch Nevis to Mallaig at the end of the day. There is a public telephone box at Inverie for you to summon the ferryman when you arrive. The crossing takes about forty-five minutes and provides an ideal though unusual end to a magnificent day's

walking. As the sun disappears behind the Cuillin of Skye and the western horizon is alight with a greenish glow you can enjoy perfect peace and happiness as you chug back to civilization across Loch Nevis.

From Kinlochhourn walk along the south side of the loch until, just past the jetty, the road ends and a narrow switchback path continues west hugging the steep hillside. It is six miles to Barrisdale but the way is full of interest. You pass a cottage at Skiary, which in the nineteenth century used to offer accommodation and another one at Runival, both in idyllic settings. You have wonderful views of the Loch Hourn coast line and the bird life that inhabits it and, since Upper Loch Hourn is so narrow, the hills on the north side are very close. The effect is similar to that of a Norwegian fjord.

Glen Barrisdale is flat and you will probably see cattle and sheep grazing the bright green grass just above the high-tide mark. Barrisdale House is now a farm but I was once startled by a light plane which landed on the rough road in front of the house. It was the Laird coming to visit his property. We were able to report an exhausted and emaciated stag which we had just pulled bodily from a deep bog beside the path. The wretched beast had been immersed up to its chest, but even when rescued it had no strength and just lay heaving on the firmer ground.

Barrisdale is a beautiful and lonesome spot. Across Loch Hourn, Ben Sgriol rises gently behind the fishing village of Arnisdale, while to the west Ladhar Bheinn rises dramatically above Coire Dhorrcail. It is sheltered from the worst of the weather and I have swum in Barrisdale Bay during a March heat wave. Even in bad weather there is majestic splendour in the storm clouds and curtains of rain which sweep up Loch Hourn.

Starting from the west side of the Barrisdale River, below the bridge, an old stalker's path can be seen snaking across the hillside. This path should be followed into Coire Dhorrcail, which ranks amongst the most impressive in Scotland. The head of the corrie is ringed by 1,000ft. cliffs falling straight down from the summit ridge of Ladhar Bheinn, while a steep buttress of rock, Stob Dhorrcail, encloses the corrie on the south side and divides it from the smaller eastern Coire na Cabaig.

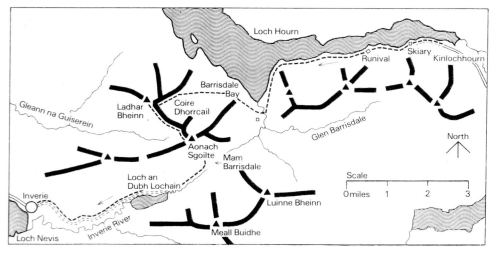

Top: A camp by the side of Barrisdale Bay. The summit ridges of Ladhar Bheinn are 3000ft. above. *Photo: Ken Andrew*

Bottom: Ladhar Bheinn from the slopes of Druim Fhada on the north side of Loch Hourn. The route described ascends diagonally from the left, skirting the base of Coire Dhorrcail, to gain and ascend the rounded ridge on its right. From the summit the walk continues along the skyline above the corrie to the obvious bealach. *Photo: Robert Adam*

Cross the corrie burn and ascend the steep but grassy slopes of Druim a' Choire Odhair on the north side of Coire Dhorrcail. A narrow ridge now leads to the summit cairn of Ladhar Bheinn at 3,343ft. It is a fine summit with cliffs falling away on the north and east sides, and there is an excellent view across the Sound of Sleat to the Cuillin of Skye.

Follow the summit ridge of Ladhar Bheinn for half a mile in a south-easterly direction until it descends to a low bealach at 2,300ft. The ridge is narrow, with a sheer drop on the north side to the floor of Coire Dhorrcail. From the bealach, traverse the western slopes of Aonach Sgoilte, the 2,786ft. subsidiary peak lying on the south-east side, until you meet the crest of the ridge above Glen an Dubh Lochain. You will see the loch below and, after a steep descent of nearly 2,000ft., you will reach a Land-Rover track which in four miles leads to Inverie. Half-way down the track you pass an imposing monument to the family of Lord Brocket.

Inverie is a delightful settlement of about 200 people, with a school, a church and a post office. Above the village there are woods and a luxuriant growth of rhododendrons and, on one occasion, I was lucky to see a golden eagle being harried by a pair of peregrin falcons. You should find plenty of interest while you wait for your boat to Mallaig.

12   Glen Dessarry and Sgurr na Ciche

For this walk, which takes you across one of the wildest and most untamed areas of Scotland, you will need to organize transport at each end. Between the upper reaches of Loch Hourn and Glenfinnan there exists a vast tract of quite uninhabited country containing Loch Quoich, Glen Kingie and Upper Glen Dessarry.

The walk is a serious undertaking, for there are no escape routes and help is a long way off. The terrain is rough but not too difficult and any hazards are likely to be caused entirely by natural occurrences. The weather is unpredictable and is often extremely bad. Before it was submerged by the rising waters of the newly dammed Loch Quoich, a rain-gauge was sited at Kinlochquoich at the west end of the loch. It recorded an average annual rainfall of 159 inches, making Kinlochquoich the wettest place in the British Isles. I have never experienced a fine day in this part of Scotland, so, whatever the forecast, be prepared for the worst. There are no bridges and the rivers and burns rise very quickly to flood level and become unfordable. The northern section of this walk is particularly vulnerable to this danger and you should bear in mind the possibility of having to make long detours late in the day, or even of being benighted. This once happened to me in March with near disastrous results.

Do not be discouraged by this introduction, for the walk includes the ascent of Sgurr na Ciche, one of the most remote and dramatic peaks in Scotland, and the traverse of the most rugged area to be found anywhere in Britain today.

Arrange transport to Strathan farm, at the extreme west end of Loch Arkaig, and walk along the rough Land-Rover track for a mile to Glen Dessarry House. The track now deteriorates badly, but you should continue for another mile to the cottage at Upper Glendessarry. On the south side of the wide and open glen you will notice the splendid open bothy of A'Chuil which has been renovated by the Mountain Bothies Association. One and a half miles further on, the glen divides and the path climbs to 1,000ft. before swinging westwards to Lochan a' Mhaim and eventually to Finiskaig, a ruined cottage beside Loch Nevis.

Just after the division at the highest point of the path, strike northwards up the steep grassy slopes to reach the bealach under Sgurr nan Coireachan. An old wall with iron stakes let into the stone at intervals runs along the rocky and undulating Sgurr nan Coireachan to Sgurr na Ciche ridge, and you should follow this westwards to Garbh Chioch Mhor. Now descend steeply to a lochan under the eastern abutment of Sgurr na Ciche.

Sgurr na Ciche rises symmetrically on all sides to a height of 3,410ft. It is one of the most spectacular mountains on the Scottish mainland eclipsing even Sgurr Mor in the Fannichs for dramatic sharpness of form. The ascent from the east looks forbidding but a way through the rocks can be found by traversing round to the south side before scrambling up the final 500ft. The actual summit is quite sharp and there is barely room for the trig point.

In clear weather the view must be magnificent, particularly to the west down Loch Hourn and Loch Nevis and across the Knoydart peninsula to Ladhar Bheinn. All I have ever seen, however, despite several visits, has been an occasional glimpse down to the grey waters of Loch Nevis and Loch Quoich.

From the summit cairn you must descend north-eastwards, down slopes which are very steep and rocky at first, but after 500ft. flatten out to a distinct ridge. When you have descended 1,500ft. you reach a bealach under the subsidiary summit of Meall a' Choire Dhuibh. Now drop down for another 1,000ft. to the floor of Coire nan Gall on the east side. Here you pick up an old stalker's path which

Walk Glen Dessarry and Sgurr na Ciche.
Maps O.S. 1:50,000 Sheet 33
Start from Strathan (ref. 978915).
Finish at Kinlochhourn road (ref. 998030).
Grading A long and serious walk over uninhabited and mountainous country.
Time 10 hours.
Distance 17 miles.
Escape Routes Refuge may be found in open bothies at A'Chuil in Glen Dessarry and at Sourlies beside Loch Nevis. From the bealach between Garbh Chioch Mhor and Sgurr na Ciche a scree gully leads S.W. towards Loch Nevis side.
Telephones Murlaggan beside Loch Arkaig; Kinlochhourn.
Transport There is no public transport alongside Loch Arkaig. On Mondays, Wednesdays and Fridays a mini-bus service runs from Invergarry to Kinlochhourn.
Accommodation Hotels at Spean Bridge, Gairlochy and Tomdoun.
Guidebooks S.M.T. Guide *The Western Highlands*.

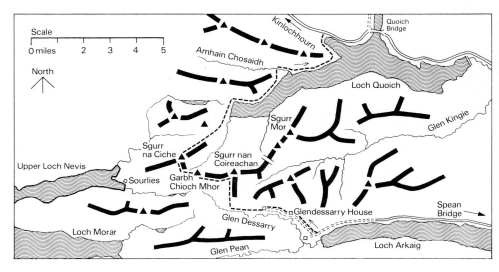

Left: Sgurr na Ciche from Mam Meadail near the head of Loch Nevis. *Photo: Irvine Butterfield*

Right: Looking back from Sgurr na Ciche, along the rugged ridge to Garbh Chioch Mhor and Sgurr nan Coireachan. *Photo: Irvine Butterfield*

leads to the regulating dam at the western end of Loch Quoich.

Cross the dam to reach the north bank of Loch Quoich and you will be surprised to find an old road. This is a continuation of the road which served Kinlochquoich in the days before the loch was dammed and the level raised. The road keeps disappearing into the loch in a most maddening way, leaving you to fight your way across the rough, morained and trackless hillside. Continue eastwards in this way for three miles until you round a corner and meet the big burn, the Amhain Chosaidh, across your path.

It was in March, 1963, when three friends and I crossed Sgurr na Ciche and Sgurr nan Coireachan from Loch Nevis, and dropped down to Loch Quoich on a day of non-stop torrential rain. The hillsides were white with water and the tiniest burns were raging torrents.

The Amhain Chosaidh was a foaming, roaring cataract, fully 120ft. wide, hurtling into Loch Quoich. The top branches of trees were sticking out of the water in places and beyond, tantalisingly, we could see the path continuing. Soaked, frozen and exhausted we plodded up Glen Chosaidh, hoping to cross further up; but even after three miles and a division of the burn, the flow was still far too great. We tried a crossing with the use of a safety rope but were swept away. Darkness fell, we camped for the night and somehow rode out the storm until morning, when the water level had dropped sufficiently for us to make a safe crossing. We had been carrying full equipment and tents, for we had been on the march for four days and this probably saved our lives.

These conditions were of course exceptional, but do not underestimate the difficulty of crossing the Amhain Chosaidh in wet weather. This obstacle passed, it is only three more miles along the track before you meet the Quoich Bridge to Kinlochhourn road, where your transport should be waiting.

Right: A break in the perpetual rain clouds wreathing Loch Quoich allows a view towards Sgurr na Ciche (right) and Sgurr Mor (centre). The described route traverses the skyline ridge from just right of Sgurr Mor to Sgurr na Ciche. It then drops down to the loch and follows its north bank, to link up with the road at Quoich Bridge, directly below this viewpoint on Gleouraich. *Photo: Ken Andrew*

13   The Rois Bheinn Ridge of Moidart

Walk   The Rois Bheinn Ridge of Moidart.
Maps   O.S. 1:50,000 Sheet 40
Start from Glenfinnan (ref. 897810).
Finish at Lochailort (ref. 767824).
Grading   A mountain traverse of intermediate standard. The ridge is mainly broad and grassy but becomes rocky in the later stages.
Time   9 hours.
Distance   18 miles.
Escape Routes   Many of the bealachs provide easy routes down glens and corries N. of the main ridge. The low bealach W. of Beinn Odhar Bheag provides an escape route before the main massif is reached.
Telephones   Glenfinnan; Lochailort.
Transport   A regular passenger train service runs between Glenfinnan and Lochailort stations on the Fort William to Mallaig line.
Accommodation   Hotels and Bed and Breakfast in Glenfinnan and Lochailort. Youth Hostels at Glen Nevis and Garramore near Arisaig.
Guidebooks   S.M.T. Guide *The Western Highlands*.

Many years ago I was privileged to attend, as a guest, the Easter meet of the SMC. We stayed at the Stage House Hotel in Glenfinnan and the weather, as is so often the case in this area, was diabolical. On Sgurr nan Coireachan the snow devils filled my pockets, boots and shirt with spicules of ice, and Bill Murray was thrown to the ground by a lightning strike on nearby Sgurr Thuilm. When the weather finally abated I was off once more to the Munros but the President, Robert Grieve, and a select party of climbers, announced that at last Rois Bheinn, the pick of the Moidart Hills, could be attempted. They returned late in the evening, glowing with success and over malt whiskies recounted the day's adventures. From that day onwards I determined to acquaint myself with the Rois Bheinn range in the wilds of Moidart.

Moidart is unfashionable country for the climber and hill walker. It is out on a limb, wet and rough, and it boasts no Munros. Knoydart, too, is rough and remote but as such it is famous and Ladhar Bheinn attracts the ambitious walker.

South of the railway line between Glenfinnan and Lochailort lie two ranges of mountains. On the west side there is the Rois Bheinn/Druim Fiaclach group, which is linked to the Beinn Odhar Mhor and Bheag group, overlooking Loch Shiel, by a bealach at 1250ft. I began making plans: a traverse of both ridges would involve a long day in rugged and trackless hill country; the location would give superb views of the western seaboard and the Inner Hebrides, and the Highland Line would

provide speedy transport back to the starting point.

My first chance arose one day in early November. The hillsides were saturated and the burns brimming; it was a dismal day of low cloud but I have always been an optimist and I was hoping for an improvement. My son, Tim, and I crossed the swollen Shlatach river by the railway bridge, one and a half miles west of the Stage House Hotel, and plodded our way up An-t-Sleubhaich, the first point on the ridge. The slopes were of coarse grass (a sure sign of permanent saturation), scrub birch and rocky outcrops. We bypassed Lochan nan Sleubhaich on the east side and continued up into the clouds.

The rain poured down and streams filled every indentation; we caught the occasional glimpse down the precipitous east slopes to Loch Shiel, but the weather was deteriorating minute by minute. The broad ridge, dotted with perched boulders, led to the trig point on Beinn Odhar Mhor. Heads down, we battled on for a further mile south to Beinn Odhar Bheag, at 2,895ft., the highest point of the walk. Even at this height there were vast slabs of rock, evidence of the extensive glacier system which formed these mountains and carved out Loch Shiel. The buffets of wind were now of sufficient force to blow Tim over, so we beat a hasty retreat down to Bealach a' Choire Bhuidhe and thence to Loch Eilt.

Although the ridge had defeated us, I had seen enough to encourage me to return. The mountains were a true wilderness and, with the absence of paths, you needed to use your own experience and judgement to select your line of attack.

My second attempt was made the following April. Back in Glenfinnan, the monument built to commemorate the 1745 uprising rose into a clear blue sky and, plastered in fresh snow, Beinn Odhar Mhor and Bheag provided a stupendous spectacle towering straight up above Loch Shiel.

I made good speed over the Beinn Odhar range and, after crossing the Bealach a' Choire Bhuidhe, I was on new ground. A straight-forward ridge led to the pointed summit of the isolated peak, Beinn Mhic Cedidh. Leaving the attractive narrow north ridge for another day I descended to the low bealach under Druim Fiaclach. The lochans marked on the

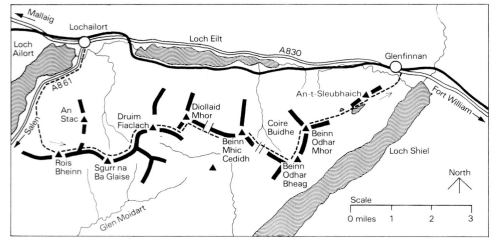

map were buried under deep snow and, as the going was tough, I traversed round the south side of Diollaid Mhor to gain the summit ridge of Druim Fiaclach.

The peaks of Glenfinnan, Loch Arkaig and Knoydart were particularly prominent, but my eyes were constantly drawn down to the dark waters of Loch Eilt, with its pine-covered islands. The lochs and the green glens were a pleasant contrast to the glare of the snow on the high ridges. Through the still air came the hoot of the midday diesel to Mallaig.

Druim Fiaclach is a sharply pointed mountain, with a fine east-west ridge that falls away steeply on either side. Two miles further on, the north face of Sgurr na Ba Glaise gave the biggest cornices of the day, but then the ridge dropped gently to the bealach under Rois Bheinn.

The shapely peak standing aloof, a mile north of the main ridge, is An Stac. An old wall runs up from the bealach under An Stac to the bealach under Sgurr na Ba Glaise, and continues over both summits of Rois Bheinn.

Sitting on the rounded trig point of Rois Bheinn's eastern summit, I surveyed the magnificent view. Steep cliffs fell away to the north, the old wall continued across the saddle to the west peak, and Loch Sunart glinted ten miles away to the south; but it was the seascape that commanded most of my attention. Prominent, out to the west, was the Sgurr of Eigg, with the snow covered Cuillin of Rhum beyond, and a faint outline of the Cuillin of Skye visible across the Sound of Sleat. Closer at hand was Loch Ailort and the Sound of Arisaig, with their low rocky islands and rafts used for the farming of salmon and sea trout.

I ambled across to the west summit of Rois Bheinn and glissaded down a steep tongue of snow towards the Alisary burn. After negotiating a deer fence, I reached the road beside Loch Ailort in double quick time.

An alternative method of descent from Rois Bheinn would be to follow the long west ridge down to Roshven Farm, where there is a licensed restaurant and tea room. But this would mean a four and a half mile road walk to the railway station at Lochailort, whereas the descent to Alisary is two miles less.

This is one of the finest hill walks in Britain. It is rich in variety and tradition and it commands panoramic views. The walk is long but not too arduous and, in my opinion, ranks very highly in this book.

Above: A view to the west along the Rois Bheinn ridge from Druim Fiaclach. Rois Bheinn is in the centre and the mountain on the left is Sgurr Na Ba Glaise. *Photo: Donald Bennet*

SCOTLAND   Isle of Skye, Inverness-shire

14   The Round of Coire Lagan

by Tom Weir

Walk   The Round of Coire Lagan
Maps   Scottish Mountaineering Trust special map of the Cuillin, about 3 inches to a mile, outline contour; O.S. 1:25,000 Outdoor Leisure Map — The Cuillin and Torridon Hills.
Start and finish at Glen Brittle Memorial Hut (ref. 411216).
Grading   Very Difficult rock climbing is necessary to complete the described route, but this can be reduced to Moderate if the difficulties are bypassed.
Time   8 hours.
Distance   8 miles.
Escape Routes   The Alasdair Stone Chute and the An Stac screes lead easily down into Coire Lagan.
Telephones   Glen Brittle House
Transport   Regular week-day bus services from Kyleakin to Sligachan and Carbost. Infrequent service from Carbost to Glen Brittle.
Accommodation   Sligachan Hotel, Glen Brittle Lodge, Post Office, Youth Hostel, Camp Site, B.M.C. Climbing Hut, Glen Brittle.
Guidebooks   S.M.T. Guide *The Island of Skye; Scottish Climbs.* Vol. 2 by Hamish MacInnes; S.M.C. *Cuillin of Skye* Vol. 1 by J. W. Simpson.

If I tell you that we had never heard of a rope sling, and that three of us were tied on 80ft. of stout hemp rope, you will know that we were pretty innocent on that first visit to the Cuillin in the 1930s. We were in Coire Lagan, high up on Collie's Climb, and a bit overpowered by the perpendicularity of the blank wall of rock jutting into the mist above us and the big plunge below to the hidden lochan from where we had started.

We were intent on doing the round of Coire Lagan and now were regretting not having taken the easy way by the Sgumain Stone Chute, instead of a direct ascent to Sgurr Alasdair. Our 'Bible' was the SMC Isle of Skye guidebook, its red covers already dog-eared and the pages matted by the rain which had drenched us on the pinnacles of Sgurr nan

Gillean and the crags of Blàven.

From Glen Sligachan we had made the big mistake of shouldering our soaking camp gear over Drumhain down to Loch Coruisk, and on round the swollen burns of the soggy coast to perch our two-man tent on the only dryish spot we could find, on the edge of a sea-cliff plunging into Loch Brittle.

By morning weariness had vanished, and so had our urge to carry these bags another step. From our tent we contoured directly upward, thirsting for adventure. Collie's Climb certainly provided it. We had never seen such a daunting place. We consulted the guidebook once again. Yes, it told us of the great steepness of the climb, but said that holds were so good that anything short of an overhang could be climbed on them.

'Well,' said the boldest of our trio, who had tried the pitch and failed, 'If that's rock climbing, I'm no rock climber.' The swirling mist and the slipperiness of the grey basalt seemed to emphasize the balefulness of our dilemma. The stage was set for eighteen-year old me to try, but I had hardly scraped my clinkers on the first foothold before Matt was calling me back and attacking the pitch once more, hardly pausing in his determination to get up. In one more thrilling hour the highest point of the Cuillin was ours.

I can still see in my mind's eye the grinning faces of my jubilant companions as we perched on the tiny point of summit, named after Sheriff Alexander Nicolson of Skye in honour of the first ascent of the mountain in 1873 by way of the Great Stone Chute. A short

scramble and we were looking down that great rent in the cliffs whose other edge is Sgurr Thearlaich, which was our route. A short sharp climb on good clean holds and we were there.

Now for Sgurr Mhic Choinnich, if we could find the way from Thearlaich on slabs so smooth that we were wondering if we had gone wrong. But sudden reassurance came to us, when ahead there loomed a prow like an Atlantic liner cleaving the clouds. We stared awestruck as detail was gradually revealed. Yes, there was Collie's Ledge — an obvious corridor across the verticalities, enabling one to attain the summit from the hidden easier side. But our eyes were on King's Chimney, leading directly up the face like an arrow.

Where was our timidity now? We had tasted

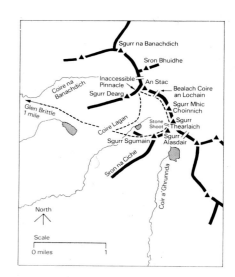

some real mountaineering and wanted more of it. We sang for pleasure up the slippery cleft, and wondered a bit about a strange flickering light that pierced the mist from time to time. We found out on top when the clouds moved and we could see the Atlantic ocean and a dark sky lit by lightning flashes. We had more eyes, however, for what was happening in front of us, with the mist parting and boiling over the corries and the knife-blade of our ridge soaring to An Stac and the Inaccessible Pinnacle.

The memory of the next bit is of sheer exhilaration as we sped along one of the narrowest ridges of the Cuillin. Energy seemed to flow from us as we rocketed over everything to get to the Pinnacle itself. How often we had

studied the guidebook photograph, wondering if we could get up the famous short side. No sign of nervousness from Matt now. He hardly paused on the awkward slab at half-way.

We didn't whoop for joy, though, until we had hitched the rope and were safely down. We'd done it, the round of Coire Lagan, or nearly all. What matter that this most difficult peak in Britain had been climbed by the Pilkington brothers as long ago as 1880? Charles Pilkington is immortalized in Sgurr Thearlaich, just as Britain's first real mountain guide, John MacKenzie, is enshrined by having Sgurr Mhic Choinnich named after him in Gaelic.

What a discovery for British alpinists to

make after the Matterhorn had been climbed, a range of true rock peaks at home, still awaiting first ascents. It was Collie and MacKenzie who discovered the Cioch in 1894, and climbed it. Collie, world wide mountain explorer, so loved the Cuillin that he settled permanently in Sligachan Hotel in 1939, and is buried with John MacKenzie in the little cemetery of Struan.

Nobody had told us of the delights of the fine screes forming a grey curtain falling to Coire Lagan and sliding us down effortlessly. Then by rock slabs and shore path we got back to the tent out on the headland. Weary and hungry, we needed no rocking to get to sleep. Later, in the small hours of the morning, we were shatteringly reminded of those menacing lightning flashes, by a crash of continuous noise that I have not heard equalled before or since.

The Cuillin corries were an echo chamber, sending back each rip of thunder, and before one had died away the next one recharged the noise. Rods of rain came through our tent as if it didn't exist. Soon we were cramming things into our rucksacks, as the floor of the tent became a raging burn, washing over our gear. For an hour and a half there was no let up, then came a lull and we started for Glen Brittle, having to use combined tactics to minimize the risk of being swept away in the more difficult burns.

Top: Looking over a cloud-sea to Blaven and Clach from Sgurr Dearg. *Photo: John Allen*

Bottom: The Inaccessible Pinnacle and Sgurr Banachdich, from the slopes of Sgurr Alasdair. *Photo: Donald Bennet.*

One of our party pulled out and went home. Matt and I went back to finish Coire Lagan, for we had still not done the bit of the ridge between Sgurr Sgumain and Sgurr Alasdair. Wise men would have stayed indoors. We scrambled up Sgumain's North Buttress in the chilling rain and were surprised by how difficult we found the 'Bad Step' on the ridge.

In numerous traverses of the round of Coire Lagan since then, I have avoided this awkward bit by descending rightward and taking the little chimney leading up back to the crest of the ridge. There is nothing harder than Very Difficult on the traverse by the route I have described. But take account of the weather. The ridge is not all rough gabbro. The smoother basalt gets slippery, and you have to maintain vigilance even though you get cold and chilled with wet.

In a poetic appreciation of the Black Cuillin, Professor Norman Collie wrote of the mountain mystery which wraps them round: 'Not the mystery of clearness such as is seen in the Alps and Himalaya, where range after range recedes into the infinite distance, till the white snow peaks cannot be distinguished from the clouds, but in the secret beauty born of the mists, the rain, and the sunshine in a quiet untroubled land, no longer vexed by the more rude and violent manifestations of the active powers of nature'.

I had this on the Inaccessible Pinnacle not so long ago, on a May morning of drifting mists playing hide-and-seek with the changing coloured rocks.

We had started at Gars Bheinn from the Loch Coruisk hut, and after six hours had been trying to shut our eyes to the fact that on both sides of us the hills had disappeared, from Torridon on one side to the Outer Hebrides on the other.

The collision of the clouds hit us on the Bealach Coire Banachdich as we swallowed a sandwich. The violence and coldness of the rain, which changed to snow, made up our minds that this was no mere spring shower. Below us was the gully which goes down easily to Loch Coruisk, and a full thousand feet of old snow invited a glissade.

We had taken the precaution of equipping ourselves with ice-axes against such a contingency. It was my third failure to complete the ridge traverse due to weather. I'll be back.

15   The Cuillin Hills of Rhum

Rhum is a very small island, only seven miles by nine, but it contains perhaps a greater variety of scenery than any similar area of land in Britain. It is rightly known as the jewel of the Inner Hebrides and I have never met a visitor to Rhum who has not fallen completely under its spell.

The Cuillin Hills of Rhum are a complex mixture of volcanic rock, red Torridonian sandstone and Lewisian gneiss. They are not as steep as the Cuillin of Skye and you can explore the high ridges in safety, without needing rock expertise. The main mountain ridge is in the south of the island and, whilst on the tops, you are constantly aware of the sea, for the waves crash against the rugged coastline below and seagulls screech and wheel overhead.

A Macbrayne's steamer from Mallaig calls at the island several times a week, but if you

wish to stay overnight you must write first to the National Trust for Scotland at 5 Charlotte Square, Edinburgh. The National Trust run a part of Kinloch Castle as a hotel. If you cannot obtain accommodation you must be prepared to camp, or walk five miles down the coast from the landing stage at Kinloch to a tiny bothy at Dibidil. If you do decide on Dibidil, you would be advised to bring a hammock and hang all food from the rafters, for the bothy is alive with rats. A rat inside one's sleeping bag at night does not make an ideal companion; this happened to a friend last time we stayed there.

The greater traverse of the Cuillin, from Barkeval to Ruinsival, may not look far on the map, but don't underestimate this walk, for at the end of the day you must return to the starting place on foot, as there is no alternative transport. The highest peak, Askival, is only

Walk   The Cuillin Hills of Rhum
Maps   O.S. 1:50,000 Sheet 39
Start and finish at Kinloch (ref. 403995).
Grading   A long and arduous mountain traverse over rough ground. Some rock scrambling involved. A rope should be carried.
Time   10-11 hours
Distance   19 miles.
Escape Routes   From the Bealach an Oir south down Glen Dibidil to Dibidil Bothy. West from Bealach an Fhuarain down to Glen Harris.
Telephones   There is only one public telephone on the island, at Kinloch.
Transport   There is no transport on Rhum. The Small Isles ferry, run by MacBraynes, leaves Mallaig several times a week. Rail services to Mallaig from Fort William and Glasgow.
Accommodation   Camping only with permission from the Nature Conservancy Warden. Bothy at Dibidil 5 miles south of Kinloch.
Guidebooks   S.M.T. Guide *The Islands of Scotland; Rhum* by Hamish Brown (Cicerone Press).

Above: Hallival and Askival from Trollaval.
Photo: Phil Cooper

61

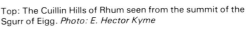

2,663ft., but it rises straight up from sea level, the bealachs on the ridge are low, and the slopes rocky and tiresome. There are few easy stretches where you can get into a rhythm.

The names of the principal mountains, Barkeval, Hallival, Askival, Trollaval and Ainshval, are of Norse origin and were given to provide landmarks for passing ships.

The Mallaig steamer anchors in Loch Scresort and you will be transported to the pier near Kinloch Castle by the estate launch! The castle was built in 1900 by Sir George Bullough, who had the red sandstone shipped in blocks from Arran. It is now used by the Nature Conservancy who own Rhum and carry out experiments on forestry and the ranching of Red Deer.

From Kinloch Castle, take the good Land-Rover track that runs due west alongside the river. After about half a mile, leave this track and strike up the rough hillside towards Barkeval. There is no path and the going is boggy, but as you climb higher a wonderful view unfolds. Across the Sound of Sleat rise the Cuillin of Skye, but it is the smaller islands that hold your gaze. Eigg, Muck, Canna, Sanday and, if you are lucky, the skerries of Oigh-sgeir and Umaolo, islets way out to the west which warrant grazing for five sheep and one sheep respectively. One bright November morning I leant into a tearing wind on Barkeval; my eyes were streaming but I could see the waves dashing over the skerries — I felt for that lonely sheep on Umaolo! Nearer the coast the little Mallaig prawners were riding out the gale, since it was far too rough for any creels to be lifted.

From Barkeval summit descend gently to the bealach and then climb up again to the Hallival-Askival ridge. The turf on each side of this ridge is riddled with holes, the breeding ground of colonies of Manx shearwaters. In September the young birds leave their holes and walk, stumble and flutter their way down to the sea.

The rocky ridge of Askival looms above and looks quite forbidding. The famous Askival Pinnacle, which is made much of in some guidebooks, is really only an airy step and it can easily be turned, by the faint-hearted, on the east side. Askival, too, is a superb view-point and I have twice seen golden eagles from the summit trig point. Scramble down the rocks on the west side until you can see the obvious ridge leading to the Bealach an Oir (Pass of Gold). From here there is an easy escape route down Glen Dibidil to the bothy, and thence back to Kinloch by the coast path.

For the main ridge, however, you must ascend the rocky slopes directly ahead, which take you to the twin summits of Trollaval. Below, to the west, is Glen Harris to which you will descend much later in the day! Another steep scramble down the slopes due south takes you to the Bealach an Fhuaran, an imposing defile between rocky hillsides. Now climb up 800ft. of difficult slopes with some awkward buttresses to be avoided near the top. You should be able to pick out a reasonable route as you descend Trollaval. This, the last steep ascent of the day, takes you to Ainshval and a broad level ridge leading round to Sgurr nan Gillean.

The main ridge swings away due west about half a mile before the summit of Sgurr nan Gillean, but it is well worth-while to make this short detour. Sgurr nan Gillean is one of the most prominent peaks of the Cuillin and is also an excellent view-point. Below the peak is a break in the high cliffs of the coast, and behind a shingle beach stands Papadil Lodge. Papadil must be one of the most unusual and beautifully situated shooting lodges in all Scotland. It

was built by the Bulloughs on a level site, well sheltered by a copse of trees and giant rhododendrons, and it enjoys perfect peace and solitude. In 1970 the lodge still boasted wicker and cane chairs, a chaise-longue, panelled rooms and a dinner service emblazoned with coat of arms — clearly it had been vacated in a hurry. Two years later, however, the roof had given away and rhododendron tendrils were growing through the windows, but in spite of the decay it had not lost its aura of by-gone days.

Return now to the main ridge and continue west along an easy ridge for one and a half miles, until you reach Ruinsival. This is your last mountain of the day but the difficulties are not quite over. The descent from Ruinsival on the north side is complex, with numerous cliffs and rock outcrops, and should not be undertaken in darkness. Scree slopes lead down to the coast at Harris, where there are a few ruined crofts and a mausoleum and where, on my last visit, I saw a herd of wild goats with shaggy coats and long horns.

In wet weather, note that the big Rangail burn is bridged a quarter of a mile up from the sea shore. Here you will meet again the good track that leads you, in six miles, back to Kinloch.

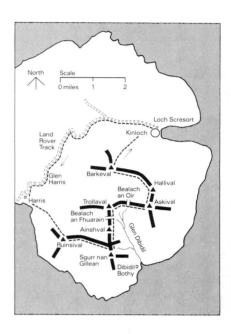

Below: The Isle of Eigg from Trollaval. *Photo: Phil Cooper*

16   Creag Meagaidh

Walk   Creag Meagaidh.
Maps   O.S. 1:50,000 Sheet 34
Start from Aberarder Farm (ref. 480870).
Finish at Glen Spean (ref. 390817).
Grading   A moderate walk over broad, boulder-strewn ridges.
Time   9 hours.
Distance   16 miles.
Escape Routes   Easy descents may be made from the Window down to Coire Ardair and from the Bealach a' Bharnish down Glen na h-Uamha to Loch Laggan side.
Telephones   Moy Lodge.
Transport   Railway Station at Tulloch (Glasgow-Fort William line). Friday bus service (Highland Omnibuses Ltd.) between Aviemore and Fort William runs alongside Loch Laggan.
Accommodation   Hotels at Roy Bridge, Loch Laggan and Newtonmore. Youth Hostel at Kingussie.
Guidebooks   S.M.T. Guide *The Central Highlands*.

I have very happy memories of the Creag Meagaidh range and, whenever I am with friends who are strangers to the Highlands, I suggest this traverse, for it is an excellent introduction to all that is best in Scottish mountaineering. The traverse of the range involves the ascent of four separate Munros, which in itself provides adequate motivation, but the route combines broad and level ridges, steep faces and extensive plateaux. The highest point of the walk is the summit of Creag Meagaidh itself, at 3,700ft., which is sufficiently high to provide views ranging from the Cairngorms to Knoydart and from Torridon to Ben Nevis. Standing in the northern section of the Central Highlands, Creag Meagaidh carries a great deal of snow, which lasts well into the summer; and in Coire Ardair it boasts one of the most magnificent winter corries anywhere in Scotland, both scenically and from a climbing point of view. Thus, as is so often the case in Scotland, the walk is best done in spring when the cliffs of Coire Ardair are still plastered in snow. I recommend that the walk be done from east to west, because that way Coire Ardair and Coire na h-Uamha of Beinn a' Chaoruinn can be seen to their best advantage.

Access to the range is simple, for the mountain traverse runs parallel to the main A86 road alongside Loch Laggan, linking Spean Bridge with Newtonmore. Escape from any of the four summits to the road is relatively simple if the need arises, but the walk is not too arduous and is one to be thoroughly enjoyed.

Start the walk from Aberarder Farm, on the north side and about midway along Loch Laggan. A good track leaves from behind the farm buildings and runs beside the Allt Coire Ardair burn. This track leads to Coire Ardair, and you follow it for a mile as it passes some twisted and bent birch trees and steadily ascends the southern slopes of Carn Liath. When the track levels off you should leave it and climb the steep hillside in a northerly direction to gain the boulder-strewn summit of Carn Liath, where there is a large cairn.

One beautifully sunny and warm day in mid March, my wife and I climbed up to Carn Liath, passing dozens of lizards basking on the rocks. It was one of those perfect days, which started with a keen frost icing the puddles and stilling the burns; yet, when the sun got up it was warm enough for shirt sleeves.

From Carn Liath the broad ridge stretches west, passing a subsidiary summit at 3,180ft., before narrowing and bending towards the south-west. You pass Coire Chriochairein, which sports a semi-circle of cliffs facing south and two minor corries which face north, before you reach your second Munro, Poite Coire Ardair, at 3,460ft. This summit overlooks Coire Ardair and the lochan which nestles under the 1,500ft. high buttresses. Many idyllic camp sites can be found on the shores of this lochan.

The cliffs of Coire Ardair are one and a half miles in length and they provide dozens of mountaineering routes. The gullies, known as 'posts', provide winter climbs of the highest standard.

The only break in the defences of Coire Ardair lies on the north side. The cliffs of the main corrie and those of Poite Coire Ardair fall away steeply to give an abrupt break or window, which can easily be ascended on either side. This window in the cliffs was probably used by Bonnie Prince Charlie in 1746, during the months after the battle of Culloden, when he was relentlessly pursued by the Redcoats. Prince Charlie finally escaped by boat to France in September of that year.

To gain the summit plateau of Creag Meagaidh from the Window, it is necessary to scramble up a steep slope for 500ft., and in spring when the snow is hard this can involve step-cutting or the use of crampons. Follow the line of the cliffs above Coire Ardair for half a mile and then turn westwards across gently

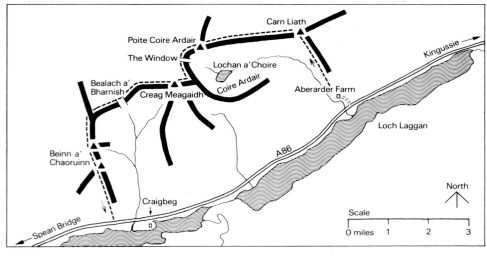

sloping ground. After another half mile you will reach the Creag Meagaidh cairn at 3,700ft.

Due south across Loch Laggan you have wonderful views of the high corrie on Beinn a' Chlachair, and beyond to the long ridge of Beinn Eibhinn, Aonach Beag and Geal Charn; a walk described elsewhere in this book. To the west the view is dominated by the great east face of Beinn a' Chaoruinn, your next objective.

Continue walking west for one and a half miles, until you reach the Bealach a' Bharnish, a gentle descent of 1,000ft. If, however, you wish to cut the walk short after Creag Meagaidh, proceed west from the summit for only half a mile and then descend the broad and easy ridge which runs south and leads in to Glen Spean, at Moy.

The great Coire na h'Uamha of Beinn a'

Chaoruinn curves round eastwards on the north side, and this east ridge provides an easy route to the almost flat summit of the mountain. The corrie, although a mile long, is not as steep and is much more broken than Coire Ardair; in winter, though, it looks very fine as you approach it from Creag Meagaidh.

Beinn a' Chaoruinn is a whale-backed mountain running north-south for one and a half miles, and the true summit, at 3,437ft., lies at the southern extremity.

It is a very short and simple descent down the continuation of the summit ridge to reach the main road in Glen Spean near Craigbeg. Unless you have been able to arrange a lift you will have a further eight and a half miles to walk back along the road to your car at Aberarder Farm.

Above: The extensive cliffs of Creag Meagaidh grouped around the bowl of Coire Ardair and its small lochan. This photograph is taken from the slopes of Carn Liath near the start of the recommended walk. The walk continues to the right, over the summit of Poite Coire Ardair, to gain 'The Window' (the obvious col to the right of the cliffs) from whence the summit plateau of Creag Meagaidh is gained. Meagaidh's cliffs, vegetated and wet in the summer, provide an ideal setting for the ice-climber in the winter conditions depicted here. *Photo: Richard Gilbert*

17   The Mamores

Walk   The Mamores.
Maps   O.S. 1:50,000 Sheet 41; O.S. 1:63,360 Tourist Map — Ben Nevis and Glencoe.
Start and finish at the Youth Hostel in Glen Nevis (ref. 127718).
Grading   A long and undulating walk mainly above the 3,000 ft. level.
Time   10-11 hours.
Distance   22 miles.
Escape Routes   North down Coire Mhusgain from the bealach between Stob Ban and Sgor an Iubhair. South to Kinlochleven down Coire na Ba from the bealach between Am Bodach and Stob Coire a' Chairn.
Telephones   Glen Nevis Y.H.; Kinlochleven.
Transport   Fort William has good road and rail links with Edinburgh and Glasgow. In summer a daily bus service runs up Glen Nevis to the lower falls.
Accommodation   Hotels and Guest Houses in Fort William. Youth Hostel in Glen Nevis.
Guidebooks   S.M.T. Guide *The Central Highlands*. *The Scottish Peaks* by W. A. Poucher (Constable).

Below: The elegant hills of the Mamore Forest, seen from the summit of Carn Mor Dearg near Ben Nevis. Binnein Mor (3,700ft.), the highest peak of the group, is on the extreme left, and Sgurr a'Mhaim is the dominant peak on the right (above the sunlit col). *Photomontage: E. A. Shepherd*

As you drive up Glen Nevis and pass the Youth Hostel, the valley opens up to give a wonderful view of the hills of the Mamore Forest. Ahead of you, Sgurr a' Mhaim rises gracefully to 3,601ft., with its high north-facing corrie carrying snow until early summer. Beyond Sgurr a' Mhaim, a high and complex ridge runs in an easterly direction and provides a fine high-level walk, parallel to, but due south of, the superb Aonachs – Grey Corries ridge. Although the walk I am about to describe does not take in all the outlying summits of the Mamore Forest, it involves a continuous ridge, eight miles long, lying mainly above 2,750ft. and including seven separate Munros.

Leave the Glen Nevis road one mile beyond the Youth Hostel and walk up one of the fire breaks through the forestry plantations to gain the lower slopes of the north ridge of Sgor Chalum. This subsidiary top of 1,823ft. marks the end of the two-mile long northern spur of Mullach nan Coirean. The angle is gentle and the ascent to the Mullach is delightful, with an ever-widening vista of hills opening out to the north and east as you gain height. Mullach nan Coirean is flat-topped with good corries on

all sides, and from the summit you should follow the lip of the huge eastern corrie for one and a half miles until you reach the abrupt north ridge of Stob Ban.

Climb steeply up the white quartzite-strewn ridge, keeping the precipitous east face on your left, until you reach the sharp summit. Coire a' Mhusgain is the deep corrie below, enclosed on the east side by Sgurr a' Mhaim. The main ridge, however, bypasses Sgurr a' Mhaim, which lies one mile northwards of your next summit, Sgor an Iubhair, and is connected to it by the narrow Devil's Ridge.

From Stob Ban you can see, six miles away to the east, the broad wedge-shaped mountain of Binnein Mor (3,700ft.), rising well above the other Mamore peaks. Sgor an Iubhair is barely a mile away and you need only drop 700ft. to the intervening bealach, which is situated above a high corrie ringed with cliffs and containing a tiny lochan. If you keep to the lip of this corrie you will not go wrong.

Sgor an Iubhair (3,300ft.) has not the status of a separate Munro, for there is not sufficient drop between it and its more elevated neighbour, Am Bodach (3,382ft.), three-quarters of a mile further east. The ridge

between the two is broad and easy, and one early April day I followed the tracks of a fox, which had been raised above the general snow level. The pressure of the fox's paws had consolidated the snow and prevented it from being blown away.

Am Bodach is at the head of Coire a' Mhail and you can see down to the climbers' cottage and suspension bridge at Steall in Upper Glen Nevis. Across Glen Nevis rises the long slope of Ben Nevis, and you have a good view of the great cascade of the Allt Coire Eoghainn, rushing down vast slabs of rock on its way to the Nevis river. The north-east buttress of Ben Nevis is outlined against the sky as it plunges down from the summit plateau, whilst to the right of the Ben is the gentle curve of the Carn Mor Dearg arête. The view south from Am Bodach includes the upper reaches of Loch Leven, with the Aonach Eagach ridge and the massif of Bidean nam Bian lying beyond.

Follow the north-east ridge of Am Bodach, as it switchbacks over a subsidiary summit before rising to Stob Coire a' Chairn, the point marked 3,219ft. on the map.

The main back-bone ridge of the Mamores now swings eastwards, but two fine summits

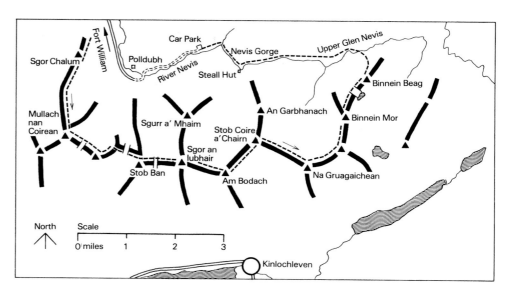

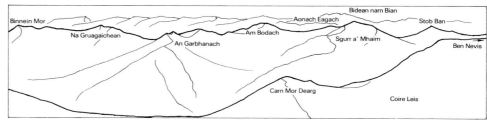

lie close by to the north: firstly, An Garbhanach (3,150ft.), then An Gearanach (3,250ft.), which is reached via a razor-sharp ridge. This ridge is less well known but, I think, more dramatic than the Devil's Ridge, but unless you want to collect the Munro of An Gearanach you should leave it for another day.

To the south of Stob Coire a' Chairn, the deep Coire na Ba falls away to end at Kinlochleven, and a good stalker's path leads from there to the bealach between your next peak, Na Gruagaichean, and Stob Coire a' Chairn. Beyond this bealach a well-defined ridge rises to Na Gruagaichean (3,442ft.), which has two tops a quarter of a mile apart. It is now only a short way to the whale-backed mountain of Binnein Mor. The south summit is reached first, then the higher north summit (3,700ft.), which is gained via a narrow ridge. Even in the company of its higher neighbours to the north

of Glen Nevis, Binnein Mor holds its own as a fine mountain. Views extend from Ben Alder to Ben Cruachan.

Below you to the north is the sharp-pointed little peak of Binnein Beag, looking barely worthy of Munro status. When you have descended the broken and bouldery north ridge of Binnein Mor, however, and are pausing at the lochan under the southern slopes of Binnein Beag, you will appreciate its

attractiveness. It is an easy climb to gain its summit and your seventh and final Munro of the day.

Descend northwards into Upper Glen Nevis and, if possible, cross the river where a good path on the north bank leads you back past the old ruin at Steall, the climbers' cottage beside the waterfall, and the magnificent Nevis gorge. It is a very rewarding seven-mile walk back to your starting point.

Above: Billowing clouds about to sweep across Binnein Mor, the highest of the Mamore peaks. This photograph is taken from the slopes of Am Bodach, showing the attractive approach ridge to the twin summits of Na Gruagaichean (middle distance), the highest of which is already swathed in cloud. *Photo: Donald Bennet*

18 Ben Nevis and the Lochaber Traverse

Walk   Ben Nevis and the Lochaber Traverse.
Maps   O.S. 1:50,000 Sheet 41; O.S. 1:63,360 Tourist Map — Ben Nevis and Glencoe.
Start from Youth Hostel in Glen Nevis (ref. 127718). Finish at Spean Bridge (ref. 221816).
Grading   An exceptionally arduous walk over the highest hills in the British Isles. In winter conditions it is a major mountaineering expedition.
Time   13 hours.
Distance   25 miles.
Escape Routes   From Carn Mor Dearg take the N.W. ridge down to the Allt a' Mhuilinn path. From Aonach Mor descend the N. ridge to the Leanachan Forest. From Stob Coire Easain descend the N. ridge over Beinn na Socaich to the Cour Glen.
Telephones   Outside the Y.H. in Glen Nevis; Torlundy near Allt a' Mhuilinn path; Spean Bridge; Emergency telephone at C.I.C. Hut.
Transport   Fort William has good road and rail links with Edinburgh and Glasgow. In summer a daily bus service runs up Glen Nevis to the lower falls.
Accommodation   Hotels and Guest Houses in Fort William and Spean Bridge. Youth Hostel in Glen Nevis.
Guidebooks   S.M.T. Guide *The Central Highlands; The Scottish Peaks* by W. A. Poucher (Constable).

Right: Ben Nevis (4,406ft.), Britain's highest mountain, dominates the neighbouring peaks — Carn Mor Dearg on the left and the summits of the Mamores in the middle distance. The walk described in the accompanying chapter follows the snowy profile of Ben Nevis and Carn Mor Dearg and then leads off to the left to Aonach Beag and the Grey Corries. *Photo: John Dewar Studios*

This considerable mountain walk takes in not only the highest mountain in Great Britain, but also two other 4,000ft. peaks and a long ridge walk across the heart of Lochaber.

During the winter months the complete walk from Glen Nevis to Spean Bridge should not be attempted in one day, because the days are too short. Even during April you can expect delays through step-cutting and cramponing, and you run the risk of being benighted. If you start from Glen Nevis, though, you can find a number of places on the Grey Corries ridge, from which you can easily escape northwards to Glen Spean. Grey Corries is the name given to the long ridge comprising Sgurr Choinnich Mor, Stob Coire Easain and Stob Choire Claurigh, whose slopes fall away in grey coloured screes.

May or June are the ideal months for this walk. The days are long and, because these hills carry an immense amount of snow, you can expect an exhilarating day, with the ridge clear yet the corries still ringed with snow, and the huge cornices on the Aonachs still in place.

From the Youth Hostel in Glen Nevis, cross the river by the footbridge and follow one of the well-worn paths in the peat steeply upwards until you meet the pony track from Achintee Farm. For the next three hours or so you must put your head down and grit your teeth as you follow this nightmare path to the summit of Ben Nevis.

The track first winds round the shoulder of

Meall an Suidhe and then zig-zags up the stony wastes to the summit plateau. At least you should be early enough to avoid the streams of tourists, because if you aren't you most probably won't make Spean Bridge that night, for Ben Nevis is but the first of seven high mountains on your day's march.

Don't delay on the summit of the Ben, because there are more remote and rewarding summits ahead. From the cairn, descend the scree slopes in a south-easterly direction until you reach a warning notice and a line of posts. If there is any old snow or ice here, be extremely careful: the slopes on either side are convex and a slip might be hard to arrest. This is a notorious place for accidents and, in December 1954, five naval cadets were killed when they slid down into Coire Leis.

After a descent of 900ft. you reach the perfect curve of the Carn Mor Dearg arête. This rocky and narrow ridge leads you round to the south side of Coire Leis and on to Carn Mor Dearg itself. Below, in the corrie, you can see the famous climbers' hut dedicated to the Scottish climber, Charles Inglis Clark. My best ever continuous standing glissade was achieved one March day from the summit cairn of Carn Mor Dearg to the CIC Hut, a vertical drop of 1,900ft.

The two bulky mountains due east of you are the Aonachs: Aonach Mor (3,999ft.) on the left and Aonach Beag (4,060ft.) on the right. The names are surprising, since the Gaelic

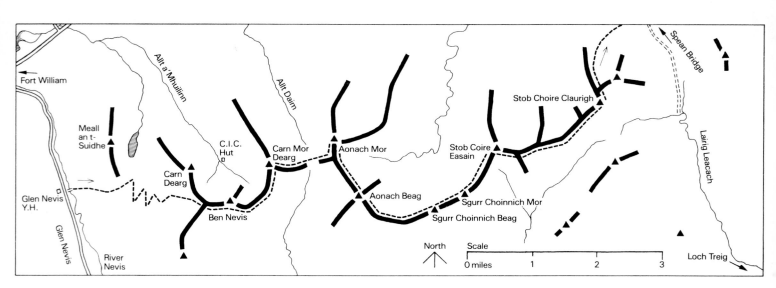

Above: The featureless, wind-swept slopes of Ben Nevis, straightforward in clear conditions, can be rapidly transformed into a dangerously hostile environment with the onset of bad weather. Many a walker and climber has battled down through the night, disorientated in this confusing terrain. *Photo: Bruce Atkins*

Previous page: Walkers set off from the summit of Carn Mor Dearg towards Ben Nevis. The fine, icy ridge that links the two mountains is one of the best sections of the Lochaber traverse, allowing views of the impressive cliffs and buttresses of the Ben. In this photograph, the North-East Buttress dominates on the right. *Photo: Ken Andrew*

word Mor means great and Beag means little.

A well-defined ridge leads steeply downwards, due east from the summit of Carn Mor Dearg, to the bealach under the main ridge of the Aonachs. Descend this ridge and then with no respite climb straight up again for 1,000ft. to gain the saddle between Aonach Mor and Aonach Beag.

Now turn south along the broad ridge which soon narrows and becomes rocky, before you reach your third 4,000ft. mountain, Aonach Beag. You have reached the half-way point of the walk and can afford to stop for a few minutes and admire the view. The high ridge of the Grey Corries stretches away to the east

and you can see your final peak, Stob Choire Claurigh, six miles away. To the south lies the Mamore Forest and beyond that the Aonach Eagach ridge and Bidean nam Bian. To the north-west lie range upon range of fine mountains: the Loch Arkaig group, the Loch Quoich group, Kintail, Glen Affric and Torridon. Away to the west you can see the perfect cone of Ben More on Mull.

Continue south to a subsidiary summit and then scramble down steeply to the col under Sgurr Choinnich Beag. In winter, when walking in the opposite direction I have been unable to surmount this rocky section due to poor quality snow and cornices. If you find

trouble here, proceed further south, where a less steep corrie under Sgurr a' Bhuic can be descended for a few hundred feet and then an easy traverse made to the Sgurr Choinnich Beag col.

The next section, over Sgurr Choinnich Mor and Stob Coire Easain, is narrow and in parts rocky and, in spite of fatigue, your interest will be maintained. After Stob Coire Easain, the ridge undulates over several subsidiary tops, before ascending to Stob Coire Claurigh, at 3,853ft., the last peak of the day. It is downhill all the way now, due north over gentle slopes of heather and rocks until you meet the Land-Rover track from Spean Bridge

to Loch Treig. Follow this down to Glen Spean, crossing the Cour River by the bridge just beyond Coire-choille, and in two miles you will reach Spean Bridge. This is a long descent but you can enjoy it to the full, knowing that you have completed one of the very best mountain walks to be found in Britain.

Top: Ben Nevis from Corpach, near Fort William. The Lochaber traverse takes the easy-angled slopes leading from Glen Nevis (right). After traversing the summit, the walker skirts round to Carn Mor Dearg, the snowy ridge to the left of the shadowy Nevis precipices. *Photo: Robert Adam*

Bottom: A view from the Mamores, showing Ben Nevis (left) and Carn Mor Dearg. *Photo: Donald Bennet*

Top left: The Grey Corries section of the Lochaber traverse. The walker is moving up the slopes of Sgurr Choinnich Beag. In the background is Sgurr a'Bhuic, a subsidiary peak of Aonach Beag which rises up on the right. *Photo: Ken Andrew*

Bottom left: Looking south across the icy slopes of Sgurr Choinnich Mor to Binnein Mor — the highest peak of the Mamores. *Photo: A. D. S. MacPherson*

Above: A view back along the whole Lochaber traverse, from Stob Choire Claurigh. The Grey Corries dominate in the foreground, and the major peaks of Aonach Beag and Ben Nevis are the prominent features in the distance. The full extent and grandeur of the walk is revealed in this detailed photograph, with the entertaining switchback ridges of the Grey Corries leading back towards the dominating bulk of the highest mountain in Britain — nearly ten miles of high-level ridge walking. *Photo: Ken Andrew*

19   Balmoral Forest and Lochnagar

Walk   Balmoral Forest and Lochnagar.
Maps   O.S. 1:50,000 Sheets 43 and 44; O.S. 1:63,360 Tourist Map of the Cairngorms. Start from Spittal of Glen Muick (ref. 310851). Finish at Braemar (ref. 151914).
Grading   A high and exposed mountain walk with no obvious escape routes.
Time   9 hours.
Distance   17 miles.
Escape Routes   Emergency shelter at Lochcallater Lodge. Easy descent to the Dubh Loch Glen from beallach east of Carn an t-Sagairt Mor.
Telephones   Spittal of Glen Muick; Braemar.
Transport   Ballater-Aberdeen daily bus service. Braemar-Ballater daily bus service.
Accommodation   Aberdeen University hut at Allt na-giubhsaich. Hotels, Guest Houses and Bed and Breakfast accommodation at Braemar and Ballater.
Guidebooks   S.M.T. Guide *The Cairngorms; The Scottish Peaks* by W. A. Poucher (Constable).

Top right: Near the summit of Lochnagar in summer, looking down the Black Spout into the crucible of cliffs dominating the northern slopes. *Photo: Tom Weir*

Bottom right: A view across the Lochnagar cliffs — Black Spout gully is the prominent feature in the centre of the picture. The walkers' route gains the summit by the slopes on the left. *Photo: Irvine Butterfield*

This walk takes you across the area of beautiful and spectacular mountain scenery known as the Royal Balmoral Deer Forest. It is an area steeped in tradition and romance and was a particular favourite of Queen Victoria and Prince Albert. Queen Victoria ascended Lochnagar in 1848 and wrote:

'On the summit there was thick fog, it was cold,
wet and cheerless and the wind was
blowing a hurricane.'

Byron wrote:

'England! Thy beauties are tame and
domestic
to one who has roved o'er the mountains
afar:
Oh for the crags that are wild and
majestic!
The steep frowning glories of dark
Lochnagar!'

The walk starts from the Spittal of Glen Muick, nine miles from Ballater, and unless you want to add two hours to your day you should arrange transport to take you there. The entire upper region of Glen Muick is now a Wild Life Sanctuary and camping is forbidden. The only possible accommodation is the Aberdeen University Mountaineering Club's hut across the river Muick at Allt-na-guibhsaich.

From the car-park near the small plantation at the Spittal, cross the river by a good bridge and continue along the road until you come to the Information Office on the right-hand side. On the other side of the road is the stalker's

cottage around which sizeable herds of deer congregate during the winter months. The stalker feeds them hay when the weather is severe.

Take the good track which leads across the glen to Allt-na-guibhsaich and continue along a recently bulldozed road through the trees until you reach the open hillside. This new rough road winds up through the heather, first on the south side and then on the north side of the burn. It continues on over the mountains to Deeside, but after two miles and just below the watershed you must leave this road and take the slanting path that crosses the burn and climbs up the open hillside ahead.

After an hour and 1,000ft. of ascent you arrive at the bealach between the shapely, rounded peak of Meikle Pap and the main bulk of Lochnagar. Pause here for a few minutes and look around. The corrie you see ahead is one of the finest in Scotland. In winter, the mile-long circle of cliffs, rising 1,200ft. above the corrie loch, provides climbing of all standards and, as it faces north, the snow lingers on until early summer.

The walk continues to the summit of Lochnagar which lies at the furthest (northernmost) end of the cliffs. You can either ascend the slopes of Lochnagar immediately to the south of the bealach, and walk round the edge of the cliffs for one and a half miles to reach the summit, or you can take a more sporting route. If you choose the latter, you must descend to the base of the cliffs and follow the narrow climbers' path round the corrie, until you reach the prominent wide gully called the Black Spout. Black Spout gully is Y-shaped and it can be climbed easily by either the left-hand or the right-hand branch. In summer, the gully provides a loose scramble up scree slopes, but in winter it provides a classic, though quite straightforward, snow climb. There is usually a small cornice at the top of the gully.

The summit cairn of Lochnagar is perched on the top of a huge boulder situated half a mile north of the Cac Carn Mor cairn and, at 3,786ft., it is just 18ft. higher than its near neighbour. The false summit of Cac Carn Mor is just above the cliffs near the top of the Black Spout.

The views are extensive. The huge mass of Ben Avon and Beinn a' Bhuird dominates the

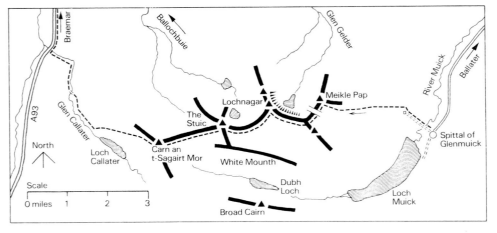

Above: The full extent of the Lochnagar cliffs, viewed from the tiny lochan in the corrie below. The Black Spout gullies are on the right, behind the large sunlit buttress. The cliffs are networked with fine winter climbs, mostly very difficult. *Photo: John Allen*

northern skyline across the valley of the Dee, but due south there is no high mountain massif, and King Arthur's Seat in Edinburgh and even the Cheviot in the border country have been sighted.

South of Lochnagar's summit lies a high barren wasteland known as the White Mounth. It makes for fast and easy walking, if you can avoid the peat hags, and in the summer the moss attracts many deer. You must now return to the Cac Carn Mor summit, half a mile south of the true summit, and then skirt the edge of another great corrie facing north-west, the Coire Lochan an Eoin. This corrie, too, guards a picturesque lochan, but the scenery is less dramatic than Lochnagar itself. Walk round to the cairn at point 3571, which overlooks the prominent rocky spur called the Stuic Buttress.

To the west of the Stuic lies a third corrie, containing two lochans. Continue along the lip of this corrie for half a mile and then turn abruptly 90° to ascend the wide north-east

ridge of Carn an t-Sagairt Mor (3,430ft.), the summit of which lies only one mile away.

Loch Callater lies due west of the summit cairn of Carn an t-Sagairt Mor, but if you descend the boulder-strewn slopes in a north-westerly direction you may be lucky enough to pick up an excellent stalkers' track that leads you down easily to Callater Lodge. When ascending Carn an t-Sagairt Mor from Callater Lodge, the stalkers' path peters out about 300ft. from the summit, near the remains of a crashed aeroplane; so, if you see wreckage, you can take heart, the path is near.

I have always found Glen Callater to be a lonesome and desolate place. The dark loch set amidst steep and bare hills has none of the romance of Loch Muick, with its stands of Caledonian pine trees, hazel and silver birch. However, a private road, sealed by a locked gate, runs up to Callater Lodge from the main A93 road. It is a comfortable two hours' walk down to Braemar for high tea or dinner in one of the excellent hotels in that village.

20 Beinn a' Bhuird and Ben Avon

The influx of visitors to the Cairngorms, following the development of Aviemore as a major tourist and skiing centre, has meant that only in the more remote hills and glens can one still experience the solitude and excitement of this unique range.

Skiers, hoisted to the summit of Cairngorm by mechanical means, wander over the plateau to Ben Macdui and beyond, while walkers make use of the numerous bothies and refuges to explore the main tops.

East of Glen Derry, however, lie two huge mountains, Beinn a' Bhuird and Ben Avon, which are very remote and consequently rarely visited. The corries of Beinn a' Bhuird rival the best that Braeriach has to offer, while the glens surpass in beauty even Glen Derry and Rothiemurchus. The walk I recommend is not the shortest way to traverse the mountains, but it is the most rewarding. It combines a long and fascinating approach march with the complete crossing of the extensive summit plateaux, and ends with another long walk through delightful glens back to civilization. The walk is equally fine in winter, when the corries are gleaming white with snow, or in the summer when the arctic flora of the high plateaux can be fully appreciated and when, with long hours of daylight, you need not feel under pressure. Transport will be needed from Braemar to the start at Linn of Dee, and at the end of the walk at Cock Bridge to take you back to Braemar.

From the bridge over the gorge at Linn of Dee, turn right along the road and after half a mile you will come to a locked gate on the left. Climb the gate and walk along the good track towards Derry Lodge. After passing through a magnificent stand of Scots Pines, you emerge into broad Glen Lui and cross the river by a wooden bridge. In winter and early spring you may see huge herds of deer in Glen Lui, for they are fed hay by the stalker from Luibeg Cottage. Half a mile beyond the bridge is another plantation and just beyond the road crosses a small burn. On the right-hand side of the burn you will find a narrow path which leads over the hillside to Glen Quoich. This path passes through a defile and skirts some beautiful shallow lochans, before emerging on to the open hillside overlooking Glen Quoich.

A wonderful scene lies before you. The combination of Beinn a' Bhuird and Ben

Avon, rising high above the old Caledonian Forests of Glen Quoich, and fast rivers sparkling over their rocky beds, cannot be bettered anywhere in Scotland. Near the banks of Quoich Water you meet a rough forestry track which you follow for half a mile north to a ford over the Dubh Ghleann tributary. Unless your visit follows a dry spell, this river will have to be waded and the crossing could be very troublesome in time of flood, so take care. The forestry track now divides and you should take the branch which leaves the bank of Quoich Water and climbs up through the trees towards the south shoulder of Beinn a' Bhuird, marked Bruach Mhor on the map. Leave the track at the point where it bends away from the burn, Alltan na Beinne, cross the burn and climb very steeply up the slopes ahead, which are heather-covered low down but rocky near the top of the broad south ridge of Beinn a' Bhuird. The cairn marking the south top of the mountain is at a height of 3,860ft., and is larger than the main top cairn one and a half miles further north.

From the south top, walk northwards, passing a granite tor, until you come to the precipitous edge of the great Coire an Dubh

Walk Beinn a' Bhuird and Ben Avon.
Maps O.S. 1:63,360 Tourist Map of the Cairngorms; O.S. 1:50,000 Sheet 36. Start from Linn of Dee (ref. 062896). Finish at Cock Bridge (ref. 257092).
Grading An exceptionally long and tough walk over high and remote mountains.
Time 13-14 hours.
Distance 29 miles.
Escape Routes There are no easy escape routes. A tiring party should not attempt to continue beyond Beinn a' Bhuird to Ben Avon but should retreat from The Sneck to Upper Glen Quoich.
Telephones Inverey; Derry Lodge; Cock Bridge.
Transport Daily bus service from Aberdeen to Braemar. There is no public transport to Cock Bridge but Grantown is connected to Elgin and Aviemore.
Accommodation Inn at Cock Bridge. Hotels and Guest Houses at Tomintoul and Braemar. Youth Hostels at Inverey, Braemar and Tomintoul.
Guidebooks S.M.T. Guide *The Cairngorms*.

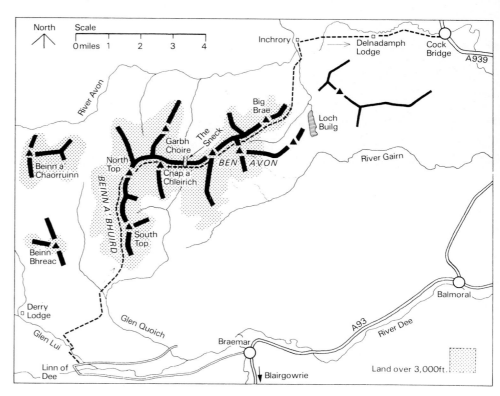

Above: Looking north-west from Glen Slugain to the eastern corries and the summit plateau of Bheinn a'Bhuird. The south top is on the left and 'The Sneck' is off-picture to the right. *Photo: John Allen*

Lochan. In misty weather watch carefully for the edge of the corrie, for cornices last well into the summer. Descend 100ft. to the head of the corrie and then climb again to the summit plateau and continue northwards. The next east-facing corrie you see is Coire nan Clach, and once again you must skirt the edge to gain the northern and highest point of Beinn a' Bhuird at 3,924ft. The summit plateau is a favourite haunt of the ptarmigan and in winter and spring their harsh croaking can be heard as they fly low over the rocks; in summer I have found a clutch of the young birds only a few yards away from the summit cairn.

Your traverse of Beinn a' Bhuird is not yet over, for you must now head east for a mile to the subsidiary summit of Cnap a' Chleirich. This is a cluster of large granite rocks above the stupendous north-facing Garbh Choire, one of the great sights of the Cairngorms. The corrie is deep and wide and is pierced by a magnificent buttress of clean rock, called the Mitre Ridge.

Continue east down easy slopes of loose, decayed, granite scree and moss to gain the bealach known as the Sneck, which at 3,100ft. divides the massifs of Beinn a' Bhuird and Ben

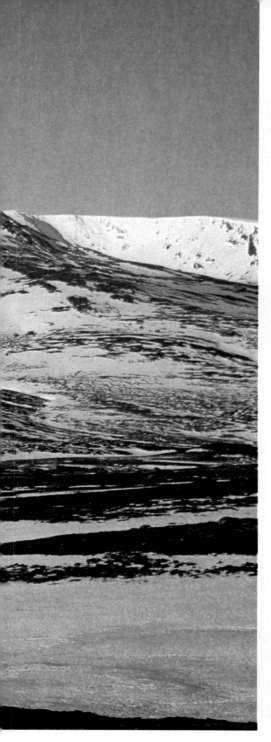

Avon.

Climb up to the plateau of Ben Avon and in less than a mile you reach the summit cairn at 3,843ft., perched on an enormous granite tor. The plateau stretches away to the east, with other granite tors dotted about at regular intervals. Follow the high ground for fully two miles in a north-easterly direction, until you reach the edge of the plateau at a rise named Big Brae. Continue in the same direction for the descent to Glen Builg, where you meet a path leading north to Inchrory Lodge. The Builg burn flows into the River Avon at Inchrory Lodge and these rivers are a fisherman's paradise. I have seen dozens of salmon resting nose to tail in the waters of the Builg burn.

Inchrory Lodge is a very well maintained white-painted shooting lodge and it is served by a Land-Rover track running east for six miles to Cock Bridge on the Braemar – Tomintoul road. Follow this track as it meanders pleasantly over the foot hills to Delnadamph Lodge and then hugs the south bank of the River Don to Cock Bridge, where the walk ends.

Top: Beinn a'Bhuird and the cliffs of Garbh Choire from the slopes of Ben Avon just above the Sneck. *Photo: Robert Adam*

Bottom: The summit tor of Ben Avon (3,843ft.). *Photo: Ken Andrew*

83

SCOTLAND   Cairngorms, Banffshire/Inverness-shire

21   The Cairngorm Four Thousanders

by Adam Watson

Walk   The Cairngorm Four Thousanders.
Maps   O.S. 1:25,000 Leisure Map — High Tops of the Cairngorms; O.S. 1:50,000 Sheet 36. Start and finish at Whitewell (ref. 917085).
Grading   An exceptionally long and arduous walk over a high and extensive plateau. It is very vulnerable and exposed to bad weather. For local weather forecast telephone Kingussie 308 or Cairngorm 261.
Time   15 hours.
Distance   29 miles.
Escape Routes   From Cairngorm down Fiacaill a' Choire Chais (easy ridge W. of Coire Cas). From Ben Macdui down to Glen Derry via Loch Etchachan. From Cairn Toul to Glen Geusachan. From Braeriach down to Gleann Einich via the slopes W. of Coire an Lochain.
Telephones   Glenmore; Coylumbridge; Cairngorm Chairlift; Derry Lodge.
Transport   Railway Station at Aviemore. Bus from Aviemore via Inverdruie to Cairngorm chairlift.
Accommodation   Hotels, Guest Houses, Bed and Breakfasts at Aviemore. Youth Hostels at Aviemore, Glenmore and Braemar. Bothies at Sinclair Hut, Corrour Bothy, Jean's Hut in Coire an Lochain of Cairngorm.
Guidebooks   S.M.T. Guide *The Cairngorms; The Scottish Peaks* by W.A. Poucher (Constable).

To me the Cairngorms are the finest hills in the world. I have seen hundreds of mountains in other countries that far surpass them in height, size, steepness and spectacular form. But nowhere else have I experienced the extraordinary variety and deep appeal that the Cairngorms have for those fortunate enough to come under their spell. When you step off the train at Aviemore and look up to them, you will catch a glimpse of their magic.

Old, smooth, rounded hills of rough pink granite, they brood above the great pine carpet of Rothiemurchus. They have an air of aloofness, timelessness and ancient mystery that far transcends our self-centred, technological modern world. If you read something of the local people's history and their recent Gaelic culture, and better still if you speak to them, you will find this adds much to the mystery

and appeal of the region. And when you finally set foot on the hills, you will find them a never-ending source of wonder. Do not hurry. Any fit person can run round these hills in a few short hours, but the Cairngorms offer so much that it is a wasted opportunity to hurry and not enjoy their potential fully.

For variety of hill-scene the Cairngorms are unsurpassed in Britain, from their big, arctic-like plateaux and scores of high corries and crags, to their many lochs, pine-clad slopes, wild glens and wind-swept moors. The variety of plant and animal life is greater than anywhere else in the British Isles. We still have here one of the most precious wilderness areas in these islands, in spite of the developers with their bulldozed roads and other schemes that have disfigured and damaged this magnificent heritage of ours.

Above: The Cairngorm plateau from near the summit of Cairn Gorm, looking south-west towards Cairn Lochan. Ben Macdui is on the left, beyond the trough of Glen Avon, and Cairn Toul and Braeriach are in the distance. *Photomontage: John Cleare*

Finest of all the hill walks in this marvellous piece of country is the tour of the four high 4,000-footers, Ben Macdui (4,296ft.), Cairn Gorm (4,084ft.), Braeriach (4,248ft.) and Cairn Toul (4,241ft.). Nowhere else in these islands can you be so high for so long; the wind-swept high plateaux roll on for miles under spacious skies. And nowhere else can you be in such arctic-like surroundings, where many snow-fields last through the summer. From July to October (mid May onwards if the thaw comes early), you need no more experience than for any hill walk where mist or other bad weather may come suddenly. But note that this is a long walk with much climbing, that your navigation in mist should be good as the plateaux are featureless and remote, and that in sudden cold weather you can experience fresh snowfalls and bitter winds

in any summer month. May and June vary greatly; the hills are largely clear of snow by mid May in an early year but still lie under an almost complete blanket till the end of June in a late year. If you have no experience of steep snow, do not start this tour when the top parts of the Cairngorms appear more than half snow-covered. Respect these hills, and realize how puny man is.

The easiest — and worst — route is to drive up the Cairn Gorm road and ride the chair lift, but you will also see crowds, litter, and a disfigured hillside. You then walk south to Ben Macdui, descend to cross the Dee at Corrour, climb Cairn Toul and Braeriach, down to the Sinclair Hut in the Lairig Ghru, and northeast by a path through a rocky gap to the Cairn Gorm car-park. The finest route begins at Glen Lui, east of the Linn of Dee. You go by

Top right: A view from Braeriach to Cairn Toul on a crisp, sunny winter's day with the plateau cloaked in deep snow. The superb weather shown in this view belies the normal Cairngorm winter conditions of high winds, poor visibility and arctic temperatures. A walker who embarks on any major Cairngorm itinerary in winter must be fully prepared, in terms of mountaineering and navigational skill and suitable equipment, to cope with the full range of hostile mountain conditions. *Photo: Irvine Butterfield*

Bottom right: A Cairngorm summer scene showing deer grazing on the slopes of Beinn Mheadhoin, with the cliffs at the head of Glen Avon in the background. The walk traverses the skyline plateau from right to left, heading towards Ben Macdui. *Photo: Ken Andrew*

Glen Derry to Ben Macdui and Cairn Gorm, back to the March Burn, across the Lairig Ghru to Braeriach and Cairn Toul, and then down the magnificent Glen Geusachan to Glen Dee and the Linn of Dee. But, as most visitors now come to the Spey Valley, I will emphasise the Speyside route. It begins south-east of Inverdruie near Aviemore, at Whitewell, a place giving one of the finest views of the Cairngorms. A magnificent approach walk follows through Rothiemurchus, first up the old cattle drove-route of the Lairig Ghru, almost to the Sinclair Hut. You then climb to the top of Creag an Leth-choin, which offers a spectacular airy perch above the Lairig's great screes below. Then up round the crags of Coire an Lochain above a big pink slab, where avalanches pour down every summer, to the plateau of Carn Lochain with its wonderful feeling of space. You now follow the cliff edge round Coire an t-Sneachda to the top of Coire Cas. Here you look down to the busy car-park far below, and on a clear day you will get a grand view to the hills beyond Inverness. From Cairn Gorm the easiest way to Ben Macdui goes by the path above the beautiful green

basins of Coire Domhain and Feith Buidhe to Lochan Buidhe, one of Scotland's highest tarns, and then south to Ben Macdui. On Ben Macdui the climate is so severe that scarcely any plants grow, and bare gravel and stones cover most of the ground. Old legends say the great spectre Am Fear Liath Mor (pronounced 'um fer lee-a more', meaning 'the big grey man') frequents the top of Ben Macdui. I have always found the summit exciting for other reasons, as it is such a fine view-point; the indicator will show you most of the main summits.

From Ben Macdui you go south-east, past the top of Allt Clach nan Taillear, but it is worth making a slight diversion to look down a spectacular drop to Lochan Uaine from the highest point above. The route then leads down the broad flank south of Allt Clach nan Taillear to the col connecting to Carn a' Mhaim, and down to the Lairig Ghru path. On the way to Corrour you pass on the left a group of ribbed granite boulders called Clach nan Taillear, or 'stone of the tailors'. Three tailors died in the snow here one New Year's eve, having wagered they would dance a reel on the same night in Speyside and Mar. From Corrour Bothy you take the zig-zag path up Coire Odhar behind, and then climb to the fine peak of Cairn Toul. The route now turns west along the cliff edge high above Lochan Uaine (a different Lochan Uaine from the one on Ben Macdui), and round to the crags of Garbh Choire Mor. Here lies Britain's most permanent snow which has melted only twice this century. There now follows a magnificent walk along a high plateau where the Dee pours out in a beautiful clear spring at 4,000ft., before plunging in a fine waterfall down the face of Garbh Choire Dhaidh on the first part of its swift journey to the sea at Aberdeen. Finally you stride round to the summit cairn of Braeriach, perched at the top of the grand 750ft. cliffs of Coire Bhrochain. An old legend has it that some cattle from Rothiemurchus once died falling over these crags.

From Braeriach your best homeward route lies along the green flat top of Sron na Lairig, down below Braeriach's beautiful trio of northern corries, into the hauntingly lovely Gleann Einich. You may now be feeling tired after a long day, but the scenery is grand. Nothing can be finer at this stage on a summer

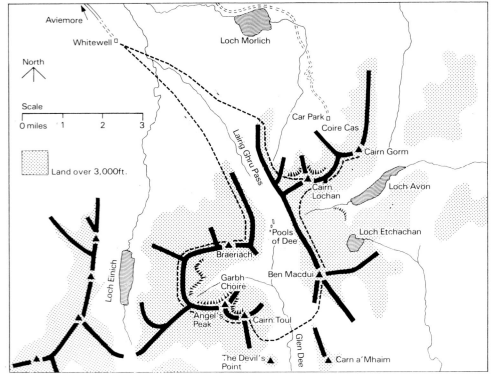

Top right: Huge cornice formations along the rim of Braeriach's cliffs testify to the fierce blizzards that sweep across the Cairngorm plateau in winter. In such conditions the route-finding between Cairn Toul and Braeriach demands the highest standard of navigational skill. Any mishap in this remote spot could easily prove fatal: the nearest road is six miles away, it is difficult to lose height quickly, and the low temperatures and high winds would quickly finish off any unsheltered casualty. *Photo: Donald Bennet*

Below right: A view into Glen Avon from the Cairngorm plateau near Feith Buidhe. This was the scene of the Cairngorm tragedy in 1971, when a group of teenagers, floundering in blizzard conditions while attempting to find the Curran Bothy, was forced to bivouac on the open slope. Six died, and only the leader and a fifteen-year-old boy survived. *Photomontage: John Cleare*

evening than to lie down for a moment in springy heather among the first pines, listening to the soothing rush of the burn and looking back to Braeriach and the Sgoran Dubh, serene against the summer sky.

Back at Whitewell in the evening light, you will see a vast area of velvety dark hills sweeping north to Lochindorb and west to the Monadh Liath. You become aware that the electric lights of Aviemore below and the cocoon-world of man that you are soon to enter again are mere flickering, temporary outposts compared with the age, serenity and mystery of this hill country. The granite screes of the Cairngorms that you have just crossed turn red, bathed in the low sun, and you realize that

the old name for these hills — Am Monadh Ruadh, or the 'red hill-range' — fits them well. The water of Am Beanaidh murmurs distantly through the dark forest of Rothiemurchus as it has done for thousands of years. A curlew calls above its home on the heather moor, a piece of wild magic to end what for you will have been one of the finest big hill walks in Britain.

22   Ben Alder Forest

Walk   Ben Alder Forest.
Maps   O.S. 1:50,000 Sheets 41 and 42.
Start from Corrour Station (ref. 356665).
Finish at Dalwhinnie (ref. 634849).
Grading   An exceptionally long and serious walk over remote mountainous country.
Time   11-12 hours.
Distance   28 miles.
Escape Routes   From the Beinn Eibhinn-Aonach Beag ridge descend steeply S. to the Bealach Dubh and seek shelter at either Corrour Lodge or Culra Lodge which is an open bothy.
Telephones   In an emergency help might be sought from Ben Alder Lodge or Corrour Lodge. Public telephones at Corrour and Dalwhinnie.
Transport   By train to Corrour Station which is a request stop. Dalwhinnie is served by the Perth-Inverness train and long distance bus services.
Accommodation   Youth Hostels at Loch Ossian and Kingussie. Hotel at Dalwhinnie.
Guidebooks   S.M.T. Guide *The Central Highlands.*

The Ben Alder Forest is a large and remote area of the Highlands, bounded by Rannoch Moor, Loch Laggan and Loch Ericht. To enter the heart of the region entails a long approach march, for there is no public road within ten miles of Ben Alder itself.

The walk I am going to describe starts from the isolated station of Corrour Siding on Rannoch Moor, traverses the high ridge of mountains situated north of Ben Alder and ends up at Dalwhinnie in Drumochter. The total distance is twenty-eight miles and there is no escape route, although a bothy called Culra Lodge, which is reached at the far end of the ridge, could be used as an emergency shelter.

The walk is only for a strong, fit and well-equipped party. I have experienced extremes of weather conditions in this area. In late May it was once so intensely hot, without a breath of wind, that I had to sit in the burn to cool off, with a tea towel over my head to keep off the sun. On the other hand, I have been turned back on Ben Alder in April by blizzards and waist-deep snow. In December, 1951, a party of four experienced climbers died in a severe blizzard near Corrour Lodge. A detailed account of this horrific accident can be found in the SMC Journal for 1952.

The West Highland Railway provides an excellent way on to Rannoch Moor. The Railway was opened in 1894 and parts of it are floated over the bog on brushwood. The early morning train from Glasgow to Fort William arrives at Corrour Siding soon after 9.00 a.m. and it can be conveniently boarded at Tyndrum or Bridge of Orchy, but since Corrour is a 'request' stop the guard must be

told of your destination beforehand. It is particularly satisfying for a walker to be whisked over those miles of bog and peat hag whilst sitting comfortably in the restaurant car finishing a hearty breakfast.

From Corrour Siding, walk along the Land-Rover track towards the western edge of Loch Ossian, but after three-quarters of a mile, and before you reach the water's edge, take the left-hand branch that leads to the north side of the loch. It is an elevating experience to walk along the open track beside Loch Ossian, with herons and many varieties of wader feeding at the loch side. As you approach the eastern end of the loch, the track passes through sweetly smelling woods of larch, and you skirt round Corrour Lodge which is almost hidden in the trees.

You must now leave the Land-Rover track, which turns off north and winds a tortuous

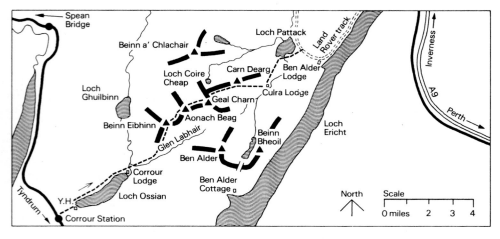

way for ten miles to Glen Spean, and take the small path straight ahead up Glen Labhair. Cross the big burn, the Uisge Labhair, by a bridge near Corrour Lodge and proceed up the glen for about two miles. Your first objective, Beinn Eibhinn, is on the left, and the quickest way of ascent is to climb the steep shoulder that rises on the far side (east) of the Glas Coire and takes you straight to the summit cairn at 3,611ft. The massive bulk of Ben Alder dominates the view east, while to the west, across Loch Treig, rise the twin summits of Stob Coire Easain and Stob a' Coire Mheadhoin. To the north, across Loch Laggan, is the long ridge of the Creag Meagaidh range.

The ridge ahead of you is broad and easy, although the slopes are rough and bouldery. From the summit of Beinn Eibhinn you descend quite gently for 500ft. to the bealach under Aonach Beag. The slopes are easy-angled on the south side, but, as is common in Scotland, they fall away steeply to the north, with broken cliffs above wide corries.

Aonach Beag (3,647ft.) is certainly the finest mountain of the group and it looks particularly shapely when viewed from the east, with its steep symmetrical sides and small flat-topped summit. You can catch the occasional glimpse of Loch Ericht round the southern flanks of Ben Alder.

Beyond Aonach Beag, the ridge narrows and drops to another bealach under the flat-topped Geal Charn (3,688ft.), whose name is not marked on the one-inch map. This is good, fast walking country at a high altitude with magnificent views. Don't stray too far to the east or north when you are on the Geal Charn plateau, or you will end up above cliffs. You must head due north-east, where there is a

Above: The rounded, glaciated peaks of the Ben Alder group — looking back to Aonach Beag and Beinn Eibhinn from Geal Charn. *Photo: Irvine Butterfield*

Top: A view up Loch Ossian to Bealach Dubh, the pass that leads through the Ben Alder Forest to Dalwhinnie. Beinn Eibhinn, the first main summit of the recommended walk, is on the left. *Photo: Robert Adam*

Bottom: Geal Charn and Aonach Beag from Beinn a'Chlachair to the north. The walk runs along the skyline from right to left. *Photo: Irvine Butterfield*

break in the cliffs and a steep and narrow spur leads down to a low bealach between two lochans.

The ridge remains narrow as you climb over a subsidiary summit and then gain Carn Dearg (3,391ft.). This mountain has two summits, the eastern one being the highest.

It is now downhill all the way to Dalwhinnie. First descend the easy grassy slopes in a south-easterly direction to Culra Lodge, beside the Allt a' Chaoil-reidhe. This is a superb bothy, solid and dry, and it contains box bunks. These bunks are useful in keeping off the rats and, if you stay overnight, I advise you to hang your food from a nail in the rafters to prevent it being scavenged. The main disadvantage of Culra Lodge is the lack of fire-wood.

An excellent stalker's track leads down the glen towards Loch Pattack. Cross the river by the bridge which is situated half a mile downstream from Culra Lodge, and follow the track until you meet the Land-Rover track near the small plantation beside Loch Pattack.

From Loch Pattack you can look back to the impressive east-facing corries of Ben Alder, which are often ringed with snow throughout the summer months. This view has been denied you whilst you have been traversing the Aonach Beag ridge.

The Land-Rover track leads in one and a half miles to Benalder Lodge on Loch Ericht side, and you are left with six long but satisfying miles along a rough switchback road beside the loch to Dalwhinnie.

It would be possible for a fit party to leave Glasgow for Corrour by the 6.00a.m. train, complete the walk, catch an evening train from Dalwhinnie and be back in Glasgow by midnight.

23 The Aonach Eagach Ridge

by Donald Bennet

The reputation of Glencoe as a sombre, gloom-filled glen is partly due to the steep and forbidding nature of the mountains which enclose it, and partly to the weather which invests these mountains with their many colours and moods. There can be no denying, however, that when dark clouds are low on the mountains and rain sheets down (conditions which some might regard as typical), then Glencoe lives up to its most formidable reputation.

The north side of Glencoe, along its whole length from the upper gorges to the flat lands below Clachaig, is enclosed by a single long ridge. From the floor of the glen its flanks rise in ever-steepening slopes, riven by scree-filled gullies and broken high up into many shattered buttresses and towers. There are no corries to give shape to the mountain as there are on Bidean opposite, just a great barrier culminating three thousand feet up in a narrow pinnacled ridge. This is the Aonach Eagach — the 'notched ridge'.

The Aonach Eagach has the reputation of being the narrowest mountain ridge on the Scottish mainland, a reputation which Liathach and An Teallach might challenge. Any decision on this must be subjective, but there can be no doubting the appeal of the Aonach Eagach. Hill-walkers aspire to traverse it, and rock-climbers do not consider it beneath their dignity to get their exercise scrambling along its crest on days when the rocks are too wet or cold for harder stuff. It is a climb for all climbers and all seasons. Often in winter on the days immediately after a heavy snowfall, when the gullies of Bidean and Stob Coire nan Lochan are full of unconsolidated snow ready to avalanche, the Aonach Eagach is at its best, for there is seldom a serious avalanche risk on its crest, and when the ridge is snow-covered then the traverse is at its most challenging — and beautiful.

The name, Aonach Eagach, applies only to the two-mile ridge between Sgor nam Fiannaidh (3,168ft.) and Am Bodach (3,085ft.). This is the highest and narrowest part of the ridge, but beyond the two end peaks it continues westwards and eastwards for a few miles so that the whole ridge from the Devil's Staircase to the Pap of Glencoe is over six miles long. It is perfectly feasible to traverse this entire ridge, but it is relatively seldom done;

the Aonach Eagach is the classic expedition and for most people it is enough.

The traverse may be made equally well in either direction, but the east to west choice has the slight advantage that the ascent to Am Bodach from the cottage at Allt-na-Reigh, near the Meeting of Three Waters, is shorter by a few hundred feet in height than the long pull uphill to Sgor nam Fiannaidh from Loch Achtriochtan, or the slightly less direct ascent from Clachaig Inn by the path up the west side of Clachaig Gully.

Going from east to west, the ridge is best reached by the shoulder of Am Bodach, which rises on the west side of the deep gully above Allt-na-Reigh. An ill-defined path leads up this grassy shoulder and zig-zags through rocky outcrops higher up. One cannot stray too far right, for there is a sudden and very steep drop into the gully on that side of the route. An hour and a half is enough to reach the summit of Am Bodach and the start of the ridge.

If a guidebook author were to write a route description for the Aonach Eagach traverse it might simply be: 'Follow the crest of the ridge for two miles from Am Bodach to Sgor nam Fiannaidh, or vice versa'. Such a description would be concise and accurate, two good features of any guidebook, but it would hardly hint at the exhilaration of the traverse or the delightful scrambling up and down over towers and pinnacles, across knife-edged gaps and round impending corners by narrow ledges. In summer there are no difficulties more than Moderate in standard, and anyone with a good head for heights will romp along, enjoying the exposure of the airy crest and the steeply plunging cliffs on either side.

In winter the traverse is a very different proposition, and pitches which in summer cause little hesitation can present many a tricky problem when covered in snow. The first of these comes soon after leaving Am Bodach, where there is an exposed descent of a hundred feet or so. A slip at this point could have nasty results. It is on pitches such as this that fast climbers will scramble down unroped in a minute or two, while others more cautiously rope-up and may take twenty minutes to get a party of three or four down. This difference in speed on the awkward pitches can make the difference between a two-hour traverse and one lasting six hours or more, and that is a long

Walk The Aonach Eagach Ridge.
Maps O.S. 1:50,000 Sheet 41; O.S. 1:63,360 Tourist Map — Ben Nevis and Glencoe.
Start from Meeting of Three Waters, Glencoe (ref. 175566).
Finish at Glencoe Village (ref. 105590).
Grading A moderate scramble in summer, it may be much harder in winter. A rope should be carried.
Time 4-5 hours in summer. 8-10 hours for a slow party in winter.
Distance 6 miles.
Escape Routes It is inadvisable to try to descend from the ridge except at its ends. This is particularly true in bad visibility or darkness.
Telephones At Clachaig Hotel.
Transport The Fort William to Glasgow bus service goes through Glencoe.
Accommodation Clachaig Hotel and Glencoe Hotel. Bed and Breakfast in Glencoe village. Bunk house at Leacantuim. S.M.C. hut at Lagangarbh. Youth Hostel in Glencoe village.
Guidebooks S.M.T. Guide *The Central Highlands; Scottish Climbs* Vol. I. by Hamish MacInnes (Constable); *Undiscovered Scotland* by W. H. Murray (Diadem, 1979).

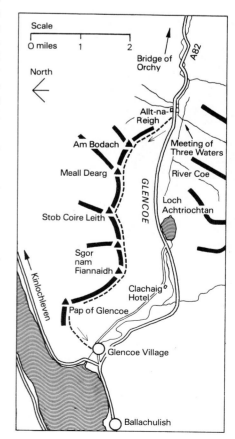

Above: Storm clouds linger at the eastern end of the Aonach Eagach ridge in this summer view from Sgor nam Fiannaidh, the last main peak at the western end of the ridge. The summits are (from left to right) Stob Coire Leith, Meall Dearg and Am Bodach. *Photo: Ken Andrew*

Top right: The ridge in winter from the same viewpoint, but showing its dominating position above Glencoe. Buachaille Etive Mor is in the distance on the right. *Photo: Ken Andrew*

time on a short winter's day.

Once past this pitch there are few difficulties as far as the flat top of Meall Dearg (3,118ft.), then the ridge drops like a switchback over a series of little towers and pinnacles towards the col below Stob Coire Leith (3,080ft.). This is the best part of the traverse: the narrow snow crest is often carved by the wind into fluted edges and cornices, steep gullies plunge hundreds of feet on both sides, and there are many sporting little pitches up and down. The

highlight is the traverse across two small pinnacles where the ridge is at its narrowest. The situation is exposed, but there are good holds which may need a bit of excavating if the pinnacles are smothered in snow.

Once the col is reached, all difficulties are past. There is an easy climb to Stob Coire Leith followed by a broad ridge to Sgor nam Fiannaidh. The fastest way off this peak, and one that is usually quite easy, is the direct descent to Loch Achtriochtan. This is a long

uniform slope which may give a good glissade; however, in hard conditions it would be better to keep crampons on, and it is not a good route if the snow seems liable to avalanche, in which case it is better to continue for a mile towards the Pap before descending to Glencoe.

No one should underestimate the Aonach Eagach in winter. It can take longer than one expects, and attempts to escape from the ridge by descending its flanks are to be discouraged. Certainly it would be foolish to commit oneself

in failing light to a gully whose lower reaches are invisible from above, and it is better to keep going to the end of the ridge and an easy descent route.

It is not surprising in view of this that the Aonach Eagach has something of a reputation for parties finding themselves benighted. My own recollections are of Freshers' Meets of a University Mountaineering Club which I will not embarrass by naming. These meets were always at the end of October, and certain of the

Above: A section of the ridge between Stob Coire Leith (left) and Meall Dearg (right) seen across the deep trench of Glencoe from the summit of Bidean nam Bian. Ben Nevis dominates the distant view across the Mamore Forest. *Photo: Tom Weir*

senior members saw it as their duty to show newcomers the ropes on the Aonach Eagach. The results were always the same: 7.00 p.m. on Sunday evening, as teams were assembling for the homeward bus, torch lights would be seen flickering high up on the ridge. Another late-night epic. Nothing for it but to return to the Clachaig, in the guise of *bona fide* travellers, for another couple of pints.

The ultimate in Aonach Eagach expeditions is the moonlight traverse. Bill Murray's writings must have inspired many an attempt, but the coincidence of a full moon, good snow and good weather is rare. It seemed to have come, I remember, one weekend in January, 1952. The JMCS bus had dropped its load of climbers at Alltnafeadh, and as we walked across to Lagangarbh under a full moon the idea was born. After supper we were off, five of us, climbing up the Devil's Staircase to start the 'long' traverse. Conditions were perfect as far as Am Bodach, but a change was in the sky; filmy mist veiled the moon and shrouded the mountains. We continued in an eerie

opalescent gloom, flitting ghostlike along the ridge, each one of us solitary and silent in a totally silent, isolated world. Then the snow started; at first a few frozen crystals floating out of the mist, then a maelstrom of swirling flakes that blotted out the moon and enveloped us on Sgor nam Fiannaidh.

Of the return journey to Lagangarbh, through the dark, wet valley of Glencoe, I remember little, for memory is selective and one recalls nothing of sleep-walking. Only the image of that strange, silent beauty of moonlight, mist and snow on the Aonach Eagach remains.

Left: At the col below Stob Coire Leith. *Photo:* Donald Bennet

Above: It is advisable to carry ropes to safeguard the tricky sections of the Aonach Eagach in winter. Many sections that could cause undue anxiety to an unroped party, can be rendered relatively harmless by conventional alpine rope technique. Here four climbers are seen enjoying the route, having just made the awkward descent from Am Bodach. *Photo:* John Allen

24   Ben Lawers and the Tarmachans

Walk   Ben Lawers and the Tarmachans.
Maps   O.S. 1:50,000 Sheet 51.
Start from Lawers village (ref. 680399).
Finish at Killin (ref. 572326).
Grading   A long walk over mainly easy ground, although the Tarmachans are rough and bouldery and much ascent and descent is necessary.
Time   11 hours.
Distance   20 miles.
Escape Routes   Descents from bealachs on the main ridge down easy grassy slopes to the south are possible in many places.
Telephones   Lawers; Killin; Bridge of Balgie.
Transport   Bus connections from Killin to Callander, Stirling and Aberfeldy. Railway stations at Lochearnhead and Crianlarich.
Accommodation   Killin is the centre for this walk where there are Hotels and Guest Houses and a Youth Hostel.
Guidebooks   S.M.T. Guide *The Southern Highlands.*

North of Loch Tay in central Perthshire, and extending from east to west for seven miles, lies the Ben Lawers range of mountains. Ben Lawers itself is 3,984ft. high, but because of its huge bulk it does not always get the respect which is its due; it is after all the highest mountain in Britain, south of Ben Nevis.

The long and easy-angled south-facing slopes of Ben Lawers make it a popular mountain with skiers, particularly since it is readily accessible from Edinburgh, Glasgow and Stirling. I am very glad to say, though, that only limited commercial development has been allowed, and Ben Lawers is still relatively unspoilt. In spring and early summer Ben Lawers is a botanist's paradise; the underlying rock is metamorphic schist, rich in lime, and the mountain has been declared a National Nature Reserve. In spring the lower slopes are bright with orchids and mountain pansies, and on the upper slopes you should find the beautiful snow gentian, alpine forget-me-not, alpine speedwell, moss campion and many rare saxifrages.

The walk I am going to describe is from Lawers village on the north side of Loch Tay to Killin. The walk includes not only the principal summits of the Lawers range but also the adjacent and more rocky Meall nan Tarmachan. The descent from Meall nan Tarmachan is direct to Killin, where you can obtain tea or dinner before catching the Aberfeldy bus to Lawers. This will save you an eight and a half mile walk back along the road.

Save this walk for a fine summer's day, when you can wander lazily along the broad ridges, picking bilberries and enjoying the flowers and the view. Perthshire has a greater variety of scenery than any other Scottish county and from Ben Lawers you have a bird's-eye view.

From Lawers village take the path which runs up the east side of the Lawers burn. After a mile, leave the path and ascend the broad south ridge of Meall Greigh. The grassy slopes ascend relentlessly for nearly 2,000ft., but half-way up, on the right, you will pass some rock outcrops.

From the summit of Meall Greigh (3,280ft.), you have a very easy two-mile walk due west along the ridge to Meall Garbh. The lowest point on the ridge is the bealach under the east ridge of Meall Garbh, at 2,800ft., after which it is an 800ft. pull up to the cairn on the summit. You can see the ridge curving away ahead of you over the subsidiary peaks of An Stuc and Creag an Fhithich, which are not named on the one-inch map, to Ben Lawers. Below is a deep corrie holding a curious lochan, shaped like a sitting cat, called Lochan nan Cat. Beyond stretches the beautiful Loch Tay with its wooded banks, fifteen miles long from Killin to Kenmore and never more than a mile across.

An Stuc is quite a sharply pointed peak with steep and broken sides. There is a small pile of stones on the summit, and beyond the ridge turns almost due south and descends for 500ft. The next summit, Creag an Fhithich, is merely a hiccup in the ridge and you very soon reach the final steep slopes of Ben Lawers. The north ridge rises for nearly 1,000ft., but the going is easy although steep; keep the precipitous east face on your left.

The summit of Ben Lawers is dominated by the huge pile of stones and the considerable cairn. The height, 3,984ft., is so nearly 4,000ft. that in 1878 an enormous cairn was built. It had a circumference of 50ft. at the base and a height of at least 12ft., thus a man standing on the cairn would have his head and shoulders above 4,000ft. Unfortunately this large cairn collapsed many years ago.

The view from Ben Lawers is so extensive that it was used as a sighting centre during the 1852 survey of the Highlands. Direct sights were taken of Ben Nevis, Ben Macdui, Ben More on Mull and the Merrick in Galloway.

Descend the steep slopes from the summit in a south-westerly direction until you reach the

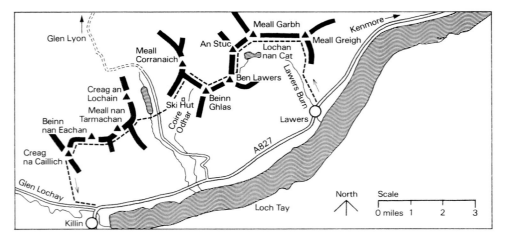

bealach under Beinn Ghlas. Beinn Ghlas is another shapely peak, 3,740ft. high and only one mile from its loftier neighbour. The western end of the Lawers range is rockier than the eastern end, and you will find a steep and broken ridge descending north-west from Beinn Ghlas to another bealach and hence to the flat-topped Meall Corranaich, another Munro at 3,530ft. Below Meall Corranaich to the south is Coire Odhar, a popular ski area where there is a hut and a ski tow.

From Meall Corranaich, an easy ridge descends in a south-westerly direction to the road at the south end of Lochan na Lairige. I was on this ridge one April day when, hearing a piercing shriek, I rounded a rock to see a golden eagle at grips with a white mountain hare. As I appeared, the eagle soared away

Above: Ben Lawers and Beinn Ghlas from the slopes of An Stuc. *Photo: Ken Andrew*

Right: Looking back to Ben Lawers from Beinn Ghlas. *Photo: Donald Bennet*

Above: A view to the north from Meall Corranaich, towards the satellite munro — Meall a Choire Leith, which lies off the main Lawers — Tarmachan walk, but is easily included in the itinerary. *Photo: Ken Andrew*

Top right: The Ben Lawers ridges seen from Meall Corranaich. *Photo: Donald Bennet*

into the sky, leaving its prey to scurry off into the rocks.

The mountain massif on the west side of the road is Meall nan Tarmachan. You will notice the rocky bluffs and lines of broken cliffs, which are uncharacteristic of the Lawers range, but make a pleasant contrast.

Cross the river by a bridge situated just below the Lochan na Lairige dam, and climb the steep stony slopes beyond. Head in a north-westerly direction and find a way through the complex of rock outcrops. At a height of about 2,750ft., you emerge on the north ridge of Meall nan Tarmachan and it is a short walk to the summit cairn at 3,421ft.

You now have a two-mile high-level walk along a complicated ridge, before you drop down to the finish at Killin. The ridge south-west of Meall nan Tarmachan continues to be easy, and you pass several small lochans before

climbing quite steeply to Meall Garbh (3,369ft.), which is not named on the one-inch map.

From the pointed summit of Meall Garbh descend a sharp ridge due west, and then follow the ridge north-west to a bealach under Beinn nan Eachan. The slopes on the south side fall away precipitously but, keeping them on your left, climb the broad and hummocky east ridge to the summit of Beinn nan Eachan.

Now descend grassy slopes on the south-west side of the mountain for 450ft., and then climb up again to Creag na Caillich (2,990ft.), which has three small summits. Follow the edge of the cliffs as you descend the mountain in a westerly direction, until you can find a way through to the more gentle grassy slopes to the south. You meet the Glen Lochay road only about a mile west of Killin.

Above: Meall nan Tarmachan from the summit of Ben Lawers. Beinn Ghlas (left) and Meall Corranaich (right) are the mountains in the middle distance. *Photo: Ken Andrew*

101

25   The Ben Lui Horseshoe

Walk   The Ben Lui Horseshoe.
Maps   O.S. 1:50,000 Sheet 50
Start from Tyndrum (ref. 330302).
Finish at Dalmally (ref. 161272).
Grading   A moderate walk over a compact group of
mountains. Several steep and rocky sections are
included.
Time   9-10 hours.
Distance   17 miles.
Escape Routes   From the Ben Oss—Ben Lui
bealach descend N. down Coire Laoigh to Cononish
Farm. From the Ben Lui—Beinn a' Chleibh bealach
descend N.W. to the main road, A85, through Glen
Lochy.
Telephones   Tyndrum; Dalmally.
Transport   Good rail and bus services connect
Tyndrum and Dalmally with Glasgow, Oban and Fort
William.
Accommodation   Hotels at Tyndrum and Dalmally.
Youth Hostel at Crianlarich.
Guidebooks   S.M.T. Guide *The Southern
Highlands; The Scottish Peaks* by W. A. Poucher
(Constable).

Ben Lui is the principal peak of a compact group of four Munros on the Perthshire – Argyllshire border. It rises gracefully to a conical summit 3,708ft. high, and it is clearly visible from the A82 between Crianlarich and Tyndrum. In winter, the high north-east corrie collects much snow and it provides a challenging route for the serious mountaineer. Ben Lui has been described as the most beautiful peak in Scotland and, when it is seen dazzling white in the winter sunshine, it is hard to disagree.

Ben Lui and the satellite peaks of Beinn Dubhcraig, Ben Oss and Beinn a' Chleibh can be traversed in a day from Tyndrum to Dalmally, and accommodation can be arranged in both places. The mountains are easily accessible from three sides and long approach marches are not necessary. I can strongly recommend this walk to those who cannot be confident of making an early start or who suspect their physical fitness. It is a walk to be enjoyed.

If transport is available, arrange to be dropped on the A82, one and a half miles east of Tyndrum, at the point where the Land-Rover track from Cononish Farm meets the main road. Walk along the this track, passing under the railway line, for three miles until the farm is reached. Alternatively, from Tyndrum South station a rough path leads across the hillside to reach Cononish Farm. This provides a

shorter and more direct route than the Land-Rover track, but involves more ascent.

From the farm, cross the river by a bridge and make your way up the broad north ridge of Beinn Dubhcraig. There is no path and the hillside gets rougher and more bouldery the higher you climb, but the ascent is quite straightforward. Near the top of the ridge you pass over a false summit and descend to a picturesque group of lochans, but the true summit is now only three hundred feet further on at a height of 3,204ft.

Your next objective, Ben Oss, lies one and a half miles away to the west, across a deep glen, and to reach it you must retrace your steps to the false summit by the lochans and then descend another 400ft. in a westerly direction to reach a bealach. Scramble up steep boulder-strewn slopes between small broken cliffs, to reach the easier-angled summit ridge of Ben Oss.

Ben Oss is a splendid view-point. The eastern corrie of Ben Lui dominates the view to the west, but the great north-eastern corrie is out of sight. Looking south, you can see down Glen Falloch to Loch Lomond and the Arrochar hills. Ben More and Stob Binnein rise above the Crianlarich hills to the east, while to the north rises the whole range of mountains of the Mamlorn group, stretching from Glen Lochay to Bridge of Orchy.

Descend the broad south-west shoulder of Ben Oss for 1,000ft., until you reach the bealach under Ben Lui. The hard work is now over and only delights await you for the remainder of the walk.

Ahead, lies the ever steepening south-east ridge of Ben Lui, rising 1,600ft. to the summit cairn. Keep to the edge of the ridge, where you can enjoy the feeling of space and, higher up, where the main east ridge joins your path, you will be able to look down into the dramatic north-east corrie.

I have climbed this ridge on a winter's day of arctic conditions, when the tearing wind had covered the rocks with luminous green ice, and snow devils were swirling below on the bealach. However, on the sharp summit of Ben Lui there was dead calm, and I was able to sit beside the large cairn in perfect peace and solitude and admire the cornices ringing the north face. It was mid March and the sun warmed my face and reminded me that spring

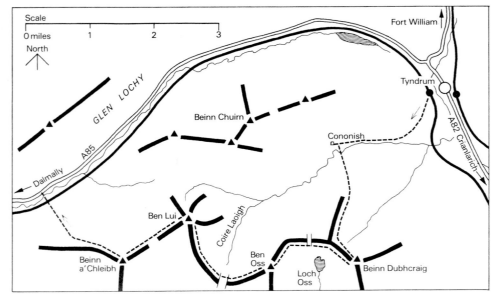

was not too far away. The air was clear as crystal and I could easily see beyond Ben Cruachan to Ben More on Mull, while to the north Ben Nevis rose above the Mamores into the blue sky.

When you have drunk your fill from the summit of Ben Lui, descend the steep and stony slopes on the south-west side of the mountain for 1,200ft., until you reach the low bealach under Beinn a' Chleibh. After Ben Lui, any mountain would seem an anti-climax and Beinn a' Chleibh is no exception. However, it is 3,008ft. high and an easy half-hour's walk up the east ridge, with some rock scrambling thrown in, will give you another Munro, your fourth of the day.

The descent to Glen Loch from Beinn a' Chleibh presents no difficulty and the broad north-west ridge leads you down in an hour to Succoth Lodge beside the railway line. From here, a good track will take you in one and a half miles to the main road at the junction of Glen Lochy and Glen Orchy, and only two more miles will see you to Dalmally. From Dalmally you can return to Tyndrum by bus or by train. There are two buses and three trains every day.

If you wish to return to Tyndrum, and cannot find suitable transport, your best plan is to leave out the ascent of Beinn a' Chleibh. Descend the northern spur of Ben Lui over a rocky nose called the Ciochan, and thence down to the glen and Cononish Farm. But this route should only be attempted in clear weather, because it is easy to mistake the main spur over the Ciochan for a smaller one that ends over the cliffs. In bad conditions the safest way is to return down the south-east ridge to the bealach, and then swing north down the glen to Cononish.

Right: The summit of Ben Lui, with a climber completing the classic Central Gully route up the North-East Face. *Photo: Donald Bennet*

Right: Ben Lui from Ben Oss, with the Ben Cruachan group in the distance. The walk follows the corniced left-hand ridge. The north-east corrie is on the right — its classic Central Gully offering a superb and direct route to the summit of this fine mountain. *Photo: Ken Andrew*

26   Ridge Wandering in Perthshire: the Crianlarich Hills

Walk Ridge Wandering in Perthshire: the Crianlarich Hills.
Maps O.S. 1:50,000 Sheets 51 and 56.
Start from Benmore Farm (ref. 414258).
Finish at Inverarnan Hotel (ref. 318185).
Grading A long walk over rocky mountainous terrain. Much ascent and descent is involved.
Time 12-13 hours.
Distance 19 miles.
Escape Routes After Stob Binnein return north down the Benmore Glen. From the low bealachs between Stob Glas and Beinn a' Chroin and between An Caisteal and Beinn Chabhair return down easy glens to the north.
Telephones Crianlarich; Inverarnan.
Transport Crianlarich is served by both the Glasgow—Oban and the Glasgow—Fort William railways. The Glasgow—Oban daily bus service connects Inveranan to Crianlarich.
Accommodation Hotels and Guest Houses in Crianlarich, Inverarnan Hotel in Glen Falloch, Youth Hostel at Crianlarich.
Guidebooks S.M.T. Guide *The Southern Highlands; The Scottish Peaks* by W. A. Poucher (Constable).

This compact group of hills lies on the southern edge of the vast Breadalbane estates. They are easily accessible from the main A82 road through Glen Falloch, which rises above Ardlui at the northern end of Loch Lomond. The principal peak is Ben More which is seen as a perfect cone, 3,843ft. high, when driving between Killin and Crianlarich.

The hills rise abruptly from deep glens and their sides are steep, though mainly grassy, with only broken bands of rock which in summer are easily negotiated. In severe winter conditions, however, the range can be transformed and, even in April, I have struggled to ascend some of the mountains, which were covered in sheets of hard ice and involved hours of step-cutting and the use of crampons. In good conditions they make ideal walking country, and the complete traverse of the range, as described below, makes a long but magnificent expedition. In spring the lower glens are carpeted with bluebells and primroses growing under the birch, alder and sycamore trees. The higher slopes of the mountains are noted for rare alpine plants.

I have described the walk from north to south, because this way the highest mountains are climbed first, when you are fresh, and late in the day you can look forward to the finish at the Inveranan Hotel, two miles north of Ardlui.

Start the walk from Benmore Farm, two miles east of Crianlarich. A path which starts

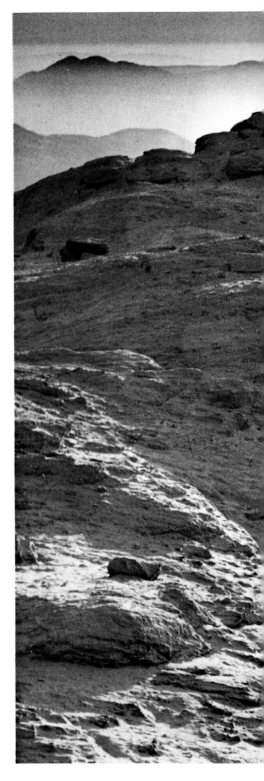

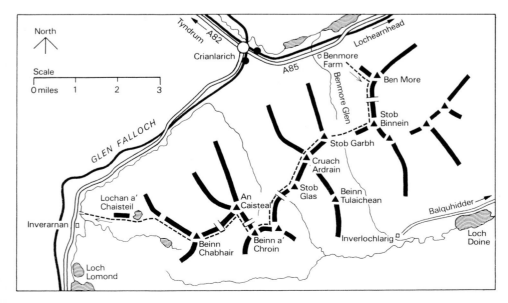

beside the burn ascends the easy slopes ahead, directly to the summit trig point of Ben More. The climb is quite simple, but it is fully 3,300ft., and it can be an awful grind on a hot summer's day. In winter, Ben More carries a great deal of snow and, in exceptional conditions, the slopes just below the cairn have been known to avalanche. The hillside becomes more rocky and boulder-strewn the higher you climb and the views open out to

Above: The broad ridge at 3,000ft. linking Stob Garbh with Cruach Ardrain (right). Beinn Tulaichean is the peak in the centre of the picture. *Photo: A. D. S. MacPherson*

provide a wonderful panorama of the Central and Western Highlands.

One mile due south, and only slightly lower at 3,821ft., lies Stob Binnein, which is another beautifully proportioned peak, a regular cone with its top cut off. To reach Stob Binnein you must descend 1,000ft. to the bealach Eadardha Beinn, meaning 'pass between two peaks', and re-ascend easily to the summit. The bealach lies at the bottom of a perfectly symmetrical sweep of the mountainside and it is seen to its best advantage from Cruach Ardrain, your next objective across the glen to the west.

From the summit cairn of Stob Binnein, steep but easy slopes descend due west to the watershed between Benmore Glen and Inverlochlarig Glen, at a height of 1,650ft. The mountain straight ahead is Stob Garbh, which is rather rocky on the east side, but you will

Above: Cruach Ardrain and Stob Garbh, from the summit of Beinn Tulaichean to the south. The walk traverses the snowy ridges from right to left. *Photo: Ken Andrew*

Top right: Ben More (3,843ft.) with its slightly lower partner, Stob Binnein, seen from Beinn Tulaichean. The walk traverses these two shapely mountains from left to right before descending the steep slopes to the col (centre left) and continuing up the rocky lower ridge of Stob Garbh (left). *Photo: Ken Andrew*

easily be able to find a way to the summit. A broad and hummocky ridge leads south to Cruach Ardrain (3,428ft.), which has twin summits close together. From the east and from Stob Binnein in particular, Cruach Ardrain looks a most impressive wedge, with a steep east face and pointed summit. It is a fine mountain and an excellent view-point for the Crianlarich group of hills.

Your next objective, half a mile away, is the subsidiary summit of Stob Glas, marking the end of the south-west spur of Cruach Ardrain. Do not confuse Stob Glas with the higher Beinn Tulaichean, which lies one mile south-east of Cruach Ardrain. The southern side of

Stob Glas is rocky and precipitous, but you can descend on the west side to a low bealach, at 1,700ft., under the east summit of Beinn a' Chroin. From the bealach you can easily gain the north ridge of Beinn a' Chroin, which leads to the gap between the west and east summits of the mountain. The east summit, at 3,104ft., is the highest.

You will probably wish to include this east summit in the day's walk, but you must then retrace your steps and ascend the west summit. The ridge drops very steeply on the north-west side to a bealach under An Caisteal, and from there you must descend again in a westerly direction to reach another bealach at 2,000ft.

under the east ridge of Beinn Chabhair.

The ground is broken and rocky and the direct route up Beinn Chabhair is barred by a line of cliffs, but by working round to the right you can avoid any difficulties, and steep grassy slopes lead to the summit at 3,053ft. Looking back to the east you can appreciate the fine individuality of An Caisteal and Beinn a' Chroin, translated aptly as the 'Castle' and 'Peak of the Cloven Hoof'. In the north-west the Ben Lui group is prominent, while Loch Lomond stretches away to the south, with the Arrochar mountains across the water.

Glen Falloch, and the end of the day's walk lies below and the north-west ridge provides a gentle and interesting descent to the glen from Beinn Chabhair. 1,000ft. down the ridge on the shoulder of Ben Glas, you pass a delightful lochan, called Lochan a' Chaisteil, surrounded by extraordinary pinnacles and castles of rock. On the south side of Ben Glas, a burn drains Lochan Beinn Chabhair and this leads down to Glen Falloch.

If you keep the burn in sight you will emerge through the trees and bracken of the lower slopes at the bridge over the Falloch river. Cross this to reach the main A82 and walk 200 yards down the road towards Loch Lomond, to the Inveranan Hotel.

Above: The Crianlarich Hills, viewed from Ben Challum to the north. The shadowy Crianlarich valley (Strath Fillan) bisects the picture horizontally in the middle distance; the peaks beyond provide the walk. From left to right they are Ben More, Stob Binnein, Stob Garbh, Cruach Ardrain and Beinn a'Chroin. *Photo: Ken Andrew*

27   Through the Grampians by Glen Tilt

A grey dawn was just breaking as I left Blair Atholl bound for Braemar by the pass of Glen Tilt. Glen Tilt is the most southerly of the three great Cairngorm passes, the other two being the Lairig Ghru and Glen Feshie. The Lairig Ghru has a fearsome reputation but it remains a popular tourist route. Glen Feshie is wide and featureless, and plans for a motor road through it, linking Speyside and Deeside, have often been mooted. Glen Feshie, too, has witnessed tragedy, for in 1970 an experienced walker was drowned whilst attempting to ford the river Eidart.

I had been told that Glen Tilt combines remoteness with dramatic and beautiful scenery, so, one day in late March, I resolved to test this statement for myself.

To enter Glen Tilt you take the road towards Old Blair and, after crossing the river by a fine stone bridge, you turn right down a rough road, marked 'Private No Cars'. This road runs through banks of rhododendrons and passes several cottages owned by the Atholl Estate, as it makes its way north, keeping for the most part high above the river.

By the time I had reached Gilbert's Bridge, it was light enough to take more interest in my surroundings. The river was the main feature, sometimes thundering through narrow banks and sometimes foaming merrily down its bouldery bed.

The clouds were beginning to disperse and patches of blue sky encouraged me to lengthen my stride. My expectations of a grand edifice at Marble Lodge were dashed, when the building turned out to be only a low grey stone cottage, apparently deserted. But the day was awakening: curlews cried overhead, while by the river dippers and oyster catchers swooped and herons stood immobile. It had been an exceptionally long and hard winter, the gullies and runnels were choked with grey ice and the vast bulk of Beinn a'Ghlo and its satellites on the east side of Glen Tilt were blanketed white down to the 1,000ft. level. A greenish tinge at the end of the willow branches was the only sign that spring was approaching.

I stopped at Forest Lodge to talk to the keeper, who was bemoaning the long winter. There was no hay nearer than Fife, and that at £2 per bale excluding cartage. Many sheep and deer had perished. On my day's walk I counted no less than six dead deer lying on the hillside or beside the river. Forest Lodge is a considerable house built of grey stone and sheltered from the north by a band of trees. It comes to life in the stalking season when it is thronged with visitors, for stalking is the principal return from the estate.

By now the sun was out and I peeled off two jerseys. The walking was easy along the broad track and interest never flagged. Pony tracks zig-zagged up the lower slopes of the mountains, beautifully constructed paths built during the last century when labour was cheap.

Four miles beyond Forest Lodge, the Land-Rover track peters out and the path passes through a deep defile clinging to the steep hillside above the river Tilt. Looking back down Glen Tilt, Beinn a' Ghlo, glistening white, completely dominated the view.

Rounding the next corner I heard the roar of water, announcing the Falls of Tarf. The river Tarf, swollen with melt-water, leapt down a rocky amphitheatre in three giant steps before joining the Tilt. The amphitheatre was covered with trees and the scene represented romantic Scotland at its best. The river Tarf is spanned by a suspension bridge, built in 1886 as a memorial to Francis Bedford, drowned in the Tarf when he was only eighteen years old.

It was now 12 o'clock; I had been walking for five hours and I stopped for an early lunch.

Walk   Through the Grampians by Glen Tilt.
Maps   O.S. 1:50,000 Sheet 43
Start from Blair Atholl (ref. 876655).
Finish at Braemar (ref. 152915).
Grading   A long but easy walk through a remote Highland glen.
Time   11-12 hours.
Distance   31 miles.
Escape Routes   None, but emergency shelter might be found at Fealar Lodge (2 miles W. of Falls of Tarf) and Bynack Lodge one mile S. of Geldie Burn.
Telephones   Blair Atholl and Muir of Inverey only. Private telephone at Forest Lodge.
Transport   Blair Atholl is well served by train and bus. Braemar is connected to Ballater and Aberdeen by bus.
Accommodation   Hotel and Guest Houses at Blair Atholl and Braemar. Youth Hotels at Inverey and Braemar.
Guidebooks   S.M.T. Guide *The Cairngorms.*

Top left: A typical view of the River Tilt, in the lower part of Glen Tilt near Blair Atholl. *Photo: Robert Adam*

Bottom left: Glen Tilt penetrates deep into the Grampian mountains, below the grassy ridges of the Beinn a'Ghlo massif (right) — a view from Meall Reamhar above Blair Atholl. *Photo: Robert Adam*

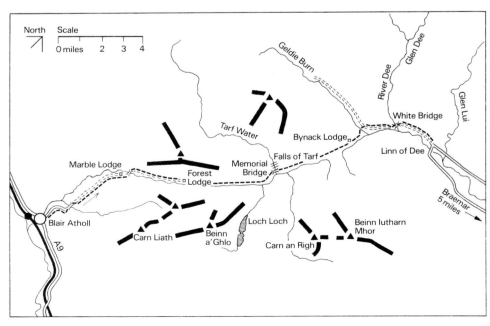

I had just reached the snow line and the next five miles across the watershed looked to be tough going.

Soon after the Falls of Tarf, the river makes an abrupt turn to the east and disappears up a deep ravine. The path divides and that to the right can be seen snaking up the hillside on its way to Fealar Lodge, which rivals Carnmore as the most remote inhabited house in Britain. The path to Deeside follows the left bank of the Allt Garbh Buidhe for another two miles, until the watershed is reached at 1,600ft. I was confronted by a white wasteland of unbroken snow. Hardly a rock emerged through the frozen surface and only several huge herds of deer, numbering many hundreds, and the occasional arctic hare scurrying across my path, broke the monotony.

In summer this broad strath is peat-hagged and boggy, but today it was level crusty snow which let me in at every step to my acute discomfort.

The enormous bulk of Ben Macdui, shining white in the sunshine and looking more Himalayan than Scottish, beckoned me onwards, and at 2.30 p.m. I was sitting eating a second lunch amidst the ruins of Bynack Lodge. The lodge is now a mere skeleton and it offers scant shelter but, surrounded by a few decayed pine trees, its situation is splendid and it carries an aura of bygone days.

Downhill now to the Geldie burn and on to White Bridge which spans the Dee. The Dee at White Bridge is a considerable river, although it rises only ten miles away on the summit plateau of Braeriach, above the Garbh Choire. It was now overcast and snowing as I trudged along the road to Inverey, but it was worth a brief stop to marvel at the Linn of Dee and the feat of Menlove Edwards who swam through that boiling cauldron in 1931.

The six miles from Muir of Inverey to Braemar make up the last lap of the walk, and I was able to meet my twelve-hour target, in spite of a call at the Mar Lodge bar.

In conclusion, it had been a tough walk in the best Highland tradition. The ancient and little known by-way of Glen Tilt had fully lived up to expectations and I felt immensely satisfied.

28   Arran's Rocky Ridges

Walk   Arran's Rocky Ridges.
Maps   O.S. 1:50,000 Sheet 91
Start and finish at Brodick (ref. 022360).
Grading   A long walk over rocky and switchback ridges. Some exposed rock scrambling is involved. A rope should be carried.
Time   12-13 hours.
Distance   21 miles.
Escape Routes   From the Bealach an Fhir-bhogha and the A'Chir-Cir Mhor bealach easy routes lead down into upper Glen Rosa.
Telephones   Sannox, Corrie and Brodick.
Transport   Regular steamer service from Ardrossan to Brodick. Summer service from Claonaig to Lochranza. The island bus service from Brodick to Lochranza passes through Sannox.
Accommodation   Hotels and Guest Houses in Brodick, Corrie and Sannox. Youth Hostel at Lochranza.
Guidebooks   S.M.T. Guide *The Islands of Scotland;* S.M.C. Guide *Arran* by W. M. M. Wallace, *Hill Walking in Arran* by Ronald L. Meek (Arran Tourist Association); *The Scottish Peaks* by W. A. Poucher (Constable).

Arran, the holiday isle set in the Clyde and overlooking Kintyre, provides ridge-walking of a standard second only to the Cuillin of Skye in the whole of Great Britain.

Access is easy. The ferry from Ardrossan to Brodick runs every day of the week and the crossing takes a mere 55 minutes. In the summer months a second ferry runs from Claonaig in Kintyre to Lochranza in the north of Arran.

The mountains form a fairly compact group in the northern part of the island. The rock is coarse-grained, weathered granite which is exceptionally rough on the hands, more so even than the Cuillin gabbro. The weathering process, combined with intrusions of basaltic dykes, has carved the rock into crazy pinnacles and deep gullies. Slopes of fine granite sand fall away from the ridges in many places and chunks of rotten rock can be pulled away by hand. Two long and beautiful glens, Glen Sannox from the north and Glen Rosa from the south, split the hills into two distinct ridges.

Either of these two ridges would make a fine excursion, but the walk I am about to describe

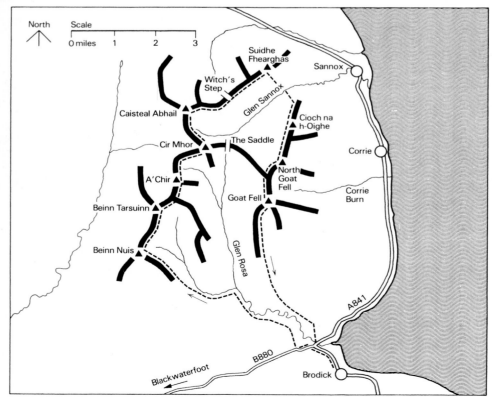

combines them both to give a long and arduous day involving some airy rock scrambling, although, in the absence of snow and ice, a rope should not be necessary.

Leave Brodick by the main road north and after half a mile, just before the bridge over the Rosa river, turn sharp left and proceed along the minor road that crosses the island to Blackwaterfoot. After 100 yards or so, you will see a narrow road on the right-hand side, signposted 'Glen Rosa'. There is a car-park three-quarters of a mile along the road, where the

tarmac ends.

Walk along the good track up Glen Rosa for a mile until you come to the bridge over the large burn which drains Coire a' Bhradain. The path to Beinn Nuis, your first objective, ascends Coire a' Bhradain via a conspicuous iron pipe, which carries water from a deep pool situated 500ft. up in the gully. The path then crosses the burn and strikes up the open grassy slopes to the summit of Beinn Nuis.

The path continues easily to Beinn Tarsuinn, a mile along the ridge to the north. The slopes

fall away precipitously on the east side, but more gently on the west.

Beinn Tarsuinn is a good view-point, as are all the Arran summits, but the most striking feature to be seen is the vast rock face of Cir Mhor, jutting out into the Fionn Coire of upper Glen Rosa. Goat Fell, your last major summit of the day, is the huge mass seen to the east across Glen Rosa, showing a line of impressive boiler-plate slabs.

Beyond Beinn Tarsuinn the ridge narrows and becomes rocky. There is some scrambling, but

Above: The craggy summit ridge of Caisteal Abhail provides a magnificent vantage point for viewing the Arran peaks. The walk described in the essay gains Cir Mhor (right) by the right-hand ridge, continues over Caisteal Abhail, crosses Glen Sannox (left) and follows the skyline ridge to Goatfell (centre). *Photo: Ken Andrew*

in general the sandy path picks an easy way through the castles of grey granite. You descend to the Bealach an Fhir-bhogha, the easiest route bypassing some impressive cliffs on the west side, and ahead of you is the rock ridge of A'Chir.

The rocks facing you are not as difficult as they look; the angle is not too great and the adhesion is excellent. The well-scratched route climbs the slabs on the west side, before making a rising traverse that leads to the crest of the ridge. Take care over this section, for although the standard is not high the climbing is exposed. The ridge, once gained, gives exhilarating scrambling, and, if a particular move looks to be too difficult, search around for there is bound to be an easier alternative. The actual summit of A'Chir is a massive boulder, which is most easily climbed from the north side.

There is one place, however, the famous

'*mauvais pas*', where only one route goes. A cairn and an arrow painted on the rock mark the place where you must leave the ridge and descend a twelve-foot wall on the east side. This leads to a groove which traverses the rocky face and provides a way down to a good path at a lower level. An exposed piece of climbing, but nowhere really hard. Having accomplished the '*mauvais pas*', you have only one more rocky tower to traverse before you reach the broad saddle under Cir Mhor.

Cir Mhor is a shapely mountain rising to 2,618ft. and it is sheer on several sides. The south-west ridge, though, is very easy and, as you plod up to the summit rocks, you can admire the stupendous Rosa Pinnacle towering up to end in a rocky prow. Cir Mhor's summit cairn is built on the top of an enormous granite tor, and you can afford a short rest to admire the view and see what lies in store for you ahead.

The long glen straight ahead is Glen Sannox and your next objective, Caisteal Abhail, or 'The Castles', is one mile due north along the edge of the corrie. About half-way up the boulder-strewn slopes of Caisteal Abhail, you will see a mound of stones, marking a spring of pure water which bubbles out of the mountainside. Like Cir Mhor, the summit of Caisteal Abhail consists of a gigantic granite tor, and from it you will be intrigued by the conspicuous gash in the ridge ahead. This is the famous 'Witch's Step', or Ceum na Caillich. The descent into the step is easy enough from the south-west, but the way out involves an awkward move across and up a steep slab.

After the Witch's Step the ridge gradually becomes easier until it broadens out into a wide shoulder under Suidhe Fhearghas. Suidhe Fhearghas is the end of the ridge, and the mouth of Glen Sannox and the sea lie

Above left: An aerial view across the 'battlements' of Caisteal Abhail towards Goatfell and Cir Mhor. *Photo: John Dewar*

Above: A view from Goatfell towards Cir Mhor (left) and Caisteal Abhail. The saddle in the centre forms the watershed between Glen Rosa and Glen Sannox. *Photo: Ken Andrew*

Left: Approaching Cir Mhor from A'Chir. The elegant buttress of the Rosa Pinnacle, picked out by the sun, offers a number of fine rock climbs. *Photo: Gordon Gadsby*

Above: Walkers descending Caisteal Abhail, heading towards Cir Mhor on a glorious summer's day. *Photo: Gordon Gadsby*

below. From here you begin the long return march to Brodick.

Steel yourself for the descent down steep heather-covered slopes into Glen Sannox and the subsequent climb up to Cioch na h-Oighe, nearly 2,000ft. The Sannox river is not bridged above the main road so it must be forded.

The west face of the Cioch is very steep and slabby and the best way of ascending it is to approach from the north and then, higher up, traverse round to the west side, where a path winds a tortuous way up through the loose rocks and heather. The impressive high corrie on the east side is the Devil's Punch Bowl which has recently been the favourite haunt of a white stag.

The south ridge of Cioch na h-Oighe is another exposed scramble if taken along the crest, but any difficulties can be bypassed. The gradual ascent of this ridge leads you to the flattish summit of Mullach Buidhe (2,688ft.). The ridge now becomes wide and leads easily to North Goat Fell, and then continues due

south for half a mile to Goat Fell itself. There is an excellent path on the east side of the granite tors that takes you to the final slopes of Goat Fell. The granite hereabouts is very rotten and decayed; pick up a piece and see how it crumbles away in your hand.

The summit trig point, 2,866ft., is perched on an area of flat granite slabs and, because Goat Fell is a popular tourist mountain, the granite has been chipped and scarred by misguided people carving their initials and other messages.

Descend the summit rocks in a south-westerly direction to reach the main south ridge that overlooks Glen Rosa. Don't attempt to descend the western slopes until you are well down the ridge, because there are vast areas of steep slabs between you and the Rosa river. Keep to the ridge until gentle grassy slopes lead down into Glen Rosa very near where you left it earlier in the day. Two and a half miles of good track and road take you back to Brodick.

29   Merrick and the Rhinns of Kells

The Galloway Hills are tucked away in the south-west corner of Scotland and, being off the north-south axis of Britain, they are little known. Mountaineers from the south speed north to the Highlands, with scarcely a thought for the extensive and beautiful area of Galloway, thirty-five miles west of Dumfries.

The hills of Galloway rise to 2,764ft. at Merrick, and there are a dozen more in excess of 2,000ft. It is an area of high moorland, outcrops of weathered granite, lochs and forests. Much of Galloway has been declared a Forest Park by the Forestry Commission, and in general the landowners allow free access on to the hills. However, the attractive open hillsides are gradually being planted with conifers on their lower slopes and the work of the Forestry Commission is evident everywhere. Only on the high tops and ridges will you be free from fencing and drainage ditches, but apart from this the Galloway Forest is sheer delight and a paradise for hill walkers.

Galloway is rich in tradition, legend and history and many of the place names have a magical and unusual sound. Where else would you find mountains called 'Rig of the Jarkness' or 'Curleywee' and lochs such as 'Long Loch of the Dungeon' or 'Clatteringshaw's Loch'? Read up about Galloway before you go, and you will get much more pleasure from your walk. The Forestry Commission publish an excellent guide which can be obtained from HMSO or bookshops in Glen Trool or Newton Stewart.

The walk I recommend starts from Glen Trool, ascends Merrick and Corserine, the two highest mountains in Galloway, and then traverses the high ridge known as the Rhinns of Kells.

Start from the car-park at the end of the road in Glen Trool and take the path northwards, which is signposted to Merrick. At first, the path follows the west bank of the Buchan burn and then passes through a plantation, before breaking out on the hillside near a ruined cottage called Culsharg. Now climb the slopes ahead, keeping parallel to the edge of the plantation, until you reach the col on the broad south shoulder of Benyellary, where you will meet a dry-stone wall. Follow the wall up to the summit of Benyellary, which is marked by a huge pile of stones. Immediately after the summit the wall makes

an abrupt turn left, and in misty conditions you can follow it for the next mile along a ridge which leads to the main massif of Merrick. On Merrick itself, the path becomes rather indistinct, but if you follow the rising ground which becomes increasingly stony underfoot you cannot miss the whitewashed trig point, which is built on a large plinth of boulders at the edge of an escarpment.

Merrick is the highest point of a group of mountains connected by ridges which together make the shape of a hand. The range is known as Merrick-Shalloch Rhinns, or 'Range of the Awful Hand'. The view from Merrick must be extensive, but I was unlucky and at 8.00 a.m. thick morning mist obscured all but nearby features. The north and east sides of Merrick are very steep, almost precipitous, but north-east of the summit plateau, 200 yards from the cairn, a ridge descends to lower ground. At first this ridge is steep and very loose, but the rocks soon give way to grassy hummocks and there are no real difficulties. As you descend the lower parts of

Walk   Merrick and the Rhinns of Kells.
Maps   O.S. 1:50,000 Sheet 77.
Start and finish at Glen Trool car park (ref. 415803).
Grading   A long walk over rough and tussocky ground. In wet weather river crossings could be hazardous.
Time   9-10 hours.
Distance   24 miles.
Escape Routes   From Gala Lane walk north to Loch Doon. From Corserine descend the S.E. ridge to Dukieston.
Telephones   Glen Trool and Dukieston.
Transport   Railway stations at Dumfries and Stranraer.
Western S.M.T. buses run between Dumfries and Newton Stewart and the Newton Stewart to Ayr service passes through Glen Trool Forest.
Accommodation   Hotels at Newton Stewart 13 miles from Loch Trool. Camp site at Caldons, west end of Loch Trool. Youth Hostels at Minnigaff, Newton Stewart and Kendoon, near Dalry.
Guidebooks   *Galloway Forest Park* a Forestry Commission Guide published by H.M.S.O.; *Romantic Galloway* by John McCulloch (Galloway Publicity Association, Castle Douglas); S.M.T. Guide *The Southern Uplands.*

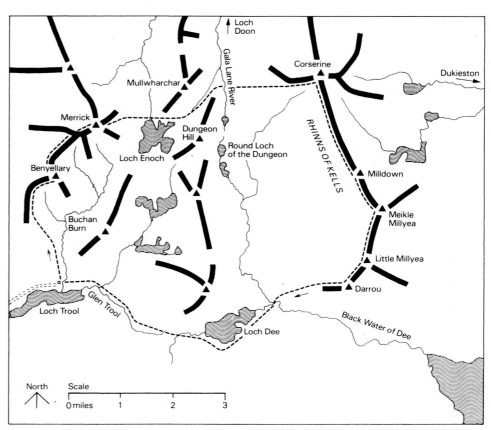

the ridge, make your way as far as possible eastwards towards Loch Enoch which you will see below.

Loch Enoch is a delightful expanse of water with many inlets, sandy bays and islands, and you should skirt it on the north side, making for the defile between Mullwharchar and Dungeon Hill. The going is arduous, across thick tussocky grass and over numerous knobbles of clean granite, for there is no vestige of a path. The long loch, stretching away north for seven miles, is Loch Doon, whose exit stream is immortalized by Burns in his poem which begins 'Ye banks and braes o' bonnie Doon'. The Atomic Energy Authority are seeking permission to 'test bore' the fine granite hill of Mullwharchar for possible disposal of radioactive waste. If this outlandish scheme goes ahead the bonny banks of Loch Doon will change to industrial wasteland.

Eventually you reach the valley bottom under the western spur of Corserine and,

unless it is exceptionally wet, you will have no trouble crossing the burn. Ahead you will see a new plantation rising up the hillside for 500ft., and there is no way round it. Cross the fence and tackle the deep heather and grass which, not being grazed, is very deep and coarse. Note that the drainage ditches are at right angles and that many of them will be covered by the long grass.

The western spur of Corserine leads gently to the summit plateau and a simple white trig point at 2,669ft. I was able to see the coastline of Northern Ireland and the Arran hills from Corserine, and it is a particularly fine view-point for the Galloway hills.

South of Corserine stretches the broad ridge of the Rhinns of Kells. Soon after leaving Corserine you descend to the lowest part of the ridge, where you will see several stone cairns, a lake on your left and the forestry plantation reaching almost to the ridge on your right. At Milldown, an old wall is met which continues

Top: The ravages of the Forestry Commission have transformed the valley between Merrick and the Rhinns of Kells into a scene of regimented monotony. The Kells ridge remains clear of the devastation; Corserine, the highest top, is on the left in this view from Dungeon Hill. *Photo: Ken Andrew*

Bottom: Looking from Craignaw across Loch Enoch towards Merrick's northern ridges. *Photo: Tom Weir*

Top: The northern slopes of Merrick, looking towards Loch Doon (top right). *Photo: Ken Andrew*

Bottom: Curleywee and Lamachan seen from the slopes of Darrou at the end of the Kells ridge. A new forestry road services plantations that will soon change the character of this lonely Galloway valley. *Photo: Ken Andrew*

along the crest of the ridge to Meikle Millyea (2,438ft.) and Little Millyea. Under Meikle Millyea, you will pass a group of tiny lochans, where I had lunch amongst the harebells and cotton grass. Meikle Millyea is predominantly stony, but the stones are flat and the going is excellent.

The last summit on the Rhinns is Darrou, after which it is an easy descent south-west to the valley of the Black Water of Dee. The Forestry Commission is active in this valley and a brand new bridge, not marked on the map, spans the river. On the south side of the Dee, an excellent track leads to Loch Dee, passes the remote farm at Black Laggan and continues to the watershed between Glen Dee and Glen Trool. Here the Land-Rover track stops and a narrow footpath takes you down into Upper Glen Trool.

As I passed the farmstead at Glenhead, I spoke to a farmer who was busy shearing sheep. He was complaining that year after year he can keep fewer sheep as more grazing is fenced off by the Forestry Commission and soon he would give up sheep farming altogether.

The last mile back to the Glen Trool car-park is part of a forest trail and it passes through woods of sycamore and oak and crosses some spectacular gorges. Perched high above Loch Trool you will see a large stone; this is a memorial to Robert the Bruce and directly behind the stone is the car-park. Your walk is over, but if you did not already know Galloway I am sure you will return to this remarkable area.

30   Borderland: the Cheviot Hills

I always enjoy driving north to Edinburgh. Both the A68 through Corbridge and Jedburgh and the A697 through Wooler and Coldstream, pass under the open slopes of the Cheviot hills, the A68 on the west side and the A697 on the east. Snow on the Cheviots augurs well for winter conditions in the Highlands, and the view east from the road summit at Carter Bar of countless miles of rolling hills is uplifting to the mountaineer.

The Cheviots were thrown up by volcanic action millions of years ago, but now they are worn down to rounded summits with steep sides and deep valleys. They are mostly smooth and grassy hills, and since to date the Forestry Commission has kept clear they provide hill walking *par excellence*. To the south the streams drain into the Coquet and to the north into the Tweed, both superb salmon rivers.

Apart from a few walkers making for Kirk Yetholm on the last lap of the Pennine Way, all you are likely to meet are sheep of the Scottish Blackfaced or the Cheviot variety which have white faces.

The highest ridge of the Cheviots marks the border between Scotland and England, the actual boundary line being a low sheep fence. The walk described below is from the ancient Northumbrian market town of Wooler to Carter Bar on the A68, where the road crosses the Scottish border. Much of the walk follows the border fence. You should arrange transport to meet you at Carter Bar, unless you can arrange your schedule to meet the Newcastle to Edinburgh bus. If you decide to start your walk from Carter Bar, there is plenty of good accommodation in Wooler.

Leave Wooler by the narrow road that climbs steeply up to the village of Earle. At Middleton Hall turn sharp right along the road signposted to Langleeford. This road soon plunges down to the valley bottom and crosses the Carey burn by a substantial bridge. Take the rough track which is marked to Broadstruther and climb up the hillside, passing a small plantation on the left, until the track levels out. Now strike out in a south-westerly direction across the short heather and rough grass towards Cold Law, whose white-painted trig point can easily be seen against the sky.

From Cold Law descend south-west to the col under Broadhope Hill. On the col you will meet a fence and a standing boundary stone carved with the letters SH. Don't ascend Broadhope Hill, but swing round south to Scald Hill; if you make for the huge bulk of Cheviot, which dominates the view west, you will not go wrong. The going is tough, through deep coarse grass and heather, but look out for clumps of white heather which grows hereabouts.

On Scald Hill you will meet a fence and a dreadfully eroded path through the peat, which leads to the summit plateau of Cheviot. This plateau is one of my least favourite places anywhere. Although it is a superb view-point for the Farne Islands, Lindisfarne and the distant Highlands of Scotland, it is composed of saturated peat bogs and progress is seriously hampered by deep pools of standing water. Only in the depths of winter, when all is frozen hard, is the summit of Cheviot at all tolerable. The trig point at 2,674ft. is situated on a plinth of turf at the western end of the plateau, but it is completely surrounded by quagmire. If you want to reach the trig point after a spell of wet weather you will need either snow-shoes or a swimming costume. The last time I made the effort, the black bog went over my knees.

Leave Cheviot in a south-westerly direction and cross some more deep peat hags, until you meet a fence which you should follow over a subsidiary summit until, after a mile, you reach a Pennine Way marker-post. Just to the north is a conspicuous mound and rock outcrop, called Auchope Cairn. The Pennine Way path, which you have just met, goes over

Walk   Borderland: the Cheviot Hills.
Maps   O.S. 1:50,000 Sheets 75 and 80. Start from Wooler (ref. 993280). Finish at Carter Bar (ref. 698068).
Grading   A long walk over remote but grassy hills. Can be boggy in wet weather.
Time   11-12 hours.
Distance   32 miles.
Escape Routes   From Auchope Cairn follow the Pennine Way northwards to Kirk Yetholm, 8 miles. From Mazie Law descend the Heatherhope Valley to Hownam, 5 miles. From Chew Green take the metalled access road south to Byrness, 6 miles.
Telephones   Kirk Yetholm; Hownam; Byrness; R.A.C. box at Carter Bar.
Transport   Wooler has good bus connections to Newcastle, Edinburgh, Alnwick, Berwick and Kelso. Railway Station at Berwick. The Newcastle—Edinburgh and Newcastle—Glasgow express bus services pass over Carter Bar.
Accommodation   Hotels at Wooler and Byrness. Youth Hostels at Wooler, Kirk Yetholm and Byrness.
Guidebooks   *The Northumberland National Park* (H.M.S.O.); *The Scottish Borders and Northumberland* by John Talbot White (Methuen). S.M.T. Guide *The Southern Uplands*.

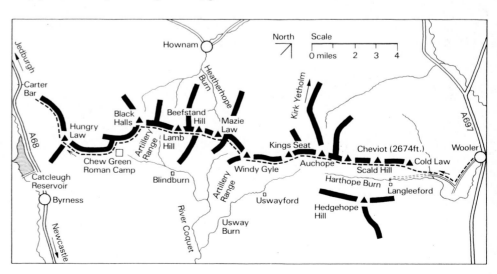

Auchope Cairn on its way to Kirk Yetholm.

The next thirteen-mile section of the walk to Chew Green is along the Pennine Way. The path is unmistakable, not only because thousands of feet have worn away the grass and exposed the peat, but because marker-posts set in peat cairns have been erected at regular intervals. These posts are an eyesore, spoiling the natural contours of the hills; they could have been put to better use laid horizontally across the worst of the bogs.

Nevertheless, the switchback path over the high backbone of the Cheviots is always delightful, and in places the ground is carpeted with cloudberries. The area is steeped in history and the path passes Bronze Age burial mounds, standing stones, and ancient drove roads, and looks down on the sites of Roman forts. The border fence between England and Scotland is your constant companion and occasional glimpses of remote farmsteads set at the head of deep grassy valleys are your only contact with civilization on the Scottish side. On the English side, a vast area of the Cheviots has been given over to the army as a firing range, and danger notices and red flags are evident, while the booming of guns echoes round the valleys.

Traverse Kings Seat, Windy Gyle, Mazie Law, Beefstand Hill, Lamb Hill and Black Halls and, if the weather is bad, note that a substantial wooden shelter has been erected

half a mile beyond Lamb Hill. Soon after leaving Black Halls the path becomes grassy, wide and well-constructed. This is the Roman road of Dere Street which runs from York to Trimontium. The path now descends to the Roman Camp of Chew Green, which is dramatically set amidst the hills and has suffered little at the hands of man. The camp was first occupied by the Romans in the first century AD; much later it was a medieval settlement, and even in the eighteenth century it was a well known meeting-place and shelter for cattle drovers. Now, all that is visible are the turf covered ramparts and ditches.

Stay on the Pennine Way for a further mile beyond Chew Green, while the path makes a dog-leg detour to avoid a danger area. But when the path reaches the forestry plantation, branch off across the heather and keep to the northern boundary fence of the plantation, which is of Lodge Pole Pine at first, giving way to Sitka Spruce. You will find it a relief to be off the peat bogs of the Pennine Way, but once again you should follow the border fence as it cross Hungry Law, Catcleuch, Leap Hill and Arks Edge to Carter Bar. With no path and much new forestry not marked on the map, take care not to lose sight of the fence.

Note that there is no shelter at Carter Bar and no telephone, unless you bring a key to use the one in the RAC box which stands in the lay-by.

Top: Looking east towards Cheviot, from the Pennine Way at Windy Gyle Hill. *Photo: Ken Andrew*

Left: The valley of Harthope Burn, with Cheviot in the distance. *Photo: Leonard and Marjorie Gayton*

Above: Hedgehope Hill from Cheviot, looking south-east. *Photo: Leonard and Marjorie Gayton*

Across the Southern Uplands: Peebles to Moffat

Walk Across the Southern Uplands: Peebles to Moffat.
Maps O.S. 1:50,000 Sheets 72, 73, 78, 79. Start from Peebles (ref. 240402). Finish at Moffat (ref. 083055).
Grading An exceptionally long walk over remote and undulating hills.
Time 14-15 hours.
Distance 35 miles.
Escape Routes The route crosses the Tweedsmuir to St. Mary's Loch road at the Megget Stone. Decend to Loch Skeen and take good path to Grey Mare's Tail. From Hart Fell descend S.W. to Ericstane.
Telephones Peebles; Glen House; Cappercleuch; Tweedsmuir; Capplegill; Moffat.
Transport Peebles is well connected by bus to the other Border towns and to Edinburgh. Peebles to Moffat bus service on Fridays, Saturdays and Sundays. Carlisle to Glasgow train service to Lockerbie then bus to Moffat.
Accommodation Wide selection of Hotels and Guest Houses in Peebles and Moffatt.
Guidebooks *Guide to Walks and Climbs in Dumfries and Galloway* by R. D. Walton (Dinwiddie's, Dumfries); S.M.T. Guide *The Southern Uplands*.

The Southern Uplands sweep north from the Scottish Border to the Pentland Hills south of Edinburgh. They form a region of exquisite beauty, with wooded valleys, tumbling rivers, rolling fells, ruined abbeys and severe, solid towns built of grey stone.

Go to the Border Country while there is still time. As yet, the hills are undiscovered by the masses and you will find solitude, peace and trackless fells awaiting your exploration.

In appearance the Southern Uplands resemble the Cheviots, but they are wilder, the grass is rougher, the heather deeper and the tops lonelier. It is easy to understand how the Border region inspired Wordsworth and Sir Walter Scott to write their romantic poetry, and it has been the source of many legends and ballads.

For this walk I have chosen the isolated range of hills between Peebles and Moffat, because they are mainly untouched by the Forestry Commission. Their valleys, draining north to the River Tweed, are particularly fine and the two towns provide first class accommodation and communications.

'Peebles for Pleasure' is a well-known Scottish expression and the walk starts from this proud and stylish old town. From the centre of Peebles walk south over Tweed Bridge and at the edge of the town fork right into Glen Sax. Soon after Haystoun Farm, the tarmac gives way to a rough track leading gently up this delightful glen towards the folded, heather-covered hills. At Upper Newby, leave the road and start climbing up the open fell side, south of Newby Kipps forestry plantation. Ahead of you lies 30 miles of peat and heather moorland, before you descend below the 1,400ft. level at Moffat.

Follow the wall over Preston Law to Hundleshope Heights which, at 2,240ft., is your first real summit of the day. The heather is deep and, as is their wont, the sheep tracks contour the hills and are little help, but the higher you climb the easier the walking becomes.

Proceed south over Glenrath Heights, where the peat is firm and even and makes for fast walking; thick, tussocky grass and bog are again encountered, though, on Blackhouse Heights and Black Law. The old boundary fence aids navigation in misty weather, and throughout the rest of the walk either fence-posts or dry-stone walls are your constant guides.

Your route keeps strictly to the high tops, but your gaze will be drawn down to the hidden valleys which penetrate these fells. Tantalizing glimpses of waterfalls, cascades, idyllic camp sites and the blue waters of St. Mary's Loch await the eye.

From Water Head, swing north to Notman Law and skirt the head of the Cramalt Burn; this brings you to the Dun Law – Dollar Law ridge. At once the only man-made intrusion into these hills comes into sight, the radio beacon on Broad Law, two miles away to the south-west and your next objective.

The radio beacon is a squat construction of white mushroom-shaped baffles set in a circle. It emits a low but menacing hum, and I preferred to pause 100 yards away at the white-painted trig point on Broad Law, the highest point of the entire walk, at 2,754ft. The authorities have done a good job in making the beacon unobtrusive: the power cables travel underground and the aerials cannot be seen at all from the south.

A good fast stretch over close-cropped grass leads you over the aptly named hill of Cairn Law, whose summit is speckled with fat, well-constructed cairns of grey stone, thence to the psychologically important landmark of the Megget Stone.

The Megget Stone is a small lichen-encrusted boulder, set beside the narrow road linking Tweedsmuir with St. Mary's Loch. The road carries very little traffic, but since it is beside the only tarmac of the walk the Megget Stone makes an ideal rendezvous for a motorized support party. With many miles now under your belt, you can look with confidence across Megget Dale to the huge massifs ahead. These are White Coomb and Hart Fell, beyond which it is downhill all the way to Moffat.

Cross the road at the cattle grid, and follow the twisting fence to Lochcraig Head. It is a long haul up to the subsidiary summit of Nickie's Knowe, but a fine view opens up west to Talla Reservoir and east to the new dam and construction site at Megget Water.

Right: Typical Southern Upland scenery at Talla Linnfoot, seen from the slopes below Cairn Law. Gameshope Burn runs down the valley in the background. *Photo: Ken Andrew*

Above: The eastern slopes of White Coomb in the Moffat Hills, looking south-east to the Ettrick Hills beyond the A708. *Photo: Robert Adam*

Lochcraig Head is a shapely, rounded dome overlooking Loch Skeen. Set in a hollow to the north of White Coomb, Loch Skeen is a gem. I have camped on its shores while a full moon silvered the water and threw the tree-covered islets into sharp relief. Loch Skeen is undiscovered by the tourists and it retains a magical quality.

The direct route to Moffat lies over Firthybrig Head and Hart Fell, but if time and energy are available a detour should be made to the Grey Mare's Tail waterfall. Loch Skeen flows into Moffat Water through the Tail Burn. This considerable stream roars through a narrow gorge and then plunges over the lip of 200ft. cliffs, in a cascade of white water and foam. The falls fully justify the extravagant descriptions of the tourist brochures, for the

setting is romantic and splendid and is now under the wing of the National Trust for Scotland.

From the bottom of the falls, a narrow path winds up the south-east ridge of White Coomb, and at Firthhope Rig, just beyond the summit, you regain the marker fence.

The next stretch to Hartfell Rig is featureless and rough, with deep tussocks, black bog and peat hags. The fence and a few sheep are your only companions. I investigated a post sticking up from nowhere on the desolate moor, to find that it marked a copper rain gauge draining into a huge reservoir. It cannot often be inspected.

Hart Fell itself has a line of crags overlooking the Blackhope Burn, and looking back east you can admire the razor-sharp ridge of Saddle Yoke, an exceptional feature for this area of hills.

Descend south-east from Hart Fell summit to the col under Swatte Fell. Once again the route is simple to find, because a new fence has been erected, although it is not shown on the map. At the col, the fence gives way to a dry-stone wall for the undulating section over Swatte Fell to Greygill Head. A solid, stone-built cairn marks the summit of Greygill Head, and only easy slopes of heather and bilberry remain before you meet the road-head at Blaebeck. Greygill was used as an artillery range during the war and notices remind you not to tamper with strange objects.

Hot meals, warmth and soft beds await you at Moffat, only two miles further along a country lane, when you will have accomplished one of Britain's most demanding and exhilarating hill walks. On my Peebles to Moffat crossing, I met not a single soul.

Right: The Grey Mare's Tail, the spectacular waterfall that cascades down the gully below Loch Skeen on the southern slopes of the Moffat Hills. *Photo: Ken Andrew*

32   Highest Pennines: Upper Teesdale and Cross Fell

This long but magnificent walk takes in some of the best fell country that England has to offer. It starts at Middleton in Teesdale and proceeds up the delectable valley of the upper Tees, before climbing up to the Pennine Ridge and traversing Cross Fell, at 2,930ft. the highest summit on the backbone of England. The walk ends at Alston in Cumbria, the highest market town in England.

Much of the walk is along the Pennine Way but you are unlikely to meet many walkers. Even on a Bank Holiday Sunday I passed only about twenty back-packers throughout the entire thirty-five miles, and most of those were toiling up Cross Fell from Dufton.

Start at the bridge over the Tees at Middleton, and take the path that keeps to the south (Yorkshire) side of the river. For the next four miles this path winds through meadows and over banks and crosses numerous walls by stiles which have been specially constructed for the benefit of walkers. The path is sometimes high above the river and sometimes at the water's edge, but the scenery is always entrancing. In spring the banks are ablaze with violets, primroses, wood anemonès, cowslips and bluebells, and always there is the river close by. The Tees is a considerable river at Middleton, and in some places it sparkles over its bed of boulders and at others it glides through deep pools shaded by overhanging branches of willow and hazel. Rabbits abound and the river banks are riddled with burrows.

Three miles up-river from Middleton you pass the first bridge over the Tees, and thereafter the path remains close beside the river. Alongside the path there are tunnels in the hillside, relics of the lead-mining industry of the nineteenth century. A short distance further up-stream is a picturesque suspension bridge called Winch Bridge, and the river foams below through a narrow gorge. The path soon enters the Upper Teesdale National Nature Reserve and long stretches of duck-boarding have been laid, to prevent further erosion of the track rather than to protect your boots from the mud. After climbing a steep hillside, you pass through scrub juniper bushes and then you hear the roar of High Force, England's most spectacular waterfall. The Tees plunges

Left: The cliffs near High Cup Nick on the Pennine Way. The curious rock saddle seen here is called Nicholas' Chair. *Photo: Walt Unsworth*

70ft. into a dark whirlpool enclosed in an amphitheatre of black cliffs.

Beyond High Force you pass a large and unsightly quarry on the north bank and, after another mile, the path climbs up a hillside of gorse bushes and temporarily leaves the river side. It descends again to the farm at Cronkley and crosses the river by a road bridge. Continue now on the north side of the river and cross the Langdon Beck tributary by a bridge half a mile up-stream. The path is well signposted, as it proceeds through fields of wild pansies to the substantial whitewashed building of Widdybank Farm.

A mile further on the path passes under a line of broken cliffs, called Falcon Clints, and then the Maize Beck joins the Tees from the west. As you round a bluff of rock, a white

Walk   Highest Pennines: Upper Teesdale and Cross Fell.
Maps   O.S. 1:50,000 Sheets 91 and 82. Start from Middleton in Teesdale (ref. 946253). Finish at Alston (ref. 717465).
Grading   A very long walk over the highest of the Pennine fells. Some stretches of rough moorland but in general the going is good.
Time   12 hours.
Distance   35 miles.
Escape Routes   From High Cup Nick, 15 miles, a good path descends to Dufton in the Eden Valley. From Cross Fell summit descend W. to Kirkland, 3 miles.
Telephones   Dufton; Blencarn near Kirkland; Garrigill.
Transport   O.K. Services run a bus between Middleton in Teesdale and Alston on Fridays and Sundays only in summer. Darlington—Middleton daily bus service. Alston—Haltwhistle—Carlisle daily bus service.
Accommodation   Hotels at Middleton in Teesdale and Alston. Youth Hostels at Langdon Beck, Dufton and Alston.
Guidebooks   Since most of this walk is along the Pennine Way, any Pennine Way Guidebook, of which there are many, would be helpful; *Peak and Pennines* by W. A. Poucher (Constable).

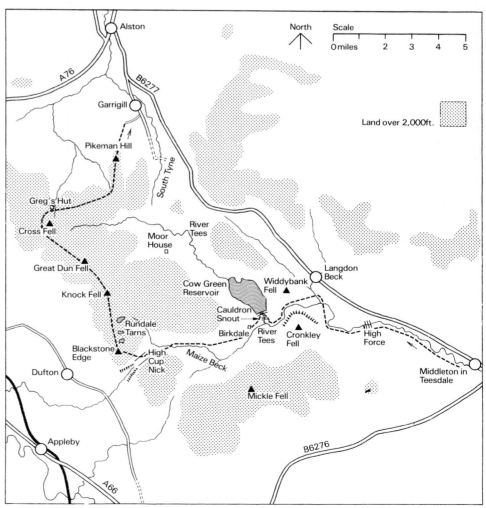

cataract of water comes into sight; this is the famous Cauldron Snout, where the Tees roars down a narrow gorge of Whin Sill rock. Scramble up the rocks on the north side of Cauldron Snout and pause at the bridge between the top of the falls and the white concrete retaining dam of the Cow Green reservoir.

The reservoir was built in 1970 in spite of much hostility from conservationists. The Cow Green area is unique for its 'sugar limestone', on which much arctic flora grows, flora which has survived the last ice age. The dam controls the flow of water down the river Tees and the dramatic flash floods which used to turn Cauldron Snout and High Force into a welter

of foam and spray will never be seen again. Although the reservoir is large, over 700 acres, you will not see it until Great Dun Fell is reached, much further along the walk.

Cross the bridge and take a rough track which branches left and climbs slowly up the fell side, passing through Birkdale Farm. The path keeps to the edge of an extensive artillery and tank firing range, which includes Mickle Fell, and you will see the warning notices erected at regular intervals.

Now descend gently to the Maize Beck which is your last reliable source of water for nearly fifteen miles. In dry weather it is easy to cross the Maize Beck, but if in doubt don't risk it, for a walker has been drowned here;

instead, keep to the north bank for a further mile where you will find a footbridge. Either way the paths meet at High Cup Nick, a wonderful geological phenomenon where the ground falls away abruptly into a vast chasm. The escarpment on the south side is particularly sheer, but you can easily walk up to the large stone cairn on the north side of this most spectacular glaciated valley.

The Pennine Way now descends to the village of Dufton in the Eden Valley, but you must make your way across three and a half miles of very rough and trackless hillside until you meet it again on Knock Fell.

From the stone cairn above High Cup Nick you can follow a line of similar cairns for a mile, until you reach an Ordnance Survey trig point built of grey stone. The ground is peat-hagged and tussocky, with deep heather and bilberry plants, but beyond the trig point it becomes easier and you can follow some recent drainage ditches. If you stray too far east you will come across a collection of small tarns. In clear weather you will easily see the radio masts on Great Dun Fell and can head for them, but in misty weather you should hug the west-facing slopes of the fells until you meet the Pennine Way track from Dufton to Knock Fell.

Half a mile beyond Knock Fell you meet the tarmac supply road for the radio station. At the locked gate take the path to the right of the

Above: Walkers descending to the Maize Beck with Murton Fell on the left and High Cup Nick — the distant skyline notch. *Photo: Dave Matthews*

133

road and this will lead you to the summit of Great Dun Fell. Ahead is the smaller rounded top of Little Dun Fell, and beyond this the huge bulk of Cross Fell. To the west the Eden Valley is spread out below, green and fertile, while to the south-east lies the vast catchment area of Upper Teesdale, draining into the now visible Cow Green reservoir.

It is easy walking in a north-easterly direction to Little Dun Fell and Cross Fell. Just before Cross Fell's summit, to the right of the path, is a spring of ice cold water which saved my life one scorching May day, but this probably dries up in the height of summer. The summit of Cross Fell is a stony plateau with the O.S. cairn and a stone wind-break built on the western edge. The views west to the Lake District hills are extensive.

Cross Fell holds patches of snow well into the summer and, when driving between Appleby and Penrith, its appearance is a good guide to the snow conditions in Lakeland.

Take careful bearings when descending Cross Fell, for the plateau is featureless and it is easy to stray on to difficult stony ground. If you descend northwards from the trig point for half a mile, following a line of cairns, you will see on your right an old cottage called Greg's Hut. This is a shelter that has been renovated by the Mountain Bothies Association and it lies on a good track running roughly east-west under the northern slopes of Cross Fell. Follow this path eastwards for two miles until you reach a collection of ruined mine dwellings. You will notice purple crystals of fluorspar, known as Blue John, lying everywhere. From the mine the track swings north and becomes wider, but it is a very rough and tiresome four-mile walk down to Garrigill village at the head of the South Tyne Valley. At Garrigill you can buy refreshments, either at the village store which is open on Sundays, or at the George and Dragon Inn.

The walk ends as it started, with a pleasant riverside stretch of four miles. The path follows the west bank of the Tyne, passing some old spoil heaps, but after two miles it crosses the river by a narrow bridge. Just beyond this bridge the path climbs up to pastures well above the river and eventually it enters Alston at the new Youth Hostel above the road bridge.

33   The Lakeland Three Thousanders

Walk   The Lakeland Three Thousanders.
Maps   O.S. 1:50,000 Sheet 90; O.S. 1:63,360 Tourist Map of the Lake District; O.S. 1:25,000 Outdoor Leisure Map — The Lake District. Start and finish at Keswick Market Place (ref. 265235).
Grading   An exceptionally long and arduous walk. Many different types of terrain are covered from roads and grassy fells to loose scree and rough boulders.
Time   16-20 hours.
Distance   46 miles.
Escape Routes   From Styhead, Lingmell Col and Mickledore descend easily to Wasdale Head. From Esk Hause descend Grains Gill to Seathwaite.
Telephones   Seathwaite; Wasdale Head; Stanah; Old Dungeon Ghyll Hotel, Langdale.
Transport   Railway Station at Penrith, 18 miles. Buses from Keswick to Ambleside, Carlisle, Whitehaven, Lancaster and Kendal.
Accommodation   Hotels in Keswick and Borrowdale. Youth Hostels at Keswick, Derwentwater and Longthwaite (Borrowdale).
Guidebooks   Guides to *The Northern, Eastern, Central* and *Southern Fells* by A. Wainwright (The Westmorland Gazette); An informative and readable Lakeland guide is *Freedom of the Hills* by A. H. Griffin (Robert Hale).

Marathon walks in the English Lake District have provided a popular challenge ever since 1911, when Dr Arthur Wakefield first completed the circuit of the four three-thousand foot peaks in twenty-four hours. Since then, extra peaks have been added by fell runners, and the best known marathon of all is the Bob Graham circuit of over forty peaks.

The framework for these marathon walks is still the ascent of the four three-thousanders, Skiddaw, Scafell, Scafell Pike and Helvellyn, starting and finishing at Keswick. The round to be completed in twenty-four hours. Thus the three-thousanders walk is challenging, not only in the ground to be covered (forty-six miles minimum) and the height to be climbed (11,000ft.), but also in the time to be taken.

Walkers might find it convenient, as I did, to enter the annual three-thousanders walk organized by the Ramblers' Association, which takes place every summer. There is a total of ten check-points on the way round, but otherwise you pick your own route and refreshments are provided where they are most needed, at Seathwaite in Borrowdale and at

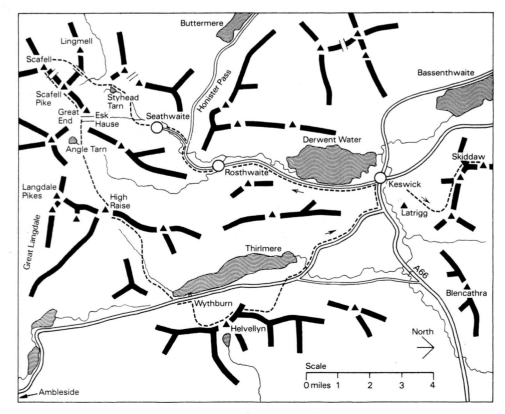

Steel End by Thirlmere. The Ramblers' Association allows you twenty-two hours to complete the circuit, but the top fell runners take only between eight and ten hours.

If you abhor organized walks, you are free of course to attempt the circuit as and when you like, but you should start and finish at the Moot Hall in Keswick market place.

It is perhaps best to make Skiddaw the first

of your four summits and to leave before dawn, because the ascent is so easy that it can be accomplished by torch light.

Leave Keswick via the railway station and then turn left along a narrow road which runs north of the railway track. After a quarter of a mile leave this road and walk up the unmade Spooney Green Lane which is signed to Latrigg and Skiddaw. This lane crosses the northern bypass of Keswick by a footbridge, and then traverses the grassy slopes of Latrigg by a delightful winding path. Beyond Latrigg you cross a tarmac road and continue up Skiddaw by a narrow path running beside a stone wall.

The path up Skiddaw is now wide and easy, and simple to follow. The slopes of the mountain are grassy until you reach the upper

Above: England's highest peaks, Scafell and Scafell Pike, seen from Bowfell. Descending from Scafell to Mickledore (the obvious col), presents the walker with one of the trickiest route-finding problems in the Lake District, as cliffs circle the whole northern flank of the mountain. The most direct route descends the right edge of Scafell's East Buttress — the dark cliff to the left of the col — by an easy rock climb called Broad Stand. This is best avoided by all except trained rock climbers. The walker has a choice of devious routes down other flanks of the mountain. *Photo: E. A. Shepherd*

Top: A view of Skiddaw (left) and Saddleback (right) from Grisedale Pike. The outskirts of Keswick can be seen on the extreme right of the picture. *Photo: John Allen*

Bottom: Looking south-east from Skiddaw's Little Man, across Lonscale Fell, to Great Dodd. *Photo: Alan Parker*

sections of the broad ridge, when they become covered with flat slatey stones. The Ordnance Survey cairn is on the northern summit.

Descend to Keswick by the same route and walk the nine miles through Borrowdale to Seathwaite. This walk along the road is not as tedious as it sounds, for the scenery is most diverse and beautiful. I was lucky to pick a glorious summer day for my walk and, apart from low clouds on Skiddaw, the sun shone throughout, and in the early morning the meadows of Borrowdale were hung with cobwebs beaded by dew.

From Seathwaite Farm continue to walk up the dale until you reach Stockley Bridge, the old packhorse bridge over Grains Gill. Cross the bridge and follow the path up to Styhead Tarn.

The main path now descends to Wasdale, but you must branch left to reach the Corridor Route to the Scafells. You will see the path winding across the slopes under Broad Crag and passing above Piers Gill. As you ascend the Corridor Route you will see the impressive

line of buttresses on Lingmell Crag straight ahead, and your path makes for the col on the left-hand side of the crag.

The main path to Scafell Pike now turns due south but you must continue in a south-westerly direction along a narrow path which eventually descends to Hollow Stones. When you have descended about 400ft. you can traverse round to meet the screes below the impressive Scafell Crag. If you attempt to keep too high, as I did, you get on to difficult ground under Pikes Crag.

The buttressed Scafell Crag which you see immediately ahead is the finest piece of clean rock in England, and its only line of weakness for the walker is the narrow cleft at the top of the scree shoot called Lord's Rake.

The ascent of Lord's Rake is horribly loose, but nowhere is it difficult, and it brings you out on the summit plateau of Scafell.

Scafell is connected to Scafell Pike by a saddle called Mickledore, at a height of 2,600ft. The descent from Scafell to Mickle-dore is tricky and you should either return

Above: On Helvellyn's summit plateau, looking south-west to the peaks of the Coniston group. Photo: Alf Gregory

down Lord's Rake and then follow the path under the west buttress which leads to Mickledore, or descend via Fox Tarn. To reach Fox Tarn from the summit cairn of Scafell you must proceed north-west for 200 yards and then descend a scree slope on the right for 300ft., until you reach a patch of bright green moss with a spring welling up through it. This is Fox Tarn, and after a further descent of 200ft. you can traverse round under the East Buttress of Scafell and gain Mickledore near the mountain-rescue box. The direct descent to Mickledore, by the series of rocky steps known as Broad Stand, is suitable only for those with some rock climbing experience. It is particularly treacherous in wet or icy conditions.

A well-scratched path leads over the boulders from Mickledore to Scafell Pike and beyond, as you switchback over Broad Crag and the south shoulder of Great End. From the slopes of Great End you descend gradually east to reach the wide plateau of Esk Hause, the most famous cross roads in the Lake District. Just before you reach Esk Hause you pass a most welcome stream of water.

Esk Hause can be a confusing place in misty weather and you must be very careful to take the correct path to your next landmark, which is Angle Tarn. Head north-west for 300 yards, until you meet a path coming up from the right (east) side. This is a path to Angle Tarn which you should reach in a mile. Cross the exit stream of Angle Tarn and then follow a rather indistinct path which traverses the hillside high above Langstrath. After one and a half miles, the path swings away east and you soon arrive at a tiny tarn which is not marked on the map. Now leave the path and strike up the grassy slopes on a bearing of 55°, to the summit of High Raise (2,500ft.), an ascent of 1,000ft. from the tarn.

From the large cairn on High Raise, you should descend the easy slopes in a north-easterly direction until you meet the path from Greenup down to Wyth Burn. It is a long and tiring three and a half mile descent down the

Above: The magnificent buttresses of Scafell Crag, picked out in the evening sun in this dramatic view from the Corridor Route beyond Lingmell. Broad Stand and Mickledore are on the left, but the best route for the walker who wishes to gain the summit of Scafell is to traverse the grassy terraces below the crag to gain the scree-filled gully of Lord's Rake (in shadow on the right). *Photo: E. A. Shepherd*

Top right: At the summit of Helvellyn, looking east across Striding Edge to the peaks of the High Street group. *Photo: Tom Parker*

Bottom right: On the Corridor Route to Scafell, with Great Gable in the background. *Photo: John Allen*

Wyth Burn valley, with bogs, peat hags and moraines to be crossed, but eventually you reach level pastures at Steel End. Helvellyn towers ahead, but you can comfort yourself with the thought that the worst is now over and it is easy going on good paths all the way to Keswick.

The minor road at Steel End is followed east for a short distance until it meets the main A591. Now walk along this road northwards for half a mile until you reach Wythburn Church. This marks the beginning of the main tourist path up Helvellyn and little description is necessary.

The path climbs steeply first through a forestry plantation and then beside a wall marking the upper boundary of the plantation. It then breaks out to the open hillside, and eventually meets the summit ridge half a mile south of the main top.

To descend Helvellyn in the direction of Keswick, follow the edge of the east-facing escarpment for 300 yards in a north-westerly direction towards the subsidiary top called Lower Man. Just before Lower Man a path branches off left and starts a gradual descent towards Thirlmere. The path steepens and becomes loose, but at the 1,750ft. level it

becomes much easier.

When you have descended to Helvellyn Gill, cross the stream and continue along the traverse path which leads to the main road at the whitewashed King's Head Inn at Thirlspot.

Unfortunately, from Thirlspot there is no alternative but to walk back to Keswick along the main road. It is a weary six miles but as you descend the hill from Castlerigg towards Keswick you can save half a mile by taking the short-cut signposted 'Keswick via Manor Brow'. At this stage of the walk, every little helps.

34   Great Langdale: the Horseshoe Walk

by Tom Price

Walk   Great Langdale: the Horseshoe Walk.
Maps   O.S. 1:63,360 Tourist Map of the Lake District; O.S. 1:50,000 Sheet 90.
Start and finish at Elterwater (ref. 328047).
Grading   A moderate walk over varied mountain terrain.
Time   9-10 hours.
Distance   18 miles.
Escape Routes   Easy routes lead down into Langdale from Red Tarn, Three Tarns, Angle Tarn via Rossett Gill, Stake Pass and Stickle Tarn.
Telephones   Elterwater; Little Langdale and the Old Dungeon Ghyll Hotel.
Transport   Railway station at Windermere (9 miles). Regular Ambleside to Langdale bus service.
Accommodation   There are numerous Hotels, Guest Houses, Bed and Breakfasts and climbing huts in Langdale. Youth Hostels at Elterwater and High Close.
Guidebooks   Guides to *The Central Fells* and *Southern Fells* by A. Wainwright (The Westmorland Gazette); *The Lakeland Peaks* by W. A. Poucher (Constable).

Langdale is, for most people, the Lake District's most accessible valley, and considering its attractions it is not surprising that it is one of the busiest. Since thirty million people live within three hours' drive of it, you might think the Langdale Horseshoe walk would be spoiled, yet, although parts of it have noticeably well-trodden footpaths, and though on a fine day you will see numbers of walkers and even on a foul day at least one or two, it is far from congested and makes one of the finest and most varied fell walks in the district.

It is usually done from near the Old or the New Dungeon Ghyll Hotel, but the walk I am going to describe is the long walk right round the Langdale skyline, starting not from the valley head but from Elterwater or Chapel Stile.

Let us begin on the south side. The first objective is Lingmoor Fell, only 1,530ft., but do not under estimate these low-lying hills, for they are sometimes surprisingly broad. It can be approached from Elterwater through woods and quarries, or by taking the lane to Little Langdale until open fellside is reached. One could spend a long time on this fascinating mine-scarred hillside, but, with the whole Horseshoe before us, we will take the most direct route to the top. Lingmoor Fell commands splendid prospects of the Langdale Pikes and the central fells, sometimes with attractive sylvan foregrounds. It is high enough to provide an extensive view, but not so high as to dwarf its neighbours.

There is a little tarn beyond the summit, and rocky Side Pike, both worth visiting, but the quickest route down takes the south side of a wooded ghyll, reaching the road by Bleatarn House. This is the place that provided the background for Wordsworth's 'The Solitary', although these days you would have to look both ways before crossing the tarmac. If you have descended this way and not by Side Pike, you may prefer to follow the road for half a mile before taking off for Pike o' Blisco, rather than strike out across the fields.

Most British hills have steep sides and flattish tops. Not so Pike o' Blisco. It is a real peak, like its taller neighbour opposite, Pike o' Stickle, steep and rocky. Again, from its summit, one can survey the route ahead, and the depth of Mickleden — Old English 'micel denu' ('the great valley') — is fully appreciated.

Pike o' Blisco presents a steep and craggy slope towards Browney Ghyll, so, on leaving the summit, keep well south of west towards Red Tarn, where the well-marked path from Wrynose to Langdale joins the equally well-marked path to Crinkle Crags. Here one is only a mile from the nearest motor road, but the col has often the quiet charm of some more remote place. The tarn clearly gets its name from the colour of the subsoil. From the rugged, heathery terrain of Pike o' Blisco there is a sudden transition to a gentler and grassier tract of country and there follows a comparatively easy ascent to the beginning of the Crinkles, where it again becomes rocky. Such is the complexity of the lavas, ashes and breccias which make up the bedrock of Central Lakeland. Those who build little cairns all over the hills should ponder on the unimaginable antiquity of the stones they are using, and leave a few of them where they are.

So from Red Tarn we come to a delightful high plateau between Cold Pike and Great Knott. For such a high fell, Crinkle Crags is really one of the easiest of access. From Wrynose Pass it is only 1,500ft. of climbing, most of it on an easy path. Soon we are on the fine, broad, lofty ridge extending south to Stonesty Pike. To the north, where we are going, the ridge narrows and steepens. After negotiating what one might call the first crinkle, we are likely to find ourselves in a narrow cleft where we must take our hands out

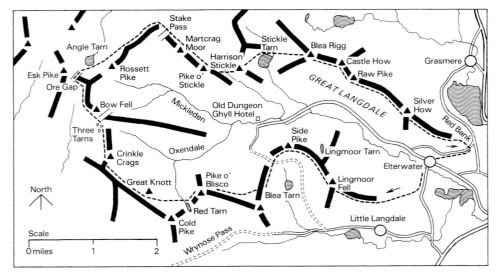

Above: Gimmer Crag and Great Langdale from Pike o'Stickle. The Langdale circuit starts by crossing Lingmoor Fell (the shadowy hill behind Gimmer Crag) and then continues past Blea Tarn (right) towards Pike o'Blisco. *Photo: W. S. Matthews*

of our pockets and scramble up a few feet, although there are other ways up to the right and left. The mile-long summit ridge is one of the pleasantest ridge walks in the district, with interesting rock formations, alpine flora persisting from the time when the area was glaciated, little tarns, and glimpses down the precipitious flank of the mountain into Oxendale. The route is not easy to follow in adverse weather, as the path winds among rocky knolls and hollows. A comparable fell top is Haystacks, but Haystacks is much lower.

It is not really for views that the fell walker toils so assiduously uphill, but for subtler and more fundamental rewards. Nevertheless let us gaze around. To the west lies that fine tract of wild country, Green Hole and Upper Eskdale, with the inspiring sky-line of the Scafells and the remarkable gash of Mickledore. To the east the main impression is of depth, particularly when mists come and go among the crags. At the end of a long downward perspective lie bright fields, dwarfed farmhouses and the familiar patterns of walls. South and west we may catch the distant gleam of water from the Duddon estuary or from the triple estuary of

the Esk, Irt and Mite, or from forgotten Devoke Water. One can also see the cooling towers of the world's first atomic power station. Surprisingly high up in the sky, so it seems, one can make out the outline of the Isle of Man with its shapely summit, Snaefell.

We blithely tread the heights and come at length to Three Tarns. Here crosses the most direct route from Eskdale to Langdale, a minor trade route in ancient times when the hills were more inhabited, although infinitely less visited than now. It is a pleasant place, a flat and quite extensive col. In mist, when the size of things is exaggerated, it seems a wilderness. From Three Tarns there is a climbers' path to Bowfell Buttress, and also a useful 'trod' below Bowfell Links, direct to Ore Gap. But our route is over Bowfell Top. It is a hill of great character, presenting a fine profile from many directions, particularly from Eskdale, whose valley head it dominates. The summit stands out as a rocky outcrop in a stony upland. You can hardly get lost approaching it but it is easy enough to do so leaving it. I remember one occasion when, even though the summit was shrouded in mist and I had no compass, I

thought I knew the ground well enough to cross it. The mist, however, concealed a covering of snow on the tops, and snow changes the appearance of things more than you would think. After leaving the summit I was soon lost, and eventually came upon a line of footprints which turned out to be my own! It took two more attempts to get successfully to Three Tarns, where I was going. Obviously it is no bad thing to carry a compass, although there are one or two places on this ridge where it will do curious things if held close to the ground. A notable landmark on Bowfell is Flat Crags, an unmistakable long, smooth slab lying at a shallow angle next to Cambridge Crag.

From Bowfell there is a pleasant, easy path down to Ore Gap, a smooth grassy col with purply red sub-soil. The slope descends blandly enough in the direction of Angle Tarn but, unless one keeps to the left, it steepens into crags, so the place needs care in poor conditions and particularly when there are plaques of old hard snow. Angle Tarn is a dramatically beautiful stretch of water, steeply hemmed in on one side and open and sandy at the other; a place to linger by and take a bite to eat.

Rossett Pike, our next stage, has a line of crags overlooking Langdale, but its northern flank is a moor, across which a path goes pleasantly and quickly to the top of Stake Pass. The purist may prefer to turn aside and follow the summit ridge, to be rewarded by views into Mickleden. Either way, we must descend to the boggy col of the Stake. Perhaps the only snag to the Langdale Horseshoe is the number of beguiling routes back to those hotels! But now the Langdale Pikes beckon and a good, steady ,stomp takes us over the back of Martcrag Moor to Pike o' Stickle. This is a splendid vantage point over the great gulf of Mickleden, and an attractive sharp summit. There are many delights hereabouts, such as the lofty moorland of High Raise with its magnificent panorama, and the imposing crag of Pavey Ark with its scrambling route, Jack's Rake. The Langdale Pike area was, in the past, a sort of Stone Age industrial estate with numerous axe factories.

Having made the short detour to the summit of Harrison Stickle, another marvellous belvedere with a fine view down Winder-

mere, we descend steeply to Stickle Tarn, a large sheet of water with an unobtrusive dam at the outlet, dominated by the mass of Pavey Ark.

At Stickle Tarn we have finished with the big hills and striking summits, but we still have a delightful ridge before us. We go first to the inlet of the tarn, turn south-east over Blea Rigg, then by a kindly, undulating, mostly descending, path by Castle How, Raw Pike, Silver How and finally Red Bank and the ribbon of tarmac that brings us back to Elterwater. These last miles are unspectacular but full of interest and beauty, and pleasant surprises. The last time I was there was on a November afternoon when shafts of light from a low westerly sun painted a warm wash of red-gold on the brackens, and the crag-bound head of Langdale showed blue and vague and precipitous. It is good to look back upon a long sky-line in the satisfaction of having walked right along it. With this feeling of assuagement one can go down to an evening's rest, and the gargantuan supper that befits the fellsman's hearty image although, for my part, I must confess exhaustion usually makes me disinclined to eat. But who cares, for we '. . . on honeydew have fed, and drunk the milk of paradise . . .'.

The full walk from Elterwater is eighteen miles, with about 6,500ft. of ascent, and without stops should take about nine and a half hours. The shorter version, starting from the Dungeon Ghyll Hotels, up Pike o' Blisco and finishing down from Stickle Tarn, is about twelve miles and 5,250ft., taking six and half hours, excluding stops.

Above: Crinkle Crags and Bowfell from near Cold Pike. *Photo: Ken Wilson*

Top left: The Langdale Pikes from Lingmoor Fell. Gimmer Crag (left) obscures Pike o'Stickle from this angle; the central peak is Harrison Stickle, flanked on the right by Pavey Ark. The Old and New Dungeon Ghyll Hotels are the white buildings in the valley on the left and right of the picture. *Photo: Tom Parker*

Bottom left: A view of the fells at the head of Langdale from Esk Hause. The Langdale Horseshoe walk descends from Ore Gap in front of Bowfell (extreme right), skirts the diminutive knoll of Rossett Pike (centre) and then heads on over the main Langdale Pikes (left), after crossing the head of Stake Pass. *Photo: Leonard and Marjorie Gayton*

35   Great Gable and the Ennerdale Horseshoe

by Roger Putnam

Walk   Great Gable and the Ennerdale Horseshoe.
Maps   O.S. 1:63,360 Tourist Map of the Lake District; O.S. 1:50,000 Sheet 90.
Start and finish at Ennerdale Scout Centre (ref. 087152).
Grading   A tough mountain walk over some of the best Lakeland fells.
Time   12-13 hours.
Distance   21 miles.
Escape Routes   From Scarth Gap to Buttermere or Black Sail. From Windy Gap to Styhead and Borrowdale. From Black Sail Pass to Ennerdale or Mosedale.
Telephones   Gillerthwaite;   Buttermere; Gatesgarth; Honister Pass; Seathwaite Farm, Borrowdale; Wasdale Head.
Transport   Railway Station at Whitehaven. Infrequent bus service from Whitehaven to Ennerdale Bridge.
Accommodation   Youth Hostels at Black Sail, Gillerthwaite and Buttermere, Hotels and Bed and Breakfasts available locally.
Guidebooks   *The Lakeland Peaks* by W. A. Poucher (Constable); *The Western Fells* by A. Wainwright (The Westmorland Gazette).

Top right: The summit bluffs of Haystacks; looking north over Buttermere to Grasmoor. *Photo: Geoffrey Wright.*

Bottom right: Walkers toil up Great Gable's interminable scree slopes. The forest-lined bowl of Ennerdale in the background is flanked on the right by High Crag and Haystacks. *Photo: Geoffrey Wright.*

To follow the watershed of a valley without deviation provides a particular fascination for the hill walker. Nowhere is this more true than on the magnificent walk marking the boundaries of Ennerdale in Cumbria.

All the Western Dales have a special quality; the sea as backdrop and reflector gives a luminescent quality of light which is lacking further inland. In addition, Ennerdale offers well-defined boundary ridges, a magnificent lake, and the most dramatic contrast with the lowland to the west, for it lies close to the forgotten industrial terrain of West Cumbria.

At daybreak, leave the car-park near the scout camp and follow the lake shore for a mile, passing the site of the lamented Anglers' Inn, razed prematurely in the latest battle of Ennerdale. This valley, so remote and wild, well illustrates the threats posed to the Lake District by 'statutory bodies' which should know better. The blanket of spruce forest is here to stay, and indeed either its maturity or the familiarity of the green mantle have blunted the sense of outrage felt by campaigners of the 'thirties, who lost their struggle to keep Ennerdale as it was. Now, conservationists prepare for the fight to preserve the lake itself, for the water authorities have designs on Ennerdale which affront all who love this valley.

From the lake shore strike north past Whins Farm, through a damp lane, two gates, and at last to the open fell. The direct route to Great Borne summit lies up the steep ridge, heathery in places, alongside the crags of Herdus Scaw.

The coastline soon appears, and the hills of Scotland, as we stop to catch the breath and tighten the laces. Herdus summit is a flat expanse of blanket peat, but the massive cairn north of Great Borne summit is an unmistakable landmark on a clear day. Cross a new post-and-wire fence bisecting the summit area to reach this cairn. A few yards beyond, an airy vantage point brings Floutern Tarn and the wet recesses of Mosedale into view and, to the east, a first glimpse of Crummock Water.

From Great Borne, fast walking over the shapely cone of Starling Dodd and Little Dodd leads to Red Pike. There is little need to worry about route-finding on this watershed. For most of the way we are guided infallibly, at first by the post-and-wire fence, and from Little Dodd onwards by a line of iron fence-posts which follow the ridge most of the way to Pillar mountain. After Scoat Fell a solid boundary wall provides an unmistakable hand-rail in poor visibility. One would prefer that these man-made features did not march so unrelentingly over the tops, but it would be ungracious to deny their usefulness on a stormy cloud-driving winter day.

At Red Pike summit the red granophyres give way to the dark and craggy landscape typical of the Borrowdale Volcanics. Below shines Bleaberry Tarn, in its perfect corrie, once thought to be the crater of an ancient volcano. And cradled in the narrows of the valley lies Buttermere, most beautiful of lakes, spoiled only by the white intrusion of the Guest House on its spur.

The next two miles provide spectacular walking above the plunging crags of Bleaberry and Birkness Combes; forget the long miles ahead and savour every downward view! High Stile succumbs easily, but how to decide which is the true summit? Ignore the implications of the map and unwrap sandwiches at the western cairn, poised above the crags. Continue gently to High Crag, which necessitates another halt, for here is the finest summit view-point of the watershed. The great Warnscale basin is shouldered by Fleetwith Pike, and on the eastern horizon spreads Helvellyn and her satellites. Skiddaw and the Scafells assert themselves and close to the south are the splendid precipices of Pillar and Gable, with the dramatic downrush of the mountain-side to Ennerdale below. High Crag calls for

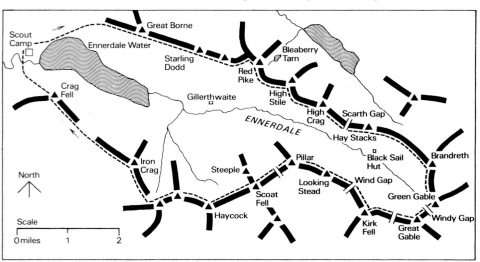

superlatives.

After a first act of such splendour, an interval is needed; a race down the scree of Gamlin End, over the Seat and across Scarth Gap, with its absurd isolated gate, and into the serrated heather garden of the Haystacks. This delightful fell, playground for a summer day, has its own tarns, crags, and delectable secret places. We cannot linger long, but must follow our guiding fence-posts up the springy slopes of Brandreth, regretting the height lost before Scarth Gap. This is not a distinguished section of the walk, but at Brandreth summit we reach the turning point, the ridge of the head of Ennerdale. And here we can look back nine miles to our starting point; the distant lake glittering and the dark forest mantling the valley floor.

At Brandreth the fence-posts strike south across a stony saddle and over the rounded summit of Green Gable. Immediately below lies Moses Trod, the legendary smuggling route from Wasdale to Honister. Above towers Gable Crag, a black north-facing precipice, forbidding even to the rock climber and surely to those folk who, for reasons unknown, built the mysterious stone enclosure on the face.

Windy Gap follows next, and then a steep climb from the col to the summit of Great Gable, ravens croaking attendance. We fetch out the hip-flask at this summit outcrop, half-way and highest point on the route, and then wander to Westmorland Cairn for the dramatic view to Wasdale Head down the scree vortex of Great Hell Gate.

The summit plateau is littered with cairns which are built again as soon as they are demolished. We follow the western edge of Gable Crag steeply down to Beck Head, where fence-posts reappear to carry us on to Pillar summit. Beck Head, a grassy saddle with two small seasonal tarns, is followed by a sharp scramble over loose rocks to twin-topped Kirkfell. These tops are separated by two more small tarns, and a stream meandering over a grassy meadow, before plunging over the escarpment two thousand feet above Burnthwaite Farm. This is a delectable bivouac spot from which to watch the evening sunlight on Scafell Crag and the shadow creeping up the shoulder of Lingmell.

However, to complete the walk within the day, we must take the direct line of descent from Kirkfell summit to Black Sail Pass, over a rocky slope rich with club mosses, and through a belt of crags. The pass, with its remnant gateway, does not detain us and we press on to Pillar, a hard slog up a steadily rising ridge. If there is time, a better alternative is to pass over Looking Stead and then desert the ridge for the High Level Route to Pillar Rock. This ingenious path, exposed and interesting throughout, threads its way across the very steep northern slope of Pillar, with dramatic views below to the dark swathes of the conifers. At Robinson's Cairn a fortress of stone, the Pillar Rock, bursts into view; one of the finest climbing grounds of the area. The 'Grand Stone' was first climbed in 1826 by John Atkinson of Ennerdale, and this ascent may have been the first true rock climb accomplished in the Lake District. The path rises from Robinson's Cairn quite steeply to attain the narrow col behind the Rock and care is needed.

It is pleasant to emerge again into sunshine on the summit of the Pillar mountain. Here we strike south-west for Wind Gap, beyond which lies Black Crag. The walker is warned that in this area the Ordnance Survey map falls below its usual standard of accuracy. Crags are misplaced, and the contours misleading. Black Crag itself is a separate summit, much more clearly defined than is indicated on the map. Then follows a grassy ridge leading to a rocky slope and a well-built wall. This remarkable structure extends over Scoat Fell and onwards, marking the very top of the watershed for almost five miles.

The top of Scoat Fell is marked by a cairn on the wall itself and here the walker must decide whether or not to take in the shapely satellite peak of the Steeple. From Scoat Fell summit, head south-west for Haycock on a wide grassy ridge, with remote and deeply carved corries to the north and more open fellside giving on to Netherbeck to the south, with dark glimpses of Wastwater beyond. At the lake edge lies Bowderdale, home of Joss Naylor, the best known fell runner in Lakeland. Joss has won the Ennerdale Horseshoe race nine times, his fastest recorded time an astonishing 3 hours 30 minutes.

Travelling more sedately we cross Haycock Hause, catching glimpses to the north of the strangely situated Tewit Tarn, and soon arrive on Haycock. Here we leave the Borrowdale

volcanic rock and, once past the rocky stepped spur of Little Gowder Crag, the character of the country changes. Caw Fell and Iron Crag are both broad topped and rounded hills, suited to fast walking if energy remains, and giving wide views to the west, with the evening light reflecting from the Irish Sea and the grim silhouette of Windscale to remind us that our day of simple pleasures is nearly over. The guiding wall of fine-grained red brown grano-phyres directs us north-west towards the lake. These great tracts of the ancient Ennerdale

Deer Forest and the Kinniside fells are wild and unfrequented now, but were well populated by Bronze Age man and still bear traces of his occupation.

At Black Pots we face the final short climb to Crag Fell; a magnificent view-point if light remains. The northern face of the fell, scoured by the pleistocene ice at Anglers' Crag, has slipped and faulted into dramatically topped profiles, adorned with tottering pinnacles poised above the water. From the summit we can savour again the energetic early morning attack on Herdus Scaw, seen across the lake, and the pleasures of the Red Pike ridge which followed.

Half an hour will be sufficient to see us back to our starting point, descending Ben Gill, through the forest, across the River Lisa and so to the car-park.

Take your time, the walk is too good to race; slower travel gives greater enjoyment on this outstanding expedition.

Above: Great Gable from Kirkfell: the cliffs of the Napes are on the right. *Photo: E. A. Shepherd*

Top left: A view from the summit of Great Gable over the flat top of Kirk Fell to Red Pike and Steeple. *Photo: Tom Parker*

Bottom left: Looking down Mosedale to Wasdale Head and the Scafell group. *Photo: E. A. Shepherd*

36   Across Lakeland: Shap to Ravenglass

by Tom Price

Walk Across Lakeland: Shap to Ravenglass.
Maps O.S. 1:63,360 Tourist Map of the Lake District; O.S. 1:50,000 Sheets 90 and 96. Start from Shap Village (ref. 563155). Finish at Ravenglas (ref. 085963).
Grading An exceptionally long and arduous mountain walk.
Time 18 hours.
Distance 42 miles.
Escape Routes Numerous.
Telephones Shap; Bridgend; Patterdale; Wythburn; West end of Hardknott Pass; Eskdale; Ravenglass.
Transport Kendal to Penrith bus service through Shap. Miniature railway from Eskdale and Boot to Ravenglass. The main West Cumberland railway passes through Ravenglass.
Accommodation Hotels and Bed and Breakfasts in Shap and Ravenglass. Youth Hostels at Kendal, Eskdale and Duddon.
Guidebooks *The Lakeland Peaks* by W. A. Poucher (Constable); Guides to *The Far Eastern, Eastern, Central* and *Southern Fells* by A. Wainwright (The Westmorland Gazette).

Only those with a powerful streak of sanity in their make-up can resist the occasional very long walk. It is that heroic dream of fluent, tireless movement over hill and dale that drives us to these excesses. The walk from Shap to Ravenglass is as long as the famous Lyke Wake walk, and much more strenuous. It can, nevertheless, be done in the daylight of a day in early summer. But whether one takes one, two, three or even four days over it, it is a superlatively good walk, through lovely country, with ever-changing scenery, and a wealth of possible variants.

H.H. Symonds in the classic, *Walking in the Lake District*, expressed the view that the best way into the Lakes was via Shap. Certainly to set off from that bleak village in the feeble light of dawn is to recapture some of the romantic solitude and wildness that attracted the earliest tourists to these hills. The country is Pennine in character, wide and open, but far ahead the long line of High Street, with the unmistakable profile of Kidsty Pike gives promise of more rugged hills.

One can go by Wet Sleddale — wetter still now with its great triangular reservoir — a long lonely trudge rising eventually to Harter Fell, but I chose Swindale and the old corpse road, in spite of having to descend right into Mardale and face the long climb out. Field

paths, minor roads and foot-paths lead through Keld and Tailbert into Swindale, then a climb up the side of the valley brings you to Mardale Common.

The head of Mardale, filled with water, is a dramatic sight, but not typical of Lakeland scenery, and one regrets losing the drowned hamlet, the Dun Bull, and the lakeside meadows. The last service in Mardale Church was on August 18, 1935, and in 1936 it was dismantled. The lakes of the Lake District are characteristically puddles on the valley floors, which they share with green meadows won from the swamps by human toil, and therein lies their charm. Imagine Wasdale Head with the water lapping the foot of Kirkfell.

I had considered going by Mardale Ill Bell, Thornthwaite Crag and John Bell's Banner to Kirkstone Pass; but from Kirkstone there is a road route straight to Ravenglass, the way the Romans went, through Galava (Ambleside) and Mediobogdum (Hardknott Fort), and this might prove a too seductive if ignominious alternative to the arduous switch-back route over Red Screes, Dove Crag and Fairfield to Dunmail Raise. So I chose instead the exhilarating narrow ridge of Caspel Gate and Long Stile, which brings you out to High Street, a natural route in ancient times when the valleys were clogged with marsh and forest, and still a

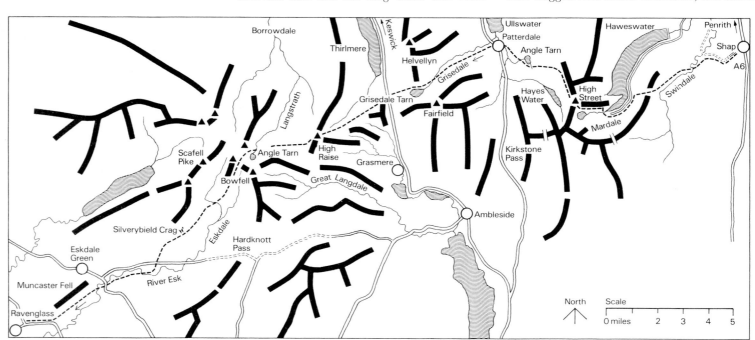

royal road for walkers. After the steep combes containing Blea Water and Small Water, the great open levels of High Street give a sense of freedom and space. From here there is a six-mile-long, wonderfully varied descent past Angle Tarn to Patterdale. Then, after a couple of hundred yards on the main road, one turns left into Grisedale.

Ahead now lie the ramparts of Nethermost Pike, Striding Edge and Helvellyn. The track leads by a pleasant wooded strath, up an increasingly rugged slope, to reveal, suddenly, the large and impressive Grisedale Tarn, in its cirque of steep grassy hills. There are usually plenty of people to be seen here for it is on the most frequented route to Helvellyn and the path is well beaten. We leave it, however, and skirting the north shore, go through a low, grassy col and down a narrow valley to Dunmail Raise, the half-way point.

Not much of a raise, Dunmail. Only the same height as Shap, in fact. But if you have

arranged for someone to be on the roadside with shots of soup and other permitted stimulants, the flank of Steel Fell will seem less daunting. Ascend by a fence and a small beck to keep clear of the bracken. There is no need to go right to the summit. You can save some 200ft. by crossing the grassy plateau to its north. Thirlmere and its forests lie below, a fine sight on a quite grandiose scale, but more like Scotland than the Lake District. This walk does nothing to endear one to the Water Boards.

The next objective is that hub of Lakeland, High White Stones. Skirting Calf Crag you follow the height of land between Wyth Burn and the Easedales. There is not much evidence of the passage of feet until you come across the Greenup Edge path. Here, above the broad hollow that marks the head of Wyth Burn, there is an iron ladder stile standing all alone. The fence it once crossed is now no more, but there are enough posts left here and there to follow in

Above: On the summit ridge of High Street above Riggindale. Backpackers toil where Roman soldiers once marched, as this interesting section of the Shap — Ravenglass walk coincides with the course of the major Roman Road called High Street. The road followed high ridges to avoid heavier going in the valleys, which at that time would have been rough, boggy and densely vegetated. *Photo: Geoffrey Berry*

*The ascent of Broad Stand is a rock-climb.

case of mist right up to High Raise. From a confused and rocky fell-side one comes out at length on a great bare upland. The Lake District lies all around in a noble panorama. On a fine day with scudding clouds it is a wonderful place to be.

A long easy descent to Stake Pass and a mercifully easy path across the back of Rossett Pike, and in a mile or two the waters of our second Angle Tarn of the day come in view, with Hanging Knotts lowering above. For anyone with the speed and stamina to do it, a fine route from here would be over Scafell Pikes, Broad Stand*, Scafell and Burnmoor, but at this stage of the walk most people will be looking for a bee-line. So Ore Gap it is. The path starts well to the right of the tarn. After the steep part there is a rather discouraging

trudge to the col, but once there one can appreciate the feeling of Cortes when he sighted the Pacific. The main ranges have all been crossed. Eskdale lies below, and beyond it the sea.

On the descent, instead of going down into boggy Green Hole, one can traverse on to Yeastyrigg and come out to cross the Esk where it changes from a sandy meandering stream to a rocky one. In times of flood this route may be impracticable, in which case Green Hole and Throstlegarth would be taken.

Across the river a slight rise up a spongy moorland brings you to the Silverybield path. Though by now the bit is no doubt between your teeth, pause to look into Upper Eskdale. The Esk is unique in the Lake District in having this high wide upper valley. Bare and

154

lonely, with the crag of Scafell and Scafell Pike towering above it, it achieves a scale and grandeur unusual in these hills.

The path goes pleasantly through two or three hollows, but don't let it take you down into Eskdale yet. Cross Cowcove Beck and find a delightful path that reaches the road at Wha House. Or go a little further west by that shyest of Lakeland tarns, Stony Tarn, to Eel Tarn and the Woolpack Inn. We are now on the Eskdale granite, with its rugged heathery terrain and colourful becks.

Near the Woolpack a side-road goes down to Doctor's Bridge on the Esk. Instead of crossing it one can take a riverside path, in delectable contrast to the open fells one has toiled over so long. Eskdale may have no lake but it is a beautiful valley. Further down, two girders

span the river, remnants of a railway bridge leading to a mine. The sure-footed can cross here — or if the river is low enough by stepping stones at Boot Church — continuing past the ancient Dalegarth Hall, through cool woods, to hit the road at Forge Bridge.

The stout-hearted will finish strongly over Muncaster Fell. The roads down Eskdale, one private and one public, are both pleasant and unfrequented. And for the weary there is always the miniature railway.

After so many miles of fells it is good to see the placid estuary, with boats lying 'like swans asleep'. The village street ends at the water's edge. Across the harbour are The Gulleries, the nesting place of black-headed gulls and terns. There is an inn, and the railway. It is journey's end.

Top: Looking towards Hawes Water and the Pennines from Harter Fell. The Shap — Ravenglass walk leaves the flooded Mardale by the long sunlit spur leading off to the left, over Rough Crag and thence to Long Stile and High Street. *Photo: Tom Parker*

Bottom: The final part of this walk of many contrasts follows the idyllic path along the banks of the River Esk, and thence over Muncaster Fell to Ravenglass. *Photo: Derek Forss*

37   Wild Boar Fell and the Howgills

Walk   Wild Boar Fell and the Howgills.
Maps   O.S. 1:50,000 Sheets 91, 97 and 98.
Start from Kirkby Stephen (ref. 775086).
Finish at Sedbergh (ref. 657922).
Grading   Easy walking over rolling and mainly grassy fells. Wild Boar Fell rougher than the Howgills.
Time   9-10 hours.
Distance   23 miles.
Escape Routes   The fells can be descended to the valley from any point except above the escarpment overlooking Cautley Spout.
Telephones   Sedbergh; Kirkby Stephen; Bullgill; Beck Side near Cautley; Nateby.
Transport   Daily bus service between Kirkby Stephen and Sedbergh operated by National Express Company.
Accommodation   Hotels in Kirkby Stephen and Sedbergh. Youth Hostels at Kirkby Stephen, Dentdale and Kendal.
Guidebooks   *Walks on the Howgill Fells* by A. Wainwright (The Westmorland Gazette).

Top right: Wild Boar Fell from Mallerstang Common. *Photo:* Geoffrey Berry

Bottom right: The Howgill range from the west: Arant Haw is the central hill. *Photomontage: Robert Brotherton*

This walk links the two Cumbrian towns of Kirkby Stephen and Sedbergh by a high-level route over the lonely and rarely visited Wild Boar Fell and the Howgill Hills.

These two areas of high open moorland are separated by the valley of the Rawthey and their features are quite different. The Wild Boar Fell country is characterized by gentle, sloping hills, with rocky bluffs of millstone grit and slopes of shale and scattered boulders. The Howgills, on the other hand, are smoothly sculptured grassy hills with steep sides enclosing deep valleys. There is a notable absence of walls and fences above 700ft. which make them ideal walking country. The western edge of the Howgills can be seen clearly from the M6 motorway as it passes through the Tebay valley, but motorists do not make walkers and the range remains inviolate.

From the market place in Kirkby Stephen take the Sedbergh road and follow it for three-quarters of a mile, until you reach an old railway track. Immediately after the railway, turn left and continue walking along an excellent farm track across the fields, keeping the River Eden on your left. After a mile the track begins to climb, crossing first a minor

road and then the railway by a narrow bridge. It continues up the fell side beside a stone wall and finally crosses another minor road. You are now on the open hillside with the north ridge of Wild Boar Fell stretching away ahead.

On the lower slopes, where the ridge is broad, the path is not very distinct, but you should aim for the first rise, Little Fell, which has an escarpment on the east side. From Little Fell you descend slightly and then make for the abrupt rocky nose known as the Nab, which has a cairned top at a height of 2,296ft. The ridge is rough and stony but nowhere particularly steep and there are good views down to the Eden Valley. From the Nab it is only a short walk to the trig point on Wild Boar Fell at 2,324ft., the actual summit lying 300 yards from a collection of smaller cairns at the edge of the eastern escarpment.

Walk to another line of small cairns half a mile south-west of the summit trig point, and descend the peaty slopes to the saddle under Swarth Fell. On the saddle there is a small tarn and you meet a wall coming up from the west side, which you can follow for half a mile to the summit of Swarth Fell (2,235ft.). There are several cairns on the summit. Continue walking in a south-easterly direction until, after three-quarters of a mile, you reach the cairns on Swarth Fell Pike. Cairns abound in this region and when you see all the stones lying on the high ground you can understand why.

Descend Swarth Fell Pike in a westerly direction until you meet a wall, and follow this down to the valley bottom where flows the River Rawthey.

The three-mile walk down beside the river to Rawthey Bridge on the main road is quite delightful. Cross the river, because the best path is on the far (west) side, and follow the ravines, cascades and waterfalls to the car-park at Rawthey Bridge. The rounded hill behind you is called Bluecaster.

Walk down the road towards Sedbergh for one mile. The valley is particularly beautiful here, with deciduous woodlands beside the rushing river, and the slopes of the Howgills beyond are green and smooth with the lower regions bracken covered. You will soon see the impressive cliff called Cautley Crag, overlooking the Cautley Valley which comes in from the right. Just before the Cross Keys Inn

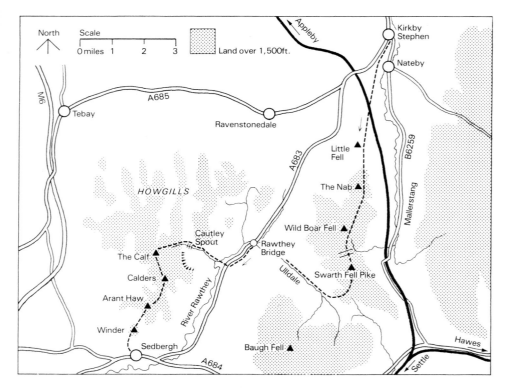

there is a gap in the wall leading to a bridge over the river. Follow the good path that keeps to the right-hand side of Cautley Beck and ascend the steep slopes beside Cautley Spout.

Cautley Spout is one of the finest waterfalls in the country and the setting could hardly be bettered. The water, descending in a series of cascades, has worn a deep groove in the rounded shoulder of the fell, while on the south side the loose cliffs of Cautley Crag contrast the grassy slopes of Great Dummacks.

The 1977 Karrimor two-day Mountain Marathon was held in the Howgills in late October, with the overnight camp site situated in the valley below Cautley Spout. The usual tranquil scene was transformed into a nylon shanty town by the arrival of over 500 teams. I lay cosily in my sleeping bag enjoying a fifth

brew of tea and watched with satisfaction the twinkling lights of the late arrivals dancing down the mountains from all sides.

Once you have climbed above Cautley Spout, the day's labours are over, for you have nothing but six miles of easy, undulating hills to cross. A rather indistinct path continues due west for nearly a mile to the summit of the Calf which, at 2,220ft., is the highest point in the Howgills, and carries an Ordnance Survey trig point. Walk south over Bram Rigg Top to Calders where there is a large cairn. The path continues south across a narrow neck between two valleys and then skirts the pointed top of Arant Haw before swinging left to the last summit, Winder (1,551ft.). From Calders to Winder is only one and three-quarter miles. Just before Winder the path divides but you

should carry straight on to include the summit. It overlooks Sedbergh, the Sedbergh School song is named after it, and it is a fine view-point for the Lune Valley and Morecambe Bay.

The best way down from Winder is to take the path that descends the south-west slopes for 800ft. until a wall is reached. Follow the wall left to Lochbank Farm, which gives access to the narrow road called Howgill Lane just below the farm. It is now only a quarter of a mile to Sedbergh's main street, where you can have tea before catching the bus back to Kirkby Stephen.

Colour photo: Another view of Wild Boar Fell from Mallerstang. *Photo: Dave Matthews*

Centre photos: Looking north across Cautley Crags to the Bowerdale valley (top). Cautley Spout (bottom). *Photos: Geoffrey Wright*

Above: Typical Howgill scenery: looking towards The Calf from the Langdale valley. *Photo: John Allen*

Left: Looking south along the escarpment of Wild Boar Fell which overlooks Mallerstang Common. *Photo: Geoffrey Wright*

38   The Lyke Wake Walk

Walk   The Lyke Wake Walk.
Mapsᐧ O.S. 1:63,360 Tourist Map of North York Moors.
Start from Osmotherley P.O. Relay Station (ref. 459998).
Finish at Ravenscar Hotel (ref. 981019).
Grading   A very long walk over undulating heather clad moors. There is a path over the entire route.
Time   13-14 hours.
Distance   40 miles.
Escape Routes   The route crosses several main roads and from high ground both N. and S. facing dales lead gently down to lower ground.
Telephones   Scugdale; Carlton; Chop Gate; Lion Inn Blakey; Wheeldale Youth Hostel; Flask Inn A171.
Transport   Osmotherley is on the Northallerton — Tees-side route (United) and on the long distance Liverpool, Manchester, Leeds to Middlesbrough route. Ravenscar is connected by bus to Scarborough.
Accommodation   Inns at Osmotherley. Ravenscar Hotel. Youth Hostels at Helmsley, Wheeldale, Westerdale and Boggle Hole.
Guidebooks   *The Lyke Wake Walk* by Bill Cowley; *The Cleveland Way* by Alan Falconer gives a good description of the first part of the walk; *A Coast to Coast Walk* by A. Wainwright describes the route as far as Rosedale Head; *A Walker on the Cleveland Way* by Colin Walker (Pendyke), gives a good photographic record of the Cleveland Hills.

This now classic walk crosses the whole of the North York Moors, from Osmotherley in the west to Ravenscar on the east coast. It includes most of the highest tops of the Cleveland Hills. The walk is a natural line and was first recognized as such by Bill Cowley, who completed the first crossing in 1955. Since then the walk has received much publicity and thousands of successful crossings are made every year by young and old. In fact, the walk has come to be recognized as a physical fitness and endurance test for aspiring outdoor types, and a crossing in under twenty-four hours entitles you to wear the Lyke Wake tie, a black tie embellished with silver coffins.

The moors on the line of the walk carry many Bronze Age burial mounds, and this gave Bill Cowley the idea of naming the walk after the Lyke Wake or coffin trail. The very moving and centuries-old dialect verse known as 'the Cleveland Lyke Wake Dirge' has been adopted most appropriately as the traditional song to be chanted, as walkers or dirgers tramp the moors by night.

The walk is forty miles long, but over the years a good track has been worn across the moor, and although still demanding, it is not as arduous as many of the walks described in this book. When I first completed the walk in 1963, the exact line was not defined and it was a case of ploughing through deep heather and bracken for much of the way, but nowadays

fellow walkers and mud are the chief hazards. I recommend the crossing from west to east, since it seems to be more natural to end at the sea, and Ravenscar is 400ft. below Osmotherley.

Try to avoid the height of the summer and the week-ends, for they are the most crowded. May is a delightful month for the walk since the heather and bracken have not yet grown and the moors abound in golden plover and curlew. September is pleasant, too, when the peat has dried out and your books kick up clouds of heather pollen.

The Lyke Wake Walk starts from the trig point, which is situated just on the west side of the wall beside the television relay station, one and a half miles north of Osmotherley. You can drive up to the relay station along a gated road which leaves the Osmotherley – Swainby road just at the end of the village.

Walk down the grassy hillside in a north-easterly direction until you meet the Osmotherley – Swainby road. Continue down the road for 100 yards, until you see a gate on the right marked with an acorn sign, the Cleveland Way emblem. The Lyke Wake Walk and the Cleveland Way follow the same route over some of the early sections. Beyond the gate is a muddy track which you follow for a mile into Scugdale. Here you cross a small stream by a footbridge and then, gaining a metalled road, you reach a telephone box and

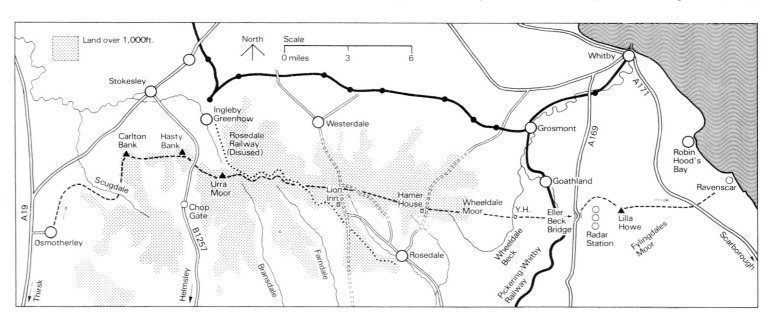

another marked gate.

The path now traverses a wooded hillside, climbs up a slimy bank of mud and leads you on to the open moorland of Holey Moor. If you are starting the walk at night or in the early hours of the morning, you will enjoy the blaze of lights and occasional shower of sparks from industrial Teeside to the north. If it is daylight, you will notice the sharply-pointed hill, Roseberry Topping, far ahead to the north-east. Later in the day, with a few more miles under your belt, you will look back to Roseberry Topping far away behind you.

At Carlton Bank you drop steeply down to the Carlton – Chop Gate road. The many spoil heaps in this area are from alum mines worked in the seventeenth century. From the road you now climb quite steeply up grassy slopes to Cringle Moor, only to descend again the other side to the col under Cold Moor. Do not be tempted to take the easy track to the

Above: Hasty Bank from the lower slopes of Urra Moor *Photo: Malcolm Boyes*

Right: Leaving Scugdale near Osmotherley, where the Lyke Wake Walk begins to gain height to reach the open moorlands. *Photo: Malcolm Boyes*

north of Cold Moor, for the proper route takes in the summits.

Your next objective is Hasty Bank and the way up involves scrambling through the sandstone outcrop of the Wainstones, but once there the path is level for a mile as it hugs the edge of the precipitous north-facing escarpment. When the path bends away south you must turn off and descend the steep muddy slopes, passing through more old spoil heaps, to reach the car-park at the top of Clay Bank on the main Helmsley to Stokesley road. You have now completed the first section of the walk and can afford a short break for refreshments. The car-park is a convenient place to meet a support party.

On the other side of the main road the path continues through a gate and keeps on the right-hand side of a stone wall which runs up the hillside on to Urra Moor. You climb gradually up the open heather-covered slopes to the cairn on Botton Head, at 1,490ft. the highest point of the Cleveland Hills. The path passes ancient boundary stones at regular intervals and then joins a wide clay fire-break, which leads to the Rosedale Railway track near Bloworth Crossing.

The Rosedale Ironstone Railway was built in 1861 and trains ran until 1928, but the old track now provides an easy and fast path for walkers. You follow it for three and a half miles as it rounds the head of Farndale, and then, soon after passing the good path leading north to Esklets in Westerdale, you turn left across the moor to hit the Blakey Ridge road, one mile south of Rosedale Head. Walk north along the road towards Ralph Cross at Rosedale Head, and then turn off right at the T-junction and continue for another mile. You pass a large white stone on the left of the road, called Fat Betty. Just after a minor road comes in on the left, you take to the moor again and follow the line of boundary stones for three miles until you meet the Rosedale – Glaisdale road near Hamer House. This section of the walk is very wet and boggy, but as you approach the prominent tumulus, marked Shunner Howe, you reach a horrid new track bulldozed out of the heather during the disastrous fire that followed the great drought of 1976. Hamer House marks the end of the second main section of the walk and you have completed more than half the distance.

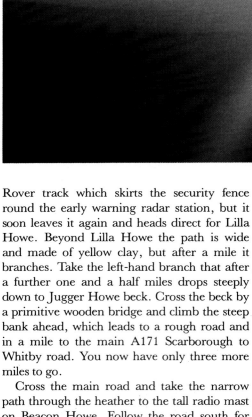

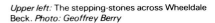

Wheeldale Moor is the next obstacle, but here again the path follows the boundary stones and you can take comfort from the sight of the three radar domes on Fylingdales Moor, only eight miles ahead. After crossing another minor road you reach the paved Wheeldale Roman Road, and almost immediately plunge down a muddy slope to the stepping stones over the stream by Wheeldale Lodge Youth Hostel. The path continues due west up to the large cairn beside Simon Howe and then descends to Eller Beck bridge, crossing the Moors Railway on its way. The railway, between Pickering and Whitby, is operated, using steam locomotives, for tourists during the summer months. This completes the third section and Eller Beck bridge is another favourite rendezvous for support parties.

From the bridge take the path that strikes up Fylingdales Moor, making for the large cairn on Lilla Howe. This path meets the Land-Rover track which skirts the security fence round the early warning radar station, but it soon leaves it again and heads direct for Lilla Howe. Beyond Lilla Howe the path is wide and made of yellow clay, but after a mile it branches. Take the left-hand branch that after a further one and a half miles drops steeply down to Jugger Howe beck. Cross the beck by a primitive wooden bridge and climb the steep bank ahead, which leads to a rough road and in a mile to the main A171 Scarborough to Whitby road. You now have only three more miles to go.

Cross the main road and take the narrow path through the heather to the tall radio mast on Beacon Howe. Follow the road south for half a mile to the old windmill, and then east again to Ravenscar village. The Lyke Wake Walk ends at the Ravenscar Hotel, which is at the east end of the village perched on the edge of the cliffs.

165

39   Ingleborough, Penyghent and Whernside

Walk   Ingleborough, Penyghent and Whernside.
Maps   O.S. 1:50,000 Sheet 98. O.S. 1:25,000 Outdoor Leisure Map — *The Three Peaks*. Start and finish at Ribblehead (ref. 765793).
Grading   A well defined walk over mainly grassy hills.
Time   9-10 hours.
Distance   23 miles.
Escape Routes   The walk crosses main roads at Chapel le Dale and Horton in Ribblesdale.
Telephones   Ribblehead; The Hill Inn; Horton in Ribblesdale.
Transport   Buses from Ingleton to Skipton, Lancaster and Kendal and from Hawes to Leyburn and Darlington. At weekends local trains between Settle and Carlisle will stop at Ribblehead.
Accommodation   Hotels in Horton, Hawes and Ingleton. Youth Hostels at Hawes, Ingleton and Stainforth.
Guidebooks   *The Yorkshire Dales National Park* (H.M.S.O.); *The Peak and Pennines* by W. A. Poucher (Constable); *The Yorkshire Three Peaks* (Dalesman Publishing Company).

Top right: Looking south-east to Penyghent from near Hunt Pot. The route from Horton ascends to the summit from the right, skirting behind the mountain to avoid the final steep screes and cliffs. The described walk continues along the skyline ridge to the left. *Photo: Shelagh Gregory*

Bottom right: A fell-runner nearing the end of the Three Peaks Race, at Hill Inn, having completed the twenty-mile circuit in under three hours. *Photo: Tom Parker*

The River Ribble, which flows into the Irish Sea at Preston, rises in the heart of the Yorkshire Dales. The river drains the great area of carboniferous limestone on which stand the separate gritstone mountains of Penyghent, Ingleborough and Whernside. The mountains themselves are mainly rounded, except in their upper parts where weathering has produced rock outcrops and boulder-strewn slopes. The valleys are fertile with good grazing and are characterized by networks of stone walls constructed of limestone, which appear dazzling white in the sunshine. Caves and potholes abound.

Try to pick a bright early summer's day for the walk when the grass is at its greenest and the flowers at their best. The air will be full of the cries of larks, curlews, redshanks, peewits and golden plovers, and you may hear the drumming of snipe.

The 'Three Peaks' round has long been a classic walk and it is now on the fell runners' calendar, the annual race being run on the last Sunday in April. The round has also been adopted by cyclo-cross enthusiasts. Inevitably commercialization has crept in, and walkers can 'clock in' and buy a certificate of achievement at the Penyghent cafe in Horton in Ribblesdale if they complete the round in less than twelve hours.

The three peaks country is extensive, and as yet the character of the walk has not been affected by its popularity. The natural features of the countryside are slow to change and walkers must be extremely careful not to alter the fine balance between man and nature. Never climb walls or pick flowers.

Much of the walk is over private land, but the route I am going to describe has been negotiated with the landowners and you will not be apprehended.

The large triangle of close-cropped grass near the Station Hotel, Ribblehead, makes a good starting and finishing point. It does not matter which way round you go, but I prefer to get Whernside behind me early on; not only is it the highest of the three peaks, at 2,415ft., but its ascent is the most tedious.

Take the rough road that passes under the giant Ribblehead viaduct and proceed through several gates to Gunner Fleet farm, where you cross Winterscales beck by a bridge and meet a narrow tarmac road. Turn right and walk along this road towards Winterscales Farm, but after 300 yards, where the road bends sharp right, follow a track beside the wall in a south-westerly direction. After 100 yards, cross the wall by a stile and so gain the open tussocky hillside.

The rather boggy path goes straight up the fell side for 1,000ft., until it crosses an old wall, which is roughly on a level with the attractive limestone outcrop called Greensett Crags away to the right. You are now under the final steep slopes of Whernside, and you should bear slightly right and take a direct route to the summit trig point. If it is misty, you can follow a wall on the left which leads to the summit ridge. The tarn which you see below you is a breeding ground for black-headed gulls.

Whernside is a high broad ridge extending from Ingleton to Dentdale. A wall runs along the ridge at its highest point so it is not easy to get lost. The summit makes a fine view-point and on a clear day you can see Blackpool Tower, Morecambe Bay, the Lake District hills, the Howgills and, of course Penyghent and Ingleborough. Follow the ridge down southwards for three-quarters of a mile, until the path turns abruptly left and descends a steep and often muddy slope leading to Bruntscar Farm and the pastures below. At Bruntscar you join a metalled road which you

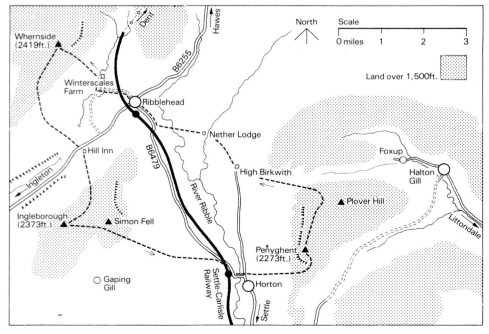

follow for a mile, negotiating several cattle grids on the way, until you reach the main Ingleton to Hawes road at the Hill Inn.

Walk past the Hill Inn towards Ribblehead, and in 200 yards you come to a gate on the right and a sign to Great Douk Cave. Go through the gate and take the path that leads across several fields in the general direction of Ingleborough. You will see a well-constructed wall coming down from Simon Fell, the hill due east of Ingleborough itself; pass this wall at the lower end and keep to the right of another good wall, which stretches away towards Ingleton and is above a vast area of limestone pavement. Quite soon a gate allows you to pass through the wall to reach the open fell and you continue along the path until it suddenly steepens and, keeping to the left of another wall, takes you on to the saddle between Ingleborough and Simon Fell. From the saddle it is an easy walk, first up some loose gritstone rocks and then across the plateau to the huge cairn and wind break on the summit of Ingleborough (2,373ft.). There are still traces of the Iron Age fort built on the flat table top of Ingleborough by the Brigantians.

Retrace your steps to the saddle under Simon Fell and then take the narrow path which traverses under Simon Fell on the south side. After one and a half miles you pass a

Top left: Penyghent from the Pennine Way near Churn Milk Hole. The route from Horton comes up the moor on the left and joins the Pennine Way where the path steepens. *Photo: Tom Parker*

Bottom left: A view along Whernside's summit ridge. *Photo: W. S. Smith*

Previous page: Ingleborough from White Scars above Ingleton. The route from Hill Inn climbs the mountain from the left, keeping just behind the steep sunlit slope. *Photo: E. A. Shepherd*

boarded-up shooting hut and then the scenery changes as you meet the limestone again. The path takes a deep runnel or gully through the limestone pavement, and then follows a dry depression known as Sulber Nick. You emerge on the lip of the valley overlooking Horton with a huge quarry on your right. The quarry lake is a beautiful turquoise colour, caused by the suspension of limestone particles. Descend the grassy slopes to a stile over the wall and then after one more slight rise you reach the railway. Cross the lines and walk down to Horton, where you can obtain refreshment either at the Penyghent cafe, which is open on Sundays, or at the Crown Hotel.

The path up Penyghent starts from the tiny settlement of Brackenbottom. From the Penyghent cafe follow the Settle road for one third of a mile until, just past the church, a minor road comes in from the left. This road hugs the bank of the Horton Beck and leads to Brackenbottom. The Penyghent path is signposted on the left and you pass through a gate and follow a wall to the open hillside. The path climbs up towards the rocky nose of Penyghent and meets the Dale Head path ascending from the south-east.

It is a rough and steep scramble over loose rocks to gain the summit of Penyghent (2,277ft.), and Ribblehead viaduct, which can be clearly seen, looks a long way off.

Continue due north towards Plover Hill by a good path which traverses the west side of the fell. You will see the Pennine Way path coming up from Hunt Pot, but do not take it; rather, keep to the smaller but distinct path which heads north-west. The fells rise and fall for several miles and the path crosses the Pennine Way and several becks before leading you to the farm at High Birkwith. Cross the beck and pick up the good farm track which goes to Nether Lodge. The track becomes rough and hard on the feet and it continues over the Ribble to Ingman Lodge, a lovely old house with mullioned windows. Just before the Lodge the path darts through a gap in the wall and, skirting the house, takes you to the main Ribblehead – Horton road. Just past Ingman Lodge you will see a spring and drinking trough of cold clear water. A drink here is exactly what you need to revitalize you for the one and a half mile march along the road to your finishing point at Ribblehead.

40   Derwent Watershed Walk

by Phil Cooper

This forty-mile circular walk encloses the water-gathering area of the River Derwent, the principal river of the High Peak. That it is rough and tough at any time of year cannot be doubted; in misty conditions navigation is tricky indeed.

Part of the route follows the well-trodden motorway of the Pennine Way across the high peat-moors, but the eastern half is in remote territory, seldom visited. The southern leg from the Derwent to Mam Tor is south of the high moors; and follows a route over shapely hills with some of the finest Peakland scenes.

The start and finish point is the crossing point of the Derwent at Yorkshire Bridge, below Ladybower dam. Whether to go clockwise or anti-clockwise is up to personal preference. Clockwise, you will complete the major ups and downs over Win Hill and Lose Hill first. Anti-clockwise, the remote and trackless area over the Howden Moors is completed at an earlier stage.

The route is described clockwise. It is a steep pull up the wooded east slope of Win Hill (1,516ft.), but this summit, long a friend of mine, commands the proverbial panoramic view in all directions. There are long views down the Derwent valley and the Eastern Edges, while much closer are the Lose Hill to Mam Tor ridge, Kinder, the southern arms of Bleaklow, the Derwent Moors and Bamford Moor. Apart from the view, Win Hill is also notable for the knoll on the top, known as Win Hill Pike, which appears as a pimple from the west and east, and as a wedge seen from north and south. The Pike makes the hill stand out from afar.

The descent is to Twitchill Farm, which has seen much better days, and down to the River Noe which is crossed just north of Hope. Our watershed includes that of several Derwent tributaries, those meriting the title 'River' being the Noe, Ashop, Alport and Westend. Lose Hill, Win's twin across the Noe, is the most shapely hill in the High Peak. From most aspects it has a graceful conical form and the pair form a gateway to the Vale of Edale.

Along the ridge from Lose Hill over Back Tor past Hollins Cross to Mam Tor is a very easy walk with good views of Kinder. The Hope Valley, containing Castleton and Peakshole water, lies just south. Mam Tor's historical associations date back a long way, for

here was an Iron Age fort whose ramparts still may be clearly seen.

The road descending into the head of the Vale of Edale is crossed at Mam Nick, where support could be arranged if required. The route continues up Rushup Edge, a whale-backed ridge whose summit, Lord's Seat, has a tumulus, and it then strikes north over Colborne. Heading on towards Brown Knoll and its trig point, a clear path runs two or three hundred yards east of the true watershed. There are several places like this where the watershed is not followed exactly, for to attempt a precise following of the 'shed all the way round would be tedious in parts, adding much extra time for little extra reward. From Colborne to Featherbed Moss at the northernmost tip of the circuit, the Derwent watershed coincides with England's main east-west watershed.

The Pennine Way alternative route avoids the best bogs of Kinder Scout's central area

Walk   The Derwent Watershed Walk.
Maps   O.S. 1:50,000 Sheet 110; O.S. 1:25,000 Outdoor Leisure Map — The Dark Peak. Start and finish at the Yorkshire Bridge (ref. 201849).
Grading   A long and rough walk over boggy and peat hagged ground.
Time   14 hours.
Distance   40 miles.
Escape Routes   Numerous. Even at its most remote the route is never more than 3 miles from a road.
Telephones   Yorkshire Bridge; Edale; Hayfield; Glossop; Crowden; A.A. box at Snake Summit.
Transport   Railway Station at Bamford (2 miles). Regular bus service from Sheffield, Glossop and Whalley Bridge.
Accommodation   Local Inns at Castleton, Bamford and Hathersage. Youth Hostels at Edale, Castleton, Hathersage, Hagg Farm Ladybower.
Guidebooks   *Walking in Derbyshire* by John Merrill. *Walks in the Derbyshire Dales* Edited by James Haworth (Derbyshire Countryside); *High Peak* by Byne and Sutton (Secker and Warburg, 1966); *The Peak and Pennines* by W. A. Poucher (Constable).

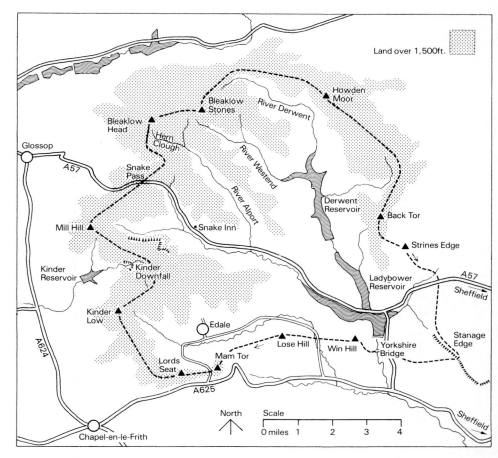

Bottom left: A view along Rushup Edge to the west of Mam Tor. *Photo: Maurice and Marion Teal*

Top left: The Woolpacks — isolated gritstone towers near Kinder Low. *Photo: Phil Ideson*

Top right: Typical Bleaklow scenery — on Alport Moor above Oyster Clough. This is to the east of the described route, a diversion that might well be chosen by the walker who wished to include a refreshment stop at the Snake Inn, between Kinder and Bleaklow. *Photo: Roger Redfern*

Bottom right: It is possible to split the Derwent Watershed walk by bivouacking in the Lower Small Clough cabin below Bleaklow Stones. *Photo: Gordon Gadsby*

Above: Sunlight and snow turn the harsh Kinder landscape into a scene of arctic beauty. *Photo: John Woodhouse*

Top right: Kinder Downfall forms a focal point for walkers on the western rim. In this wild view of the waterfall, a fierce blast of wind throws the water backwards to the plateau. *Photo: Maurice and Marion Teal*

Bottom right: Near the northern edge of the Kinder Scout plateau. *Photo: Shelagh Gregory*

and we join this route at the top of Jacob's Ladder. The Pennine Way follows the western edge of the plateau to that excellent waterfall known as Kinder Downfall, but the purist will see much more of Kinder by following the true watershed from Kinder Low to the summit at 2,088ft., the highest point in Derbyshire and the Peak District, marked by a small cairn. He will continue to Crowden Head, another barely perceptible rise on the plateau, then head north-west to skirt the north of the Downfall and along the middle of Kinder's western arm to Ashop Head, Mill Head and the Snake.

The last mile or so before the Snake is an obstacle course over the groughs. Our purist, following the true watershed, can make a quick detour to Featherbed Top and back.

Crossing the Snake Pass, we head for Bleaklow, the High Peak's second mountain and generally wilder and bleaker than Kinder. Its groughs are more eroded and there is less jumping to do. The well-trodden path deviates

slightly east from the 'shed and enables one to have a drink from Hern Clough. The Hern Stones are a couple of gritstone boulders, and the Wain Stones are a couple more at Bleaklow Head. From the south they have a resemblance to a pair of heads kissing. At this point, heading east across Bleaklow, the Pennine Way is left and a new air of remoteness, peace and seclusion enters. From here right round to Moscar are vast areas of peat and heather moorland showing few footprints. Above all, it is the air of solitude which gives Bleaklow and the Howden Moors their appeal.

Bleaklow's ridge curves in an 'S' but there are occasional parish boundary stakes to guide the walker. It is now that any navigational problems will make themselves evident. Bleaklow Stones are a collection of wind-eroded gritstone boulders, the Anvil and Trident being particularly fine. Grinah Stones are seen a mile to the east, but the watershed leaves the route to Grinah about half-way, swinging north and round Swain's Greave, where lies

the source of the River Derwent.

All the way across the Howden Moors to Back Tor is particularly arduous and largely trackless. There are occasional stakes to mark the parish boundary, coincident with our watershed, and trig points on Outer Edge and Margery Hill, highest point in South Yorkshire. Above all, the stretch round the head of Abbey Brook has the deepest tussocks of heather and moorland grass of the whole watershed, and there is simply no path, scarcely even a sheep track.

The walk may be considered cracked on reaching Back Tor (1,765ft.), for good paths now lead most of the way back. However, there is no path where the watershed lies coincident with the Derbyshire-Yorkshire boundary, from Dovestone Tor, across Strines Edge, to point 1,161 on the Strines road. This is private grouse moorland and the alternative is to follow the bridleway from Back Tor down Foulstone Delf, to join the road near Strines Inn, a handy refreshment halt.

It is an easy short climb up the grassy track from the Strines road, east then south to Moscar Lodge. Crossing the A57 again, we continue along the top of Stanage Edge which

becomes finer all the time until it is left at the 1,502ft. trig point on High Neb. Here we head back to Yorkshire Bridge, leaving Stanage Edge by one of the many paths through the bracken, joining the road at the corner of a wood on Dennis Knoll.

So there it is; the best, boggiest, bleakest, roughest, toughest, loneliest, wettest parts of the Peak District all brought into a day's walk encircling the headwaters of a fine river.

Top left: Walkers trudge across frozen Bleaklow. Hard frost conditions, with little snow, allow rapid progress across the normally arduous ground of Bleaklow and Kinder. *Photo: Gordon Gadsby*

Bottom left: Looking east from Margery Hill towards Cranberry Clough. *Photo: Gordon Gadsby*

Above: At the Cakes of Bread on Derwent Edge, looking south towards Wheel Stones. A short distance beyond this point, the true watershed route cuts down the slopes on the left to join Strines Edge. *Photo: Shelagh Gregory*

Overleaf: Looking towards the Swamp and the Alport Valley from near Bleaklow Stones. This view is taken from the Derwent Watershed route, close to the point where it leaves the Marsden to Edale section of the Pennine Way. *Photo: Phil Ideson*

41   High Peak Classic: Marsden to Edale

by Roger A. Redfern

This is unquestionably the most famous moorland traverse of the Peak District, the great classic of the southern Pennines by which all other long walks in the area are judged. It is about twenty-five miles long, and in winter conditions is thought by many to be the finest route in Peakland, taking in as it does the three highest moorlands of Black Hill, Bleaklow and Kinder Scout; three extensive gritstone plateaux at or above the 2,000ft. contour.

One of the best things about this walk is that it adheres to the gritstone and shales throughout its length. Another attractive feature is the regularity with which valleys alternate with the high tops, endowing the walk with constant interest. Marsden to Edale is not a dull route in any sense of the word. It doesn't make much difference which way it is tackled, though Edale to Marsden will often mean the prevailing wind is helping you along from behind.

The Manchester cotton merchant, Cecil Dawson, is always thought to have invented the walk at the beginning of the century, though he modestly claimed that Ross Evans did it first. There is no doubt, however, that Dawson was the greatest rambler of the southern Pennines in those pre-Great War days, adopting gym shoes for high-speed going on the high moors. Dawson it was, too, who improved on the Marsden to Edale by beginning at Colne and going by Hebden Bridge to Marsden. Later he extended it to fifty miles by starting at Colne and finishing at Buxton, the longest route in Peakland until 1919, when the Colne to Ashbourne was first completed.

In the early twenties the illustrious Fred Heardman completed the first Double Marsden to Edale. In September 1953, Courtenay and Desmond did this double walk in under thirteen hours, almost an hour of the time being spent taking refreshment at the half-way point. Of course, the route has attracted competitiveness, with athletes running it in less than four hours and some have thereby paid with their own lives; the majority, however, are mountaineers and ramblers with a genuine interest in the lonely hill ground which they traverse.

From Marsden, a track curves up beside the four reservoirs in the Wessenden Valley, and this makes the easiest route up to

the Holmfirth to Mossley road (A635) at Wessenden Head. It is a bad weather alternative for the Pennine Way. Some of the early walkers preferred a direct line south-west from Marsden, up on to Black Moss and on across White Moss. This latter line crosses the A635, two miles west of Wessenden Head then continues south-eastwards across the shallow trenches drained by the head-waters of the west-flowing Holme Clough. Three miles beyond the A635, this and the route from Wessenden Head. join at the triangulation pillar atop Black Hill (1,908ft.).

What a wilderness this moor-top can be, with acres of black, oozing peat reaching in all directions. In mist it is indeed a depressing place, but in clear conditions the tops of far hills beckon one onwards. There are three alternatives now: to follow the undefined line of the Pennine Way to the south-west down

Walk   High Peak Classic: Marsden to Edale.
Maps   O.S. 1:50,000 Sheet 110; O.S. 1:25,000 Outdoor Leisure Map — The Dark Peak.
Start from Marsden (ref. 048113).
Finish at Edale (ref. 123859).
Grading   A long and rough walk which can be difficult in bad conditions.
Time   10-11 hours.
Distance   25 miles.
Escape Routes   Wessenden Head. Woodhead—Holmfirth road at Holme Moss. A628 at Woodhead. Snake Pass summit on A57. Ashop Clough to A57 at Snake Inn.
Telephones   Holme; Woodhead; Crowden; Snake Inn; Hagg Farm Ashopton.
Transport   Edale is served by British Rail from Manchester and Sheffield. Marsden has rail connections to Manchester and Huddersfield.
Accommodation   Hotels and Bed and Breakfasts in Marsden and Edale. Youth Hostels at Marsden and at Rowland Cote, Edale.
Guidebooks   *Pennine Way Companion* by A. Wainwright (The Westmorland Gazette); *A Guide to the Pennine Way* by C. J. Wright (Constable); *Portrait of the Pennines* by R. A. Redfern (Robert Hale).

Left: On Bleaklow, looking south (see page 177).

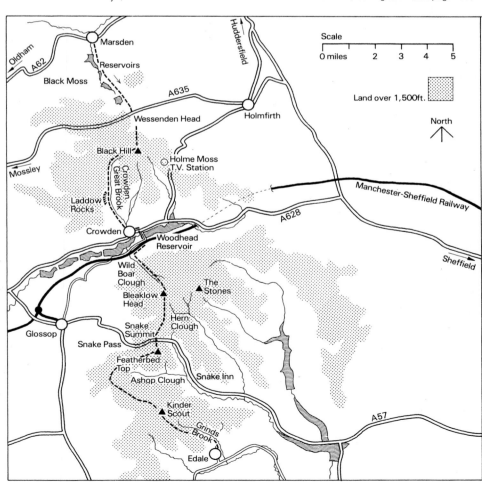

into the safety of Crowden Great Brook; to make directly to the south by Tooleyshaw Moss and Westend Moss to Crowden; or — the quickest and easiest alternative — to proceed eastwards beside the soaring television mast on Holme Moss to the A6024 hill road, and along it for four miles down to Woodhead beside Woodhead Reservoir in Longdendale. This last is a good idea in the dark or in thick mist.

Proceed down the A628 for almost a mile towards Manchester, turning across the impounding wall of Woodhead Reservoir on the B6105. Instead of following this road beside the electrified railway, turn up-stream a few yards to the former station bridge over the line. This gives access to Bleaklow, the most serious section of the route, with few escape routes and requiring careful compass work in poor visibility. There is an ascent of almost 1,400ft. to Bleaklow Head from Woodhead Reservoir, and the most interesting way is to aim now for the Rollick Stones and the lower end of Wildboar Clough (not to be confused with the Cheshire valley in the western-most extension of the National Park). The ascent of this gritstone ravine makes one of the best scrambles in the southern Pennines and, after heavy snow or rain, it is best to keep out of it and follow the moor high above.

In any event, though, it is the key to the correct route to Bleaklow Head (2,060ft.). I cannot agree with Wainwright that Bleaklow is '. . . an inhospitable wilderness of peatbogs . . . nobody loves Bleaklow. All who get on it are glad to get off'. This great, unique British desert can be a delightful place of fresh air, freedom and broad skies. In winter conditions it can, of course, be a real challenge to physique and route-finding ability.

We are now once more on the line of the Pennine Way and this goes southwards, swinging down between the tops of Hern Clough and Crooked Clough, before reaching the top of the Snake Pass (A57) by means of a carpet of plastic laid here to reduce erosion of the peat by the army of Pennine Way pilgrims who come this way annually.

While the Pennine Way slants off to the south-west we maintain a southerly course over the tussock grass and bilberry dome of Featherbed Moss (1,785ft.) and so into Upper Gate Clough. Soon down to the remains of

Ashop Clough shooting cabin, beside the young River Ashop. It is less than two miles' walk eastwards beside the river from this point to the Snake Inn on the A57 — a useful escape route to know of.

Now begins the last, long uphill pull of half a mile and 700ft. from the cabin ruins, across Black Ashop Moor and up through the grit-stone escarpment of The Edge, to the plateau of Kinder Scout. It is best now to strike to the east of south, aiming across to the Fair Brook, where it leaves the plateau surface in a steep, stepped-floor ravine (a waterfall is marked on the O.S. map here). A steady south-easterly course across the deeply dissected peat moor will deliver one to the headwaters of the Grinds Brook. By following the stream to the place where it suddenly cuts down from the rim

towards the Vale of Edale you quickly come, in clear weather, in sight of journey's end.

There is a feeling of well being on reaching this southern side of Kinder Scout, when the sunlight slants at a low angle over Rushup Edge late on a winter's afternoon, or when the descending sun brings cool air to the end of a summer's day. Down the rocky ravine now, joining the Pennine Way below the silhouette of the famous Mushroom Rock on Grindslow Knoll and so down the widening track to the fields above Edale village.

Whether you intend to do this classic walk just once, or hope to emulate Harry Buckley, who in September 1953, completed his 116th solo Marsden to Edale, doesn't really matter. Every time brings new experiences and memories of highest Peakland.

Top and centre left: Two views of the steps and pools of Wildboar Clough, the ravine that provides entertaining access from the north to the Bleaklow plateau. *Photos: Roger Redfern*

Lower left: The deep groughs that pit the surface of the Bleaklow plateau display an interesting combination of thick moorland vegetation and high, eroded banks of black peat. *Photo: Roger Redfern*

Below: Mist boils up below the rim of Kinder's southern escarpment. *Photo: Shelagh Gregory*

Top left: Walkers descend from Bleaklow, heading south towards the top of the Snake Pass. The shadowy northern slopes of Kinder Scout are in the background. *Photo: Shelagh Gregory*

Lower left: In the middle of the Kinder plateau, where oily black groughs, when not snow-filled, provide arduous and time-consuming terrain for the walker. This view is taken looking north-east towards Crowden Head. *Photo: David Higgs*

Above: The ravine at Grinds Brook. The Marsden to Edale walk drops down from Kinder into this fine rocky valley which leads towards Edale. *Photo: David Higgs*

42   Wildest Dartmoor: the North to South Traverse

by Len Copley

About five years ago two fellow walkers and I decided it was about time we tackled the Dartmoor North to South. With plenty of experience of walking on both the north and south moor, it was decided, without too much attention to detail, to tackle it on the following Sunday.

Duly arriving at Belstone Common at about 10.30 a.m. on a glorious May morning, we pointed ourselves in the right direction and set off at a cracking pace. The going underfoot was good and by 1.30 we had arrived at the Beehive Hut on the East Dart.

During lunch it slowly dawned on us that we were overheated and starting to dehydrate. As there was no chance of us finishing this walk during the hours of daylight we decided to abort.

Any further reference to a North to South walk was duly avoided until a few months ago when, at a meeting of Dartmoor Guides, three ladies in the company casually mentioned that they had accomplished the Dartmoor North to South the previous week in atrocious weather conditions, had thoroughly enjoyed it and were looking forward to tackling it again in the reverse direction. This rekindled our interest but this time we planned our walk a little more carefully.

With the decline in rural bus services, many of the villages on the Northern Moor are poorly served by regular transport, so it was decided to press-gang one of our wives to drive up to our starting point.

We arrived at Belstone at 6.30 in the morning, with the surrounding tors still wreathed in strands of early morning mist. With expressions of 'good luck', coupled with 'you must be mad', we started off.

Crossing the river Taw on a convenient wooden bridge just below Birchy Lake, we started a long slow climb towards the top of Cawsand Hill. In places the going was rough, dodging ankle-breaking clitter, but once at the top the view was tremendous. Standing atop the Bronze Age cairn we could see our route stretching before us into the distance. At this spot Dartmoor truly deserves the name 'The Last Wilderness'. To our right, below us, were the Taw Marshes and on the side of Belstone Tor we could see the remains of 'Irishman's Wall' — a relic of the 'improvers of the past'.

Our route took us past White Hill, Little

Hound Tor, through the Bronze Age Stone Circle, on to Hound Tor. This ridge-walking kept us above Galleven Mire — a place to be avoided. These mires are sometimes known as 'Dartmoor Stables', a resting place for ponies. And this would have been the last resting place for a Scottish Blackface had we not spotted him through the glasses and heaved him out.

At Wild Tor we stopped to find the letter-box hidden in a crevice on the northern side. It contained a visitors book, rubber stamp, ink-pad and pen.

This idea of letter-boxes was started during the middle of the nineteenth century by a guide in the Chagford area, named James Perrot. He took visitors to Cranmere Pool, where they would leave their visiting cards and sign the visitors book.

With the introduction of postcards, people started leaving stamped addressed cards; the next group of visitors collected these cards and posted them at the next convenient village, leaving their own cards for the following group. It was interesting to see where the cards were eventually posted and how long they took to reach their destination.

The box, book and stamp at Wild Tor are thought to have been placed there in 1977 by a group of engineering apprentices from one of the large car manufacturing groups.

By contouring the side of Hangingstone Hill and Whitehorse Hill, we dropped slowly down towards Quentin Man, crossing the Teign close to another Dartmoor letter-box at Teign Head, and headed for Stats House — an old peat cutters' dwelling, now in ruins. Close by there is a peat-pass, cut at the turn of the century by a man named Frank Philpots. There are many of these passes on the moor, enabling walkers and horsemen to negotiate their way through the heavily-rutted peat covering.

Instead of taking the peat-pass down to the river, we headed straight for Sandy Hole Pass. Here the banks of the river have been artificially narrowed by the tinners. This increased the speed of flow, enabling them to wash the crushed tin ore.

With painful memories of our previous walk in mind, we strolled along the river bank, past the waterfall to where the river takes a short right-angled bend. We arrived at the Beehive Hut at about 11.00 a.m., and after a short

Walk Wildest Dartmoor: the North to South Traverse.
Maps O.S. 1:63,360 Tourist Map of Dartmoor; O.S. 1:50,000 Sheets 191 and 202. Start from Belstone (ref. 620933). Finish at Bittaford (ref. 653569).
Grading A long walk over rough and boggy moorland.
Time 14 hours.
Distance 25 miles.
Escape Routes Main roads are crossed at Postbridge and Dartmeet.
Telephones Belstone; Postbridge; Dartmeet; Bittaford.
Transport Exeter to Okehampton bus (Western National) to Sticklepath, one mile from Belstone. From Bittaford walk one mile to Ivybridge for Western National bus to Plymouth.
Accommodation Bed and Breakfast at Sticklepath. Hotels at Ivybridge. Youth Hostels at Chagford, Bellever and Tavistock.
Guidebooks *Dartmoor* by Crispin Gill (David and Charles); *Crossings Guide to Dartmoor* (David and Charles); *Dartmoor* by L. Harvey and D. St. Leger-Gordon (Collins); *Walks in the Dartmoor National Park*, No. 1 by Elizabeth Prince (Dartmoor National Park).

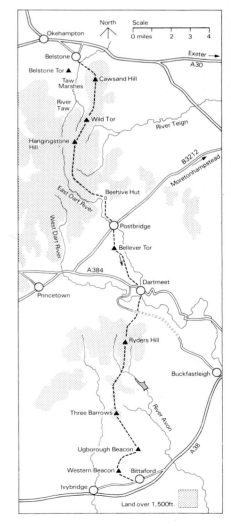

Previous page left: Belstone Tor — typical of the many granite outcrops to be found all over Dartmoor. *Photo: Leonard and Marjorie Gayton*

Top: Looking west from White Hill. *Photo: Viv Wilson*

Bottom: An ancient clapper bridge at Teign Head. *Photo: Dartmoor National Park*

Right: Looking towards Belstone and Wild Tors from Taw Marshes, *en-route* to Cawsand Hill. *Photo: Len Copley*

spell we crossed the river at the take-off point of the Powder Mills leat and followed the path alongside the dried-up leat beneath Broadun Ring, where the Bridle Path cuts across the leat. We turned and followed the Bridle Path on to Postbridge, where in the distance we could see the 'grockles' (tourists) gathering by the car-load at Postbridge.

Quickly crossing the main Princetown to Mortonhampstead road, we disappeared into Bellever Forest, taking the track leading up to Bellever Tor. The time was now 12.30 and we had covered thirteen miles of what we considered to be the worst territory; we decided it was time for lunch, knowing that time and weather were on our side.

At 1.15 we moved off towards Huccaby Tor, taking the road down to Dartmeet — another

grockles' paradise. Leaving crowded car-parks we moved down-stream and then climbed to Combestone Tor, where ahead of us lay the next moorland stretch.

Passing Horn's Cross we headed out for Holne Ridge — this part was heavy going, especially where we walked across old peat ties. Cutting across the Sandy Way, we could see the familiar sand-hill of the old Redlake China Clay workings in the distance. We passed over the top of Ryder's Hill and down past the Tinners' huts at Fish Lake when, suddenly, disaster struck. The ground in front, on either side and behind started to move, and we realized we were on a 'Quaker'. Being 'tail end Charlie' at this particular time, I was the one to break through the crust and sink up to my waist in slush. (Quakers or Featherbeds

occur when depressions in the granite fill with water, and vegetation forms over the top, resulting in a deep stinking mass of rotting vegetation covered with a crust of bright green moss). For the next few miles, until we reached a convenient stream, my companions refused to walk with me.

After a quick wash down and a ten-minute break, we passed the deserted Red Lake China Clay pit, crossed the Abbot's Way (sometimes referred to as 'The Jobbers Path') at Crossways and picked up the track of the old Red Lake Railway. Here we had the choice of following the track right down to our destination at Bittaford (a convenient route if the mist closed in) or following the river Erme down to Harford, contouring around Weatherdon Hill, Western Beacon, and so down to Bittaford.

In the end we decided to follow the high ground and walk parallel to the old railway track, stopping to examine the Bronze Age remains at Three Barrows, Piles Hill and Ugborough Beacon.

Moving across to Butterdon Hill, in the fast fading light we could just make out the remains of the Neolithic chambered tomb at Cuckoo Ball and, below that, our final destination, the track leading to the Western Machinery Works and Bittaford.

By 9.15 p.m., after sinking the second pint at the bar of the Horse and Groom, three rather smug self-satisfied males got around to discussing where would be the best place to start the South to North, and when.

Above: The visitors' book at Wild Tor. *Photo: Len Copley*

43   The Snowdon Horseshoe

by Jo Fuller

Walk   The Snowdon Horseshoe.
Maps   O.S. 1:50,000 Sheet 115; O.S. 1:63,360 Tourist Map of Snowdonia.
Start and finish at Pen-y-pass (ref. 646557).
Grading   A classic mountain walk with some scrambling along the Crib-goch ridge. In full winter conditions this is a serious mountaineering expedition.
Time   7-8 hours.
Distance   8 miles.
Escape Routes   North or south from Bwlch Goch; down the railway track from Yr Wddfa; south from Bwlch y saethau.
Telephones   Gwastadnant; Pen-y-pass; Pen-y-Gwryd; Glanaber in Nantgwynant.
Transport   Railway stations at Bangor and Betws-y-Coed. Bus service from Caernarvon to Nant Peris and (in the summer months) Caernarvon to Pen-y-Gwryd.
Accommodation   Hotels, Guest Houses and Bed and Breakfast establishments abound. Youth Hostels at Llanberis, Pen-y-pass, Capel Curig and Idwal Cottage.
Guidebooks   *The Welsh Peaks* by W. A. Poucher (Constable). *Hill Walking in Snowdonia* by E. G. Rowland (Cicerone Press).

Occasionally the winter strikes the mountains of North Wales hard. The snows have the opportunity to accumulate in the gullies and in the steep craggy cwms, and even the screes below the cliffs on the Pass of Llanberis become smooth cones of hard-packed snow.

Craig Rhaeadr assumes a far more dominant role on the south side of the Pass. The grey, almost triangular buttress of the Nose of Dinas Mot, supreme in summer, concedes this position and reclines gracefully against the whiteness and the sharp-edged darkness of the perpendicular crags, festooned with ice, that flank it. The waterfall that usually slides over the red convex face of Craig Rhaeadr creates in time a great curving 250ft. wall of ice. Up in the heights of Cwm Glas Mawr, on the left bank of the torrent that descends from the slopes beneath Crib-y-ddysgl, the majestic upward sweeping bulk of Cyrn Las broods, its leftwards curving lines incised in thin whiteness, and the steep snow covering the head-wall of the cwm leads beyond and up to the ramparts of the ridge on the Snowdon Horseshoe.

The car-park at Pen-y-pass provides the usual starting point to the route. The footpath contours amiably above the road in a south-westerly direction, overlooking the Pass and gently climbing up towards the true crest, which it reaches at a broad col and from which suddenly most of the objective is revealed. The spikiness of Crib-goch is hidden by the buttress that lies immediately ahead, but behind its

shoulder the high white line of Crib-y-ddysgl curls round to swing up into the lovely pyramidal shape of Yr Wyddfa which falls sharply on the other side to Bwlch y saethau, and then the long graceful curves of Lliwedd's twin peaks are displayed and persuade the eye to linger. Small Glaslyn in the upper cwm of the Horseshoe is thus contained within a bowl of steep craggy sides and, when not caught up in ice, its waters tumble in cascades into Llyn Llydaw which points a long finger in the direction of Pen-y-pass and the old Gorphwysfa Hotel which is now part of a Youth Hostel.

The buttress which leads up to the start of the Crib-goch arête presents different problems according to the conditions. Sometimes the summer scrambling way provides a fine, steep

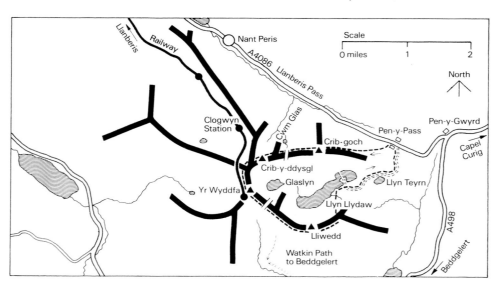

Above: Looking across the north-east face of Snowdon (Yr Wyddfa) towards Bwlch y saethau and Lliwedd. The Horseshoe walk descends to Bwlch y saethau from the summit by the Watkin Path (round the corner on the south-east face), and continues towards Lliwedd along the obvious ridge. *Photo: Basil Goodfellow*

route up firm, hard snow, and sometimes there is a greater covering of ice over the rocks, increasing its interest. Towards its summit the rocks become shattered, of reddish hue and blocky in appearance, and one becomes increasingly aware of the exposure. Standing perched on the small topmost blocky platform, there is always a tendency to pause, reflect and to absorb the scene. At times the weather has been sparklingly cold and bright with a low sun casting deep shadows, adding a glitter to the surface, emphasizing the texture of the snow and its wind-sculptured shapes. The slopes on either side fall away; far, far away down into Cwm Glas Mawr to the north and down to Llyn Llydaw in the south, whilst the arête reaches out into the distance, enticing, uncompromising and so steeply defined. More

recently on the arête, when there was a great deal of ice but in a fairly heavy mist, we were only aware of the narrow icy crest through which some of the rock pinnacles protruded. We balanced our way along, and at about the half-way stage the mist suddenly cleared from the summits, revealing only the very steep upper slopes on both sides and imparting a feeling of even greater remoteness. It was a world of white and black and we were alone in it. The graceful downward sweep of snow to the north was broken by a line of crags emerging darkly out of upward drifting mist which obliterated all the lower features, and we felt that we could have been on the highest sharpest ridge of pinnacles anywhere . . .

The end of Crib-goch is marked by at least three rocky towers, which are turned on the

Top left: Yr Wyddfa and Crib-y-ddysgl from Crib-goch, the classic view of the Snowdon Horseshoe.
Photo: Walter Poucher

Left: Y Wyddfa and Crib-y-ddysgl from the summit of Lliwedd.
Photo: Dave Alcock

Right: The final slope to the summit of Crib-y-ddysgl, with Crib-goch and Moel Siabod in the background.

Photo: David Higgs

south side, but the final one also offers an inviting problem which turns it on the north side. The mist had closed in again and we peered up at the thick ice which coated the rock, remembered that the first step up and out to the right is awkward and places one over intimidating space, and so carefully chipped out some good footholds and uncovered the rock spikes for our hands. Once on the ramp the pitch went well and on the topmost rocks we lingered, aware that this exquisite isolation would have to be soon relinquished because the short descent would bring us on to the broad flat col; the vertical airiness abruptly giving way to the easily managed flatness. We trudged past the enclosure where the natural vegetation is being allowed to grow without interruption from either man or sheep and acknowledged the inevitable reminder that man's influence on this area and his exploitation of its resources has been long-term, penetrating and deeply entrenched. The mountains of Snowdonia bear so many scars, so much human alteration and interference, and yet, when the harsh hand of winter persists and hides some of the disfigurations, the enhanced scene assumes once more a wild splendour.

The ridge continues in an almost due westerly direction and soon reverts to a narrow and craggy character. The rocks provide interesting diversions which are always worth attention, and to swing up the flakes and blocky chimneys is a bonus any time. Curving in from the north-east, the long ridge which swings north to north-north west and carries the railway line from Llanberis merges with the Horseshoe route and, as we joined it on this misty day, such was the depth of snow that there was no visible sign of sleepers, rails, cuttings or any other of the iron paraphernalia that normally litters the hillside. Huge flakes of snow were falling thickly out of the greyness, and periodically the capricious mist granted us a brief glimpse of the face directly below the summit of Yr Wyddfa, with the straight lines of the Trinity Gullies strongly marked. Snow usually emphasizes the synclinal structure of

Right: Snowdon from Yr Aran. The Watkin Path takes a diagonal line down the sunlit face just above the cloud shadow. The Horseshoe walk follows this, and then continues towards Lliwedd (off the picture on the right). *Photo: Gordon Gadsby*

Above: The Snowdon group silhouetted against an afternoon cloud sea. The magnificent conditions can often be experienced in North Wales during the Autumn months. *Photo: Alan Kimber*

this face and now, as we glimpsed it, the bedding planes, etched out by erosion and imperceptible in summer, were piled deeply with whiteness which merged in places but the shallow down-fold lines could still be traced.

The ugly squatness of the summit café, however, was evident despite the rounding off effect of the deep drifts and banks, and all its edges had grown huge jagged fringes of ice particles, because of the unrelenting frost. They had been corded and teasled by the wind over a long period, but the building provided shelter for a hot drink and food, as the flakes continued to hurtle out of the sky.

The snow was falling heavily when we left the summit and took the start of Bwlch Main which eventually leads down to Beddgelert. The definite ridge made us feel comfortable in

the total whiteness, but we soon had to leave this and cross the steep face which falls from Yr Wyddfa into Cwm Tregalan, making sure that we were heading in an easterly direction in order to reach Bwlch y saethau, the descent picking a delicate way between the lines of crags. The snow was superb and the steepness of the descent was exhilarating because the heel held fast as it was down-driven into the crisp firmness, but it is a slope that needs particular care.

The way up to the summit of Lliwedd provides a scramble but there is an awkward point which, because of the accumulation of snow on this winter's day, gave us a short vertical bank with a slightly overhanging lip, but now there were figures ahead so we tackled it with nonchalance. There is a winding rocky

ridge which leads up from the outlet of Glaslyn to Bwlch y saethau and our companions had come into our route by this way which, in such good conditions, had been a sporting ascent needful of rope and slings.

The southern slopes of Lliwedd are convex and broken by numerous rocky steps and boulders, but the northern face of the twin peaks forms magnificent cliffs of 900ft. which soar above Llyn Llydaw. The nature of the rock has resulted in a succession of long vertical ribs and grooves, more continuous at the base and holding much ice and cascading tangles of icicles, but becoming more broken towards the summit, full of hard-packed snow which curls and curves out of the cracks. The features of these great cliffs give a fascinating and dramatic sequence of vertical views as the

upward climb to the western and then to the eastern summits is made, the exertion being more than compensated for.

A speedy descent along the ridge to the point where it provides a long snow run down to the shore of Llyn Llydaw and the main track which leads round the northern shores of Llyn Teryn, and thence northwards back to the car-park at Pen-y-pass completes the circuit.

In such a winter the route takes a great deal of traffic. Snowdonia is easily accessible and there is a relatively large number of huts belonging to a wide range of organizations in the area, but a truant mid-week excursion earns one an almost empty Horseshoe and its wonderful sharpness, exposure, rich variety of experience and completeness leave fine memories.

Above: An RAF Mountain Rescue helicopter flies into the Horseshoe bowl below the cliffs of Lliwedd. This sight, all-to-frequent in winter, is a sobering reminder of the regular accidents to hill walkers on Snowdon. Notorious black spots, like the final steep sections of the Watkin and Miners' Paths, and the convex slopes above Clogwyn du'r Arddu, collect their quota of victims almost every winter. These are easy routes in summer, and, perhaps because of this, tend to be underestimated in winter by the many hundreds of walkers who embark on them without ice axes. *Photo: David Higgs*

44 Tryfan and the Bristly Ridge

Walk   Tryfan and the Bristly Ridge.
Maps   O.S. 1:50,000 Sheet 115; O.S. 1:63,360 Tourist Map of Snowdonia.
Start from E. end of Llyn Ogwen (ref. 665605).
Finish at Ogwen Cottage (ref. 650603).
Grading   A short but rough walk involving some scrambling over fine rocky ridges.
Time   5 hours.
Distance   7 miles.
Escape Routes   From Bwlch Tryfan descend westwards towards Llyn Bochlwyd and pick up a good track to Ogwen. From Glyder Fach the rough southern slopes can be descended almost anywhere to Pen-y-Gwryd.
Telephones   Ogwen Cottage; A5 one mile E. of Llyn Ogwen; Pen-y-Gwryd.
Transport   Railway Stations at Bangor and Betws-y-Coed. Bus service from Bangor to Bethesda.
Accommodation   Hotels in Capel Curig and Bethesda. Farm house accommodation in the Ogwen valley. Youth Hostels at Idwal Cottage, Capel Curig and Llanberis.
Guidebooks   *The Glyders Range* by Showell Styles (Gastons/West Col); *The Welsh Peaks* by W. A. Poucher (Constable); *Hill Walking in Snowdonia* by E. G. Rowland (Cicerone Press).

Right: Tryfan, flanked by Glyder Fach (left) and Y Garn (right), looking typically impressive in this view from near the A5, west of Capel Curig. The North Ridge leads directly to the summit from the valley. In the background the dark outline of the Bristly Ridge stands out from the bulk of Glyder Fach. *Photo: R. S. Clow*

Overleaf: A view from the summit of Glyder Fach, looking towards the Snowdon group and Glyder Fawr (right). The rock formation in the middle distance is the Castle of the Winds, and the Gribin Ridge leads off to the right beyond. *Photo: Peter Wild*

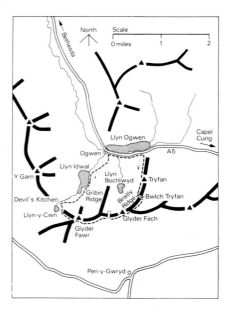

Map-distance reveals that this is one of the shortest walks in this book, but it is surely one of the steepest and most strenuous. Moreover the map-measurer, unable to make the walk more than seven miles long, takes no account of 3,500ft. of steep ascent and the same amount of descent, all amid the grandest rock scenery in Wales. Half a century ago the North Ridge of Tryfan and the North-East (Bristly) Ridge of Glyder Fach were included in a list of 'Easy Courses' for cragsmen in George Abraham's *British Mountain Climbs*; and though nowadays every summer sees thousands of men, women and children with no pretensions to be 'cragsmen' clambering up and down both ridges, the inclusion is a sufficient hint that here will be found plenty of work for hands as well as feet. By the same token, the route can become vastly more difficult in winter conditions, demanding rope and ice-axe on the steeper sections.

Perhaps because the two ridges are easier to ascend than descend, the walk is usually done with a start from the Tryfan end. In my opinion this is also the best way to do it for full appreciation of the superb views, as well as to extract the most pleasure from the unexpected clefts and corners on the ridge climbs. Two ladder-stiles a quarter of a mile apart give access from the A5 at the east end of Llyn Ogwen, to the foot of Tryfan's North Ridge. There are handy laybys for cars. Well-marked paths mounting from the stiles unite above a heathery shoulder, on the west flank of which is the ever popular Milestone Buttress, and the North Ridge begins its magnificent upward spring at once.

There are usually small cairns in place to mark the best route up an awkward boulder-scree, and the little crags at its top can be penetrated by any one of half a dozen scrambling routes. Above, a succession of rocky steps takes you up the broader lower half of the Ridge. Here, as Archer Thomson wrote in 1902, '. . . wayward humours and lively impulses may be indulged in with impunity . . .' by choosing your own line of ascent; but if you are more walker than climber it is wiser to select the ledge or cleft that shows the plainest traces of use. A few summers ago a friend and I, descending the North Ridge, paused on a heathery ledge to allow passage room for a large party of teenagers coming up. One of the

Above left: The East Face of Tryfan. The described route follows the profile of the mountain from right to left. The high mountains in the background are Elidir Fawr and Pen-yr-oleu-wen (right). *Photo: Peter Wild*

Far left: Looking up the North Ridge of Tryfan. *Photo: Shelagh Gregory*

Near left: Adam and Eve, the curious, up-ended boulders that mark the summit of Tryfan. *Photo: Shelagh Gregory*

Above: Glyder Fach from Bwlch Tryfan, with Cwm Bochlywd and the Gribin Ridge on the right. The wall on the left-hand slope leads up to the start of the Bristly Ridge. *Photo: Barry Smith*

boys, indulging a 'lively impulse', elected to try and climb to our ledge by his own original route well to one side of the proper way. The expression on his face as, clutching at the heather, he tried to reach our perch prompted us to ask if he was all right. 'No!' came the gasping reply and we grasped his wrists just as his hold gave way. He would have fallen no more than twenty feet, but his party would almost certainly have had to turn back and carry him down.

About half-way up, the Ridge narrows and rears in a fine little tower of bare rock; the hardest bit. In dry summer weather it is not difficult to climb straight up, though every hold is smooth and polished by innumerable ascents, and from its top you drop down into the Notch which is so conspicuous in views of Tryfan seen from the west. In conditions of snow and ice this little climb, which has some exposure, can be virtually impassable, and then a rather less dicey alternative may be found by clambering round on the left (east) side into the Notch. Above this the scrambling is less demanding, over delightful rock to the little plateau of the summit, where stand the twin monoliths 'Adam' and 'Eve' in lieu of a cairn. The rock of Tryfan is volcanic, and the tendency of the lavas to break off at vertical contraction joints has formed these two columnar boulders. If you step across from Adam to Eve you are deemed to have received the freedom of Tryfan. In calm dry weather it is not too hard a step but the penalties of failure

are unpleasant in the extreme.

A well-scratched, cairned route on the west side of the ridge takes you down a thousand feet to Bwlch Tryfan, and a track up the scree beyond leads to a practicable break in the eastern wall of Bristly Ridge. In the splendid scrambling that follows few variants are possible, for Bristly is narrower than North Ridge, though no harder. The rock scenery is very fine, subtly different — more pinnacles, fewer broad saddles — from that of North Ridge. You finish on a short horizontal ridge that abuts on the flank of Glyder Fach, and a cairned path leads on to the remarkable summit of that mountain and one of the finest views in all Wales. In hard winter conditions a steep but easier alternative to Bristly can be found up the scree slope under the east flank of the ridge.

The well-cairned 'highway' along the Glyder crest from Fach to Fawr is comparatively easy walking. Those who have not had their fill of hand-and-foot work can find a delectable direct route over the rock spikes of Castell y Gwynt. Beyond the undistinguished summit of Glyder Fawr, 3,279ft. up and the highest point of the walk, a cairned and much used scree path descends north and then north-west to Bwlch Blaen Cwm Idwal, the boggy saddle whence the cliffs of the Devil's Kitchen fall on its north-east side. There is a small lake, Llyn y Cwn, just to the west of the path at the bottom, and if you go north-north-west for a few hundred yards along its outlet stream you

come to where the stream plunges over the cliffs and get a memorable peep into the chasm of the Devil's Kitchen itself. But the path of descent, the only one, runs north-east from Llyn y Cwn and is cairned. Descending very steeply through the most impressive scenery yet encountered, it reaches the bottom of the Kitchen and continues down through a tilted maze of boulders into Cwm Idwal, a National Nature Reserve. On the way down a branch path to the right leads to the east shore of Llyn Idwal, passing the foot of the famous Idwal Slabs, where you will almost certainly see climbers on the classic routes; or, by bearing left, straight down to the old moraine humps above the west shore, you can finish the walk by a less populous path and find a place for a swim if it is needed. Either way will bring you down to the A5 near Idwal Youth Hostel and to the end of this walk.

To state the time occupied by a mountain walk is to invite a shower of disagreement but I would allow five hours for this route, though it could certainly be done in less. If you are a connoisseur of mountain scenery, or a geologist, or a botanist, or a lover of eminently climbable rock, you could take the whole of a fine summer day over it without wasting a single minute. You will have enjoyed to the full a superb route that rivals the 'Horseshoe of Snowdon' as the best mountain walk in England and Wales.

Top left: Looking back to Tryfan's South Ridge, from below the Bristly Ridge. *Photo: Gordon Gadsby*

Lower left: 'The Freedom of Tryfan'. *Photo: Alan Kimber*

Above: the Devil's Kitchen cliffs. The route descends the left-hand ramp to the base of the dark cleft of the Devil's Kitchen, and then continues down into Cwm Idwal by the obvious path. *Photo: Ian Wright*

Overleaf

Left page: A profile view of the Bristly Ridge from the head of Cwm Tryfan. *Photo: Gordon Gadsby*

Top right: A youth group disperses after posing for the obligatory photograph on the Cantilever Stone. This remarkable perched boulder, near the summit of Glyder Fach, has been a favourite photographic subject for generations. *Photo: David Higgs*

Lower right: Tryfan from the top of the Bristly Ridge. *Photo: Dave Matthews.*

45   The Welsh Three Thousanders

by Harold Drasdo

Walk   The Welsh Three Thousanders.
Maps   O.S. 1:50,000 Sheet 115; O.S. 1:63,360 Tourist Map of Snowdonia.
Start from Snowdon summit (ref. 609544).
Finish at Foel Fras (ref. 697682).
Grading   The classic long and challenging walk of Snowdonia. A preliminary recce is strongly advised for the route is complex.
Time   11-13 hours in good conditions.
Distance   24 miles.
Escape Routes   The walk crosses main roads at Nant Peris and Ogwen.
Telephones   Pen-y-pass; Gwastadnant; Nant Peris; Ogwen; A5 one mile E. of Llyn Ogwen.
Transport   Railway Stations at Bangor and Betws-y-Coed. Bus Service from Caernarvon to Nant Peris and (in the summer months) Caernarvon to Pen-y-Gwryd.
Accommodation   Hotels, Guest Houses and Bed and Breakfast establishments abound. Youth Hostels at Llanberis, Pen-y-pass, Capel Curig and Idwal Cottage.
Guidebooks   *The Welsh Peaks* by W. A. Poucher (Constable); *Hill Walking in Snowdonia* by E. G. Rowland (Cicerone Press).

The Himalaya put together a total of fourteen 8,000m. peaks. North Wales assembles fourteen 3,000ft. hills. But, for the mountain lover, sheer scale is often a minor consideration. You can't really love the eight-thousanders.

Future maps won't show the Fourteen Threes at a glance and, to save some dismaying sums, it's useful to know that 3,000 feet make 914 metres. However, the Threes will survive metricization. They are disposed in three distinct blocks, Snowdon, the Glyders and the Carneddau. The thousand-metre contour selects only four of the fourteen and unhappily these stand in pairs in the two outer groups. The conquerer of the metric thousanders loses on two counts. He has to bypass the summits of the fabulous Glyders, because the culminating point achieves only 999 metres. And he has to stagger over the wretched Glyders at more than 750 metres anyway, because they stand squarely across his path. The Imperial Threes make a lot more sense.

The excursion is often, perhaps usually, thought of as a race rather than as a walk and

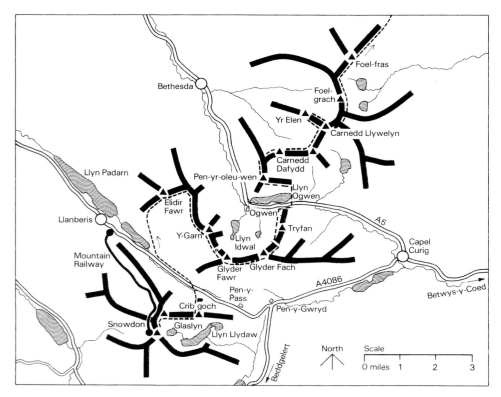

we are obliged to treat it as one in this space. It was probably first taken in one day in 1919 by Eustace Thomas, 'the greyhound of the groughs'; 'supported', as the expression has it, by Rucksack Club companions, he clocked about twenty-two and a half hours. Through the next twenty years a succession of itchy feet made subtractions until, in 1938, Capel Cure, Hamer and one Thomas Firbank recorded

eight hours twenty-five minutes, after considerable training and reconnaissance. They also made the expedition famous.

Firbank strikes the reader as an endearing character, a bit larger than life. In *I Bought a Mountain* he tells the story of the effort. A train was engaged to take the team up Snowdon and Firbank easily pardoned himself later. He makes fun of the spectators, reporters and photographers who attended the somewhat less than secret occasion, whilst clearly enjoying the attention shamelessly. Yet he is so innocent a romantic that we can only admire him. In 1947 the Threes were honoured with a sixty-page handbook, one of a series of footpath guides published by St. Catherine's Press of London. The writer, T. Firbank, laid down the law: 'The object was to stand upon the

Above: The Welsh Three Thousanders walk starts from the summit of Snowdon, reverses the Horseshoe to the sharp summit of Crib-goch (seen here), and then drops down to the Llanberis Pass, by-passing Dinas Mot. *Photo: David Higgs*

fourteen peaks of the Three Thousanders within the shortest time of which one was capable, using no mechanical aids en route'. From this it followed that one can ascend the first peak and descend the last by any approach or means, the critical time being that taken between these two summits, halts included. A search for the fastest sequence and line has long ago concluded, so that nowadays only a few eccentrics vary the same marginally downhill route from Snowdon to Foel-fras.

As a prophet, Firbank was no great shakes. Somebody special, some great day, might break seven and a half, he conceded. 'Let us say that his time might be seven hours, twenty-nine minutes, fifty-nine seconds. He would not do the trip much more quickly.'

Since then the Threes have resounded to the bump of boots and lighter foot-gear. In the early 'seventies Joss Naylor crashed the five-hour barrier. The double traverse has certainly been accomplished many times. On July 18th-19th, 1978, for reasons best known to himself, John Wagstaff ran from Snowdon to Foel-fras, then ran back to Snowdon, and then ran back to Foel-fras again. His time was twenty-two hours, forty-nine minutes, a hard day's night. Before dismissing the efforts of these psychopaths it ought in fairness to be pointed out that the number of people who have gone over the Threes without a sneaking glance at a wrist-watch at start and finish is probably pretty

small. Actually, the fell runners are a company of kings.

On the other hand, many walkers will take the Threes at a more leisurely pace, approaching it as an aesthetic experience and possibly one of great intensity. That's my inclination. Here we have to attack it like a fell-runner, looking neither to left nor right.

So, having climbed Snowdon, and perhaps having bivouacked and breakfasted there, we can begin. The bit down the railway line is easy. We arrive at the obelisk erected by John Ellis Roberts to the eternal disgrace of himself and the Park Authority. The bit up Crib-y-ddysgl is easy too. Only twelve left to go. But from here on it helps to know one's way round. The walker familiar with the descent to Bwlch Goch, the way through the Pinnacles, and the stupendous horizontal arête of Crib-goch is at an enormous advantage. Then we go steeply down the correct ridge and the slopes beneath, keeping the cliffs of Dinas Mot to our right, until the Llanberis Pass is reached. And down the road to the village of Nant Peris.

Now we can begin again. We're damn near back at sea level. The slog up Elidir Fawr is not appealing but once at the top things steadily improve. Y Garn, for me, is a friendly hill, however vile the conditions. The walk down to Llyn y Cwn is a relaxing preliminary to the trudge up Glyder Fawr. Then the curious moonscape of the Glyder and then the

Top left: The fourth Three Thousander is Elidir Fawr, a well-positioned mountain offering interesting views of Snowdonia, including this one across Bwlch Brecon towards Pen-yr-oleu-wen and the Carnedds. *Photo: Peter Wild*

Above: A reverse view to the previous picture — from Pen-yr-oleu-wen towards the whale-back of Foel Goch and Elidir Fawr (centre). The route follows the obvious ridge that links the two mountains and then heads off to the left towards Y Garn. *Photo: Maurice and Marion Teal*

Lower left: Winter snow invests the main Ogwen peaks with a real alpine character that is particularly well seen from the summit of Y Garn. Llyn Ogwen is on the left, dominated by Tryfan (centre). *Photo: Bruce Atkins*

Top photo: Looking back towards Y Garn, Foel Goch and Elidir Fawr from the summit of Tryfan. The route descends to Llyn Ogwen and continues up the slopes of Pen-yr-oleu-wen on the right. *Photo: Gordon Gadsby*

Right: Carnedd Llywelyn seen from Yr Elen. *Photo: Maurice and Marion Teal*

Above: Heading towards Craig Llugwy from Carnedd Dafydd. The massive cliffs of the Black Ladders are on the left. *Photo: Maurice and Marion Teal*

arresting landmarks, one hard upon another. Bwlch y Ddwy Glyder, the Castle of the Winds, the heaped blocks of the little Glyder, the Cantilever, the scree flank of Bristly Ridge, Bwlch Tryfan, the outmanoeuvrings of the South Ridge, Adam and Eve. Never a dull moment.

Is a hang-glider a mechanical aid, Firbank's followers might ask themselves? Over there stands Pen-yr-oleu-wen, two hundred feet above us; and here lies the intervening valley, two thousand feet below. Swiftly down to Llyn Ogwen, then, and rapidly up the Hill of the White Light. Along the ridge to Carnedd Dafydd and on to Craig Llugwy. Head for Carnedd Llywelyn, the second summit of Wales, but save it for later or climb it twice. Better to contour above Cwm Llafar, collecting Yr Elen first. Then Llywelyn and easily to Foel-grach, ignoring the refuge which signals the defeat of the National Park idea. Only a minor top and a few miles of gently descending ridge remain.

A paper by the American sociologist Jessie Bernard comes to mind — 'The Eduaemonists: human energy considered as an article of consumption'. Some people do the Threes because they can't keep still. Some people do it because it's beautiful, and it's there, and the less fit you are the more of a challenge it is. Either way, it's an event.

46   Roughest Wales: the Rhinog Ridge

by Harold Drasdo

Walk   Roughest Wales: the Rhinog Ridge.
Maps   O.S. 1:50,000 Sheet 124
Start from Trawsfynydd Nuclear Power Station (ref. 698384).
Finish at Barmouth (ref. 610160).
Grading   A long and rough walk over wild mountainous country.
Time   9-10 hours.
Distance   22 miles.
Escape Routes   Down the Roman Steps to Cwm Bychan. S.W. from Bwlch Drws Ardudwy to Cwm Nantcol.
Telephones   Pen-y-bont 3 miles W. of Rhinog Fawr; Pen-isar cwm in Cwm Nantcol 2½ miles W. of Y Llethr.
Transport   Bus service Portmadoc, Barmouth, Ffestiniog, Caernarvon, Bangor. Railway station at Blaenau-Ffestiniog.
Accommodation   Hotels at Ffestiniog (3 miles from start) and Barmouth. Youth Hostels at Ffestiniog and Gerddi Bluog near Harlech.
Guidebooks   *Hill Walking in Snowdonia* by E. G. Rowland (Cicerone Press); *Rambles in North Wales* by Roger Redfern (Robert Hale); *The Mountains of North Wales* by Showell Styles (Gollancz).

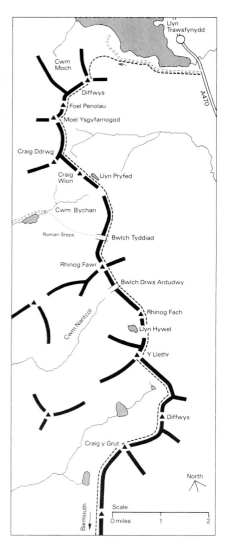

Of all the traces that men leave behind in wild country, surely a naturally developed footpath is the most acceptable. For some of us the eye and the imagination are less jarred by a quite atrociously eroded track than by the artificial walkways now colonizing our hills in the name of our Parks. The unimproved footpath stands for the golden age before the planner came. On our mountains there are ancient trackways, their purposes so obscure that only historians may read a meaning.

Yet the mountain walker has to prefer wilderness to wild country and this preference leads to his special dilemma. To keep secrecy about one's favourite places is certainly selfishness, but to enthuse about them loudly must accelerate their degradation — and we may live to see them lose the virtues for which we valued them. 'The earth is soft and impressible by the feet of men', Thoreau said, and that's only the beginning.

The fantastic chain reaching from Maentwrog in the north to Barmouth in the south — or, we might say, from Diffwys 1,850 to Diffwys 2,462 — sets this and related problems in an extreme form. It's not even easy to fix on a name. Geologists call the region the Harlech Dome. The Welsh say y Rhinogau or y Rhinogian and I don't know which to prefer. But mostly they mean only Rhinog Fawr and Rhinog Fach rather than the whole range. And those two impressive peaks, though psychologically and physically the heart of the area, are each exceeded by Y Llethr and the bigger Diffwys.

The Rhinogs give the closest copy of a mountain wilderness North Wales can offer. Parts of the Migneint, admittedly, suggest an extremer sense of desolation or remoteness and show some comparably difficult ground; but the Migneint has a moorland rather than a mountain character. The famous summits to the north match the Rhinogs in boldness of form and stand a good deal higher; but they are divided by roads into trivial parcels and they have been vulgarized by the operations of the hill farmer. In fact the Rhinogs is easily the wildest and most extensive mountain block in Gwynedd. Most of the ridge is built of Rhinog grits of the Cambrian era, an early subdivision of the next oldest system known. Say, a hundred million years older than Snowdon — but we get that by instinct the moment we set

foot here. Wherever the rock is not bare, bilberry and a sinewy heather grow, waist-high in places and rooted in boulder screes. The sparse bird-life of the ridge is that of bog and acid moorland. Few sheep graze here but the biggest flock of feral goats in Wales wanders over these hills.

The Rhinogs is a valuable and sensitive area and gets D classification by the Park authority; no improvement of access, no promotion. Most of the old tracks run in an east-west sense, over the cols; along the ridge and its flanks there exists no real path, much less any continuous right of way. It remains an arena in which those admirable British eccentrics, landowner and trespasser, may meet on their own ground. It should be mentioned that along the ridge itself access is rarely contested. However, it should also be mentioned that amongst the region's incidental beauties we have to include a necklace of massive and extensive stone walls, said to have been built by French prisoners during the Napoleonic Wars. These walls are often eight feet high and since they are showing their age now, a skilled rock-climber is pressed to cross them without disturbance. Whilst trespass is not a moral offence, damage to these walls most certainly is, aside from an unprovoked injury to the hill farmer.

Car parking, too, is limited on most approaches and pressure will bring problems. In other ways the area is not so vulnerable as might be feared. The heather on some of the finest parts of the ridge lies in only an inch or so of soil and when removed reveals a clean rock pavement extending those already used.

Most walkers will want to go from north to south in order to take the best ground while still fresh, and so as to finish at sea level amidst the fleshpots of Barmouth.

If a car has to be abandoned, the car-park at Trawsfynydd nuclear power station must be used. Three routes lead into Cwm Moch. From near the dam a leat may be followed south-west until it collects the stream by a bridge. The same point may be reached more

Top right: Craig Wion, the focal point of the northern Rhinogs. Here, the ridge is flat-topped, and characterised by deep transverse canyons and rock outcrops. *Photo: Gordon Gadsby*

Bottom right: Rhinog Fawr (left), Rhinog Fach and Y Llethr (right) seen from Cwm Nantcol. *Photo: Tom Dodd*

pleasantly by the track east of Llyn Llennyrch. Or one can enter the cwm from the west on the old bridleway passing Nant Pasgan-bach.

Once into Cwm Moch climb the steep grassy gully at its head to gain the eastern end of Diffwys. The ridge is found to consist of fine pavements with a few short heather interruptions and Foel Penolau, the true top of this little hill, is quickly reached. It is as curious a summit as Wales can show, an extensive and almost unbroken platform of rock, strongly defended on all sides. Midway along the south-western face a weakness leads down to the col. (The gritstone climber who turns back to examine this escarpment may never reach the Roman Steps, let alone Barmouth). Moel Ysgyfarnogod is now close to hand. From this modest eminence, the highest point in the northern section, an extraordinary scene may be admired. The distant peaks appear to great

advantage. And the stranger who scans his map carefully makes a barely credible discovery; the rough, long-abandoned landscape he is entering was once a great metropolis of prehistoric man. There follows a descent to a small triangular lake, crossing broad rock terraces littered with blocks disposed as the last ice age left them and not to be moved, maybe, until the next reshapes this place. On the edge of the lake, a green track leads to old manganese workings.

At this early stage a pattern starts to impose itself on the attention. Lots of unexpected ups and downs. No reason to be deduced from the map that this pattern will continue. (It will). Up over bare rock terraces and by tiny gullies. Down similar features. Another triangular lake. Along the crest of Craig Ddrwg, heading for Clip but missing it if one wishes, since it stands off the watershed. The divided ridge of Craig Wion. A horseshoe-shaped lake, looking in misty conditions alarmingly like another glimpsed a mile and a half ago. Llyn Pryfed appears and should be passed to the east. Next, a splendid mile of Celtic badlands leading to Bwlch Tyddiad, the gap of the threshold, that taken by the Steps. Every so often, a fifty-foot or hundred foot trench across the ridge. Little outcrops, rather like Dartmoor tors. At one point we reach one of the lateral canyons through a longitudinal canyon, a weird intersection in the sixty-foot blocks. A cross-roads, yes; some will have doubts already. Then down slabs and a little gully to the top of the Roman Steps, dubiously Roman but evidently steps.

The first third is completed and we have reached the big Rhinog. We take the eastern descent until we pick up a track rounding the shoulder and climbing to Llyn Du. Up Rhinog

Left: Looking towards Craig Wion and the dark bulk of Rhinog Fawr from the slopes of Clip. This photograph illustrates the tortuous, trackless terrain in sections of the northern Rhinogs that has given them their reputation as the most arduous mountains in Wales. *Photo: Gordon Gadsby*

Above: On the pavements south of Craig Wion, a marvellously complex area described by Harold Drasdo as ''a splendid mile of celtic badlands'' This photograph is taken looking south towards Rhinog Fawr and Bwlch Tyddiad. *Photo: David Higgs*

Above: Llyn Hywel and Rhinog Fach from the slopes of Y Llethr. Lake Trawsfynydd with its Nuclear Power station can be seen in the distance, beyond the right-hand slopes of Rhinog Fach.
Photo: John Cleare

Fawr. Down Rhinog Fawr. Bwlch Drws Ardudwy: from the lowlands to east and west the view of this colossal chasm has daunted prospective ridge-walkers to the degree that it encouraged the earliest travellers. 'The gap of the door to Ardudwy'; and Rhinog or rhiniog means 'doorpost'. Up Rhinog Fach. Down Rhinog Fach. Some uncertainty and some space for the use of his capacities ought not to be denied the mountain traveller, so the less said about these two fine peaks the better.

And now we arrive at a romantic and enchanting scene. Llyn Hywel, wedged tightly between the little Rhinog and Y Llethr, laps against slabby cliffs. The atmosphere verges on the sublime and must have caused some pre-romantic shudders before the long amnesia in the racial memory cleared. Up Y Llethr, the culminating point in the area. Here it turns out that we have crossed an unexpected frontier. The ground has changed character and we can lengthen' our stride on these ordinary sheep-walks. Crib-y-rhiw and Diffwys pose no obstacles and then the ridge descends very gently to Barmouth with a choice of exits on to public footpaths and roads.

A personal reminiscence. Three or four years back I got high on three days on the Rhinogs. Eventually, still high, I found myself regarding the toilet wall graffiti in a pub in the main street. One inscription was scrawled over and over again: 'Northern Soul'. It seemed packed with significance. The lonely hill-walker's mind and the gregarious disco mind got together again, still friends. Might I not relate the expression to the *genius loci* of that wild landscape too?

But, how to protect the Rhinogs? Well, it never does any harm to walk them in snow. Otherwise, keep to the pavement whenever you can. Don't run the grass slopes or the screes, and keep your rucksack light. Go alone, or go with people who would have gone there anyway. If you climb a wall and knock a stone off, replace it. If the wall collapses, rebuild it. If you can't rebuild it, please go back home: send your conscience money to the tenant farmer whose address you might obtain at the Park Office at Maentwrog.

And if you completed it and enjoyed it, no need to do it again. You can devise innumerable fine journeys through a magnificent other-world of cwm and llyn along either flank of the Rhinogs.

216

47   The Arans and Berwyns

by Jim Perrin

We are capable of the strangest actions, such as packing a rucksack on a fine autumn morning and setting out into the wilderness. Years ago I had been a walker, and had visions, soon to be dispelled, of being so again. On this autumn morning, tired leaf colour was revivified by a hint of the sere, and the sun shone softly from an eggshell-blue sky. I was Ulysses, my back once more to Ithaca, in quest of untravelled worlds.

Which is rather a grand introduction to the muddy, narrow lane leading steeply up out of the Dee valley, opposite the chapel in Glyndyfydwy. I followed this lane to a deserted quarry east of Moel Fferna, and soon, thankfully, it became quite polite and gentle in ascent. From the quarry, half a mile of deep heather on a compass bearing is not the best way to the top of Moel Fferna, and convinced me of the folly of straying from Berwyn paths. And it began to rain. I splashed along over Cerrig Coediog and Bwlch Croes y Wernen in a downpour, getting wetter and heavier-hearted by the minute. Behind me, and over to the north, hills beyond the Dee were sunlit. A wind blew in my face. Just before Nant Rhydwilym, by an incongruously green field intruded into the brown moor, the rain stopped, and I ate a sunlit lunch by the 'Wayfarer' plaque. My dog, a black labrador bitch who had frisked and busybodied across several more miles than her master by this time, sat and played Jack Sprat's wife with the apricots in a quite enormous bag of dried fruit which I had brought along. A couple of walkers crossed the Bwlch and talked of rain. To the west the Berwyns cleared of cloud; heather looked soft and warm as old tapestry. We set off at a fastish pace and in very little time were resting again on top of Moel Sych, southernmost of the major Berwyn peaks. This section of the walk really deserves to be savoured, rather than hurried. The valleys leading off east are beautiful in their blend of long perspective and intimate detail; the cwms hard under the summits are sculpted and fine; and the going on the tops is smooth and good. Sitting on top of Moel Sych in a mood of buoyant optimism, it seemed as if we might go on thus for ever. The afternoon was young, the sun shone, and the view spread wide. Within ten minutes it had changed utterly. A west wind rose, bringing rain. The path towards Milltir Gerrig

from Moel Sych petered out amongst innumerable miry and heathery knolls; you could barely see a hundred yards. From Moel Sych to Milltir Gerrig is three miles; on the map, the gently falling contours of a long ridge arouse the expectation of ease. By the time I reached Milltir Gerrig I was tired, dispirited, wet through, and time had passed. Car drivers on the Llangynog road glanced pityingly as I squelched past. Just west of spot height 464 I took a sodden track down to the right, and after a few hundred yards ducked into a copse of pine trees by a stream, where I took out my primus and brewed some tea.

Hazlitt, they say, died of drinking strong, green tea; Johnson wrote in its defence; to me, it was re-birth. With two pints of the stuff steaming inside me, I could look with equanimity upon the disintegration of my bag of dried fruit within a soaking rucksack. I set off towards Hafod Hir in something like high spirits. My plan here was to find the fork in the path over Hafod Hir to Melangell, and then to walk on compass bearings to Cyrniau Nod. It was a bad plan. No trace of a path exists over

Walk   The Arans and Berwyns
Maps   O.S. 1:50,000 Sheet 125.
Start from Glyndyfrdwy (ref. 148426).
Finish at Dinas Mawddwy (ref. 859149).
Grading   An exceptionally long and rough walk over desolate hills.
Time   14-15 hours.
Distance   34 miles.
Escape Routes   Easy routes of descent can be made from the Berwyns to the east down the valleys of Ceiriog, Gwynedd and Ffynnon. Tarmaced roads cross the line of the walk at Milltir Gerrig, Cwm Lloi and Ty Nant.
Telephones   Glyndyfrdwy; Cwm Pennant; Tyn-y-wern; Talardd; Dinas Mawddwy.
Transport   Crosville bus service from Chester through Llangollen to Bala. Railway station at Blaenau Ffestiniog then bus to Dolgellau and Dinas Mawddwy.
Accommodation   Youth Hostels at Llangollen, Cynwyd and Minllyn. Bed and Breakfast in Glyndyfrdwy, Corwen and Dinas Mawddwy.
Guidebooks   *Rambles in North Wales* by Roger Redfern (Robert Hale); *The Mountains of North Wales* by Showell Styles (Gollancz).

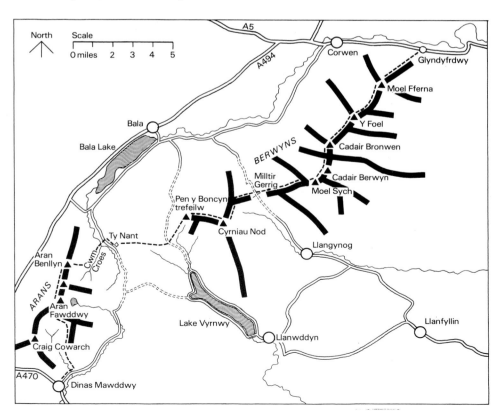

suffering under a louring heaven. From its ridge I crossed yet another boggy valley, to a shooting cabin by a shaley gully in the east flank of Cefn Gwyntog. Dry wooden benches, a few spent cartridges on the floor, and rain dinning on the roof. With an hour of daylight left I contemplated spending the night here, but instead crossed over Cefn Gwyntog to the Afon yn y Groes, kept to the west flank of a wood on its west bank, and followed a wet path down to the Hirnant road at 955258. It was quite dark by now, the wind blowing, and rain fell incessantly. The miles from Milltir Gerrig had been a version of Purgatory. A fullish moon shone through a gap in the clouds on a ruinous house. I stumbled into a wood by the junction of the Afon Cwm Lloi and the Nant Nadroedd Fawr, put down my sack, fed my very wet dog, who was by now mystified as to what was going on, and quite forlorn, made a brew of tea, got into my sleeping bag and bivouac sack, and tried to sleep. To no avail. My dog, luxurious by nature, had nosed her way to the depths of the bivi sack, and shivered, kicked, and groaned all night. The rain dripped. Occasional vituperative sallies of wind spattered drops across my head. I was wet, cold, aching; the trees gave little shelter. At the first glimmers of dawn I got up, dressed still in wet clothes, allowed myself the luxury of dry socks, and lit the stove. I can think of few sounds more welcome than the roar of a primus on a cold morning. For breakfast, a loaf, a pound of bacon, and Daddy's Sauce may not have been a balanced diet, was certainly gluttonous, but was needed and appreciated.

By seven I was away again, following the forestry track along the south bank of the Nadroedd Fawr, and then the stream itself, before crossing yet more heather to reach the stream leading down to Ty Nant. My joints by now were grating and crackling in an extraordinary manner. The body's slow decay; it is odd how you can find a little wry humour in even the most exigent of truths. Hobbling along the road like an eighty-year-old seemed like quite a good bad joke.

The way up from Cwm Cynllwd to Aran Benllyn is problematical. The farmers hereabouts are not overly inclined towards access agreements or walkers, and there are no public rights of way. There seems, however, to be no

Hafod Hir, and the terrain from Hafod Hir to Cyrniau Nod is trackless knee-deep heather, interminable, boggy. Rain and wind. My rucksack, which had weighed perhaps thirty pounds at the outset, now seemed treble that amount. Never had sky seemed so vastly indifferent, nor landscape so large, as when I struggled to gain the crest of Cyrniau Nod. Its brown and purple heathery whale-back is ingrained in my memory as the archetype of

objection to walking up to Llyn Lliwbran, beneath the fine cliff of Gist Ddu, and from here you can scramble round to the right of the cliff to gain the summit ridge. Once on this, a succession of little steps promises fulfilment which is never allowed. By contrast, the ridge between Benllyn and Fawddwy is pleasant, airy, and this day was touched once or twice by unexpected sunlight. The best descent from Aran Fawddwy is down the ridge called Drws Bach to spot height 568, whence a good path slants down the side of Hengwm into Cwm Cywarch. The walk down Cwm Cywarch to Dinas Mawddwy is truly rest after long labour, and the Red Lion in the latter village is as good an inn as this part of Wales provides

As an entity, this walk suffers from an illogical section, from Milltir Gerrig to Cwm Cynllwyd, which lies over grouse moors, is quite trackless, and is some of the hardest going you could ever wish to meet. But the compelling succession of the Berwyn summits, and the graceful isolation of the Arans, are adequate compensation for the anguish of their interim. And the general loneliness, the untrodden nature of the ground, its wide skies and your own small figure in a vast landscape, add an attraction moving towards the mystical, a liberation of soul in despite of the body's pain.

Editor's Note: Jim Perrin confirms that the walk could be completed in a single day given fine weather, a fit party and the will to succeed. Estimated time fifteen hours.

Left: The Arans from Bala Lake. *Photo: Kenneth Scowen*

48   The Black Mountains

by Phil Cooper

These gentle whale-back ridges occupy a fair slice of Welsh/English border country and, although the bulk of the area is in Wales, England claims one mountain, and there are two more summits over 2,000ft. high on the border itself. There exists a comprehensive network of easy paths all over these hills and, because of the lack of re-ascents along the main ridges, a long distance can be covered easily within a day's walk.

The main ridge runs north-south from Hay Bluff, above Hay-on-Wye in the north, to Pen Cerrig-calch above Crickhowell in the south, some twelve miles away along the ridge. Three more parallel ridges strike off south-south-east and contain lovely pastoral valleys between them. These are the valleys of the Grwyne Fechan, Grwyne Fawr, Vale of Ewyas (containing Llanthony Priory), and the Olchon in England, which marks the north-east boundary of the Black Mountains.

The walk described is thirty miles, and walkers describing themselves as 'fit' will be able comfortably to ignore the 2,000ft. of ascent per hour in Naismith's rule, and reckon on a good three miles per hour. The Black Mountains include fifteen summits over 2,000ft., and all are included. Several of the valleys are crossed to make something more like a mountaineering expedition out of these pleasant uplands. The Gospel Pass at 1,778ft., situated six miles south of Hay-on-Wye, is both the starting and finishing point. I have camped a night here in my van and made the mistake of leaving my damp boots out to dry overnight but the cloud came down low and in the morning they were completely saturated, and the van's engine didn't run properly until I had dismantled all the high-tension electrics, cleaned and re-assembled them.

The generally easy nature of Black Mountains walking can be assumed from the start, as it is only a five-hundred foot pull and under a mile west to the Twmpa, the first top. There is a choice of easy paths, but even away from them in the vegetation, walking seems reasonably easy. After the second top, Pen Rhos-dirion, a 'there-and-back' detour is necessary to Twyn Tal-y-cefn before contouring round the head of the Grwyne Fawr valley over Pen y Manllwyn (not counted as a summit, not having any separate complete contour), and heading for Waun Fach, the

highest of the Black Mountains at 2,660ft. Unimposing from any angle, this bulky mass is completely surpassed for quality of shape by its neighbour Pen y Gader-Fawr, whose flat top with short, sharp sides is akin to that of Ingleborough. However, most shapely of all in this area is the Sugar Loaf, which stands alone just south of the Black Mountains and fails to reach 2,000ft. by a short head. It is prominent in today's views and well worthy of a separate ascent.

But we leave Pen y Gader-Fawr for the moment and continue west then south along the Black Mountains' main ridge, over a pass with good access routes both sides, just before Mynydd Llysiau. Next is Pentwynglas; this part of the ridge is very nearly flat and Pentwynglas merits only one contour ring of its own. Pen Allt-mawr is a useful bit higher, and the short sharp ascent should get the lungs warmed up for the valley crossing to come.

Walk   The Black Mountains.
Maps   O.S. 1:25,000 Leisure Map of Brecon Beacons National Park, Eastern Area; O.S. 1:50,000 Sheet 161.
Start and finish at the Gospel Pass (ref. 236351).
Grading   A long but simple walk over rolling uplands.
Time   12 hours.
Distance   30 miles.
Escape Routes   The walk crosses roads at Cwm Farm after 15 miles and at Llanthony, 23 miles.
Telephones   Llanthony; Capel-y-ffin or many of the farms on the lower slopes of the mountains.
Transport   Rail connection at Abergavenny 18 miles. Bus service (Western Welsh) to Hay-on-Wye.
Accommodation   Hotels at Hay-on-Wye. Youth Hostel at Capel-y-ffin 2 miles south of the Gospel Pass.
Guidebooks   *A Companion Guide to South Wales* by Peter Howell and Elizabeth Beazley (Collins); *The Brecon Beacons National Park* (H.M.S.O.).

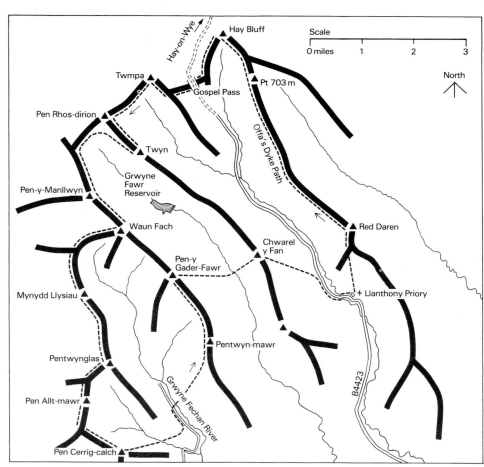

Lastly on this main ridge is Pen Cerrig-calch, from where the descent could be made straight down its east ridge to the road, but recommended is a deviation towards Crickhowell, just to see the unusual Table Mountain at 1,480ft. Not quite as distinctive as its far distant name-sake, it is nevertheless worth a visit before crossing the Grwyne Fechan valley.

Just before Cwm Farm, a track runs to the right at an acute angle and, a few yards up this, one swings sharp left and over the stream. A path goes left as soon as the stream is crossed and climbs up through the wood past Nant-yr-Ychain fawr and out of the side valley to reach the crest of your next Black Mountain ridge. On reaching the ridge, there are two summits to visit: firstly, the very minor top of Pen-twyn-mawr, then the best Black Mountain of them all, Pen y Gader-Fawr. From here the crossing of the Grwyne Fawr valley is started by a 1,200ft. descent near the edge of the forest and an easy ford of the stream.

In the unlikely event of its running too high to ford easily, the track up the valley crosses the stream half a mile up, and that bridge could be used.

This is a straight-down and straight-up crossing and the edge of more forestry is followed as you puff up to Chwarel y Fan, the highest point in the county of Gwent. We have already touched this ridge with the visit to Twyn Tal-y-cefn but that is nearly three miles away now. The next summit objective is the minor top of Red Daren, whose name on the map is a bit further south-east down the slopes. Try to find time to make the slight deviation necessary to visit Llanthony Priory, a twelfth-century Augustinian priory in a magnificent setting; there are various paths available to facilitate a descent to it. The direct route is due east, to meet a bridge over the Afon Honddu near Tafolog, from where it is a steepish ascent up the slopes of Red Daren for some 1,100ft. to the trig point marking the summit.

Red Daren is a summit evoking particularly fond memories for me, for (being on the border) this was my final English mountain summit. I had visited all the points in England above 2,000ft. and stood on the trig column looking all around me on a hot, still August day with a sense of complete satisfaction and achievement. I expect this may be similar to

what mountaineers experience on a previously virgin summit in the Himalaya, or on top of Everest. Perhaps we hill-walkers can, after several years of travelling and walking on our homeland hills and moors, have an idea how the true mountaineer may feel after a relatively short duration trip to some remote corner of the earth.

Jumping off the trig point and back down to earth, we are now on Offa's Dike and, this being a long-distance path, more people are likely to be met on the walk north to 'Point 703m.' (2,306ft.), sometimes known as Black Mountain, and the highest point in Hereford and Worcester. There is a minor diversion east to Black Hill from here; this is the only summit wholly within England, and it has a trig point. Lastly, there is Hay Bluff at the north of the circuit, and the ridge of Ffynnon y Parc leads you back to base camp at Gospel Pass.

Here is a good, longish walk really to blow away the cobwebs. Nowhere is the scenery dramatic, yet the ridges offer pleasant walking and the valleys are quite charming and full of life and interest. The colours are good in spring and autumn, but at any time of year these uplands can offer as challenging a walk as you could wish.

Top: Llanthony Priory. *Photo: John Woolverton.*

Above: Looking down to the pass of Rhiw Trumau from the ridge south-west of Waun Fach. *Photo: Maurice and Marion Teal*

223

49   Plynlimon

by Phil Cooper

Walk   Plynlimon.
Maps   O.S. 1:50,000 Sheet 135
Start and finish at Eisteddfa Gurig (ref. 797841).
Grading   An easy walk over grassy and undulating hills. The peat hags and bogs could be unpleasant in wet weather.
Time   6-7 hours.
Distance   19 miles.
Escape Routes   Descend easy slopes to the east of Plynlimon and make for the Hafren Forest.
Telephones   The Inn at Dyffryn Castell on the A44 three miles south of Eisteddfa Gurig.
Transport   The Aberystwyth to Rhayader bus passes the starting point at Eisteddfa Gurig.
Accommodation   Hotel at Ponterwyd. Youth Hostel at Ystumtuen, one mile south of Ponterwyd.
Guidebooks   *A Companion Guide to South Wales* by Peter Howell and Elizabeth Beazley (Collins); *Red Guide to the Wye Valley* (Ward Lock).

'A sodden weariness' is how one early traveller described it. Plynlimon is, however, traditionally regarded as one of Wales' principal mountains along with Snowdon and Cader Idris. My first visit took place on one of those really foul days with pouring rain and low cloud. A tatty painted sign at Eisteddfa Gurig proclaimed Plynlimon as the source of numerous rivers and pictured spectacular mountain peaks looking just like a bevy of Schiehallions. A sign read 'Foot-path to Plynlimon' and was signed by the Ponterwyd Improvement Committee. Really! I followed the path up, past a derelict mine and up the wet slimy slopes. It was marked by stakes all the way. This suited my mood that day as I was feeling particularly unambitious. I stood on the summit trig point then returned the same way. It scarcely came as a surprise to confirm that this mountain was altogether quite different from Schiehallion. My resolution was to see it under better conditions.

The following year I was working on a crazy project to visit all the Welsh summits over 2,000ft., any point having its own complete contour ring of 2,000ft. or above counting towards the total of 233. Plynlimon boasts ten such summits and it makes a jolly good day's tramp to visit them all. Many of their names are fascinating and you can spot the sources of the various rivers which are born here.

There are several possible starting and finishing points, but Eisteddfa Gurig on the A44 Aberystwyth to Rhayader road seems as good as any.

Starting from Eisteddfa, a track runs west towards the forestry. Walking up the edge of the forest, you reach the summit of a subsidiary top of Y Garn at about 2,100ft. Y Garn, western outpost of Plynlimon, lies half a mile along a grassy ridge to the west. It is necessary to retrace steps to this subsidiary top then head north for Plynlimon himself. (I could not possibly refer to this mountain as 'her'!) Plynlimon is the anglicized form and the Welsh original, given in brackets on the map, is Pumlumon Fawr. 'u' in Welsh is, of course pronounced as an 'i' in English but I remain mystified as to how the 'l' got in. On the way to the summit the stream of Nant-y-moch starts to the west, while other streams forming the Afon Tarenig, an early tributary of the Wye, run east then south.

Pumlumon's summit, 2,468ft., boasts a good view on a clear day. Best is one of those exceptionally clear days which occur during an unsettled spell, for some parts of the view are very distant. You will probably see those other mid-Wales 2,000ft. mountains a few miles south: Bryn Garw, Drygarn Fawr and Gorllwn. But, with luck, further away you could spot parts of the Black Mountain or Carmarthen Fan, Fforest Fawr, the Brecon Beacons — highest of all in South Wales — and the border country Black Mountains. 2,000ft. mountains just across the Dovey Valley are Tarrenhendre and Tarren y Gesail, and a good bit further up are Cader Idris and the Arans. That heathery compact group forming Radnor Forest lies south-east.

Our day's objective is to include all the 2,000ft. tops of Plynlimon, so we must descend to a spur above Llyn Llygad Rheidol, one of the mountain's few lakes. We'll include Bugeilyn and Glaslyn as being within its bounds. There are two small tops on this spur and views 450ft. down to the llyn. The next top lies right above the source of the River Wye, and is not named on the one-inch or 1:50,000 maps, but is shown as Pen Pumlumon Llygad-Bychan on the 6-inch.

The 2,000ft. top-collector has to make a second trek north to take in Pencerrigtewion, across Llyn Llygad Rheidol from his two

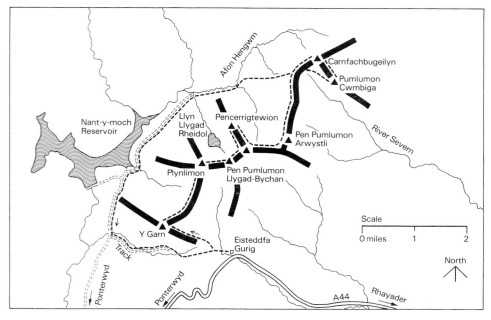

earlier minor tops. Plodding on eastwards, the beautifully named Pen Pumlumon-Arwystli is almost engulfed by the highest trees of Hafren Forest (Severn being the English for Hafren). There is a mild valley dropping away north called Cwm Gwarin, which runs into the Afon Hengwm. Just two northern outliers to go; the going seems to become tougher with increasing northing and the peat hags are bigger. It's a good half-hour's journey to what we shall name Carnfachbugeilyn (sheer magic!), although this name strictly applies to those ancient stones a short distance down from the summit north-east. The llyn of Bugeilyn is about one and a half miles north.

Pumlumon Cwmbiga only makes the ranks of the two-thousand footers by a couple of feet. There's another ancient group of stones forming Carn Biga nearby. Below here, the Afon Biga forms a major input to Llyn Clywedog. But just south of our last top is the infant Severn. To try and locate the actual source is a 'must' because of the river's importance.

Those having to return to Eisteddfa have quite a long walk back, but it is interesting and varied enough.

The most attractive return route from Pumlumon Cwmbiga runs on the north-west side of Plynlimon. Proceed due west for two miles, thereby descending into the valley of the Afon Hengwyn which is the biggest river feeding Nant-y-moch reservoir, then pick up a track when Cwm Gwarin joins Hengwm. This is followed to the Ponterwyd-Talybont scenic road.

A mile and a half south of this road takes you to Lle'r-neuaddau, then a track runs back east, through the forestry of the first leg of the walk, to Eisteddfa. The total distance taking the Nant-y-moch return is nineteen miles.

So, you won't find those rocky peaks of Snowdonia here in mid-Wales, those ice-scoured corries, the hanging valleys, dramatic crags festooned with classic rock-climbing routes — or the hordes of tourists, crocodiles of school kids, and cairns of orange peel.

Here's Wild Wales much as old Borrow saw it — give Snowdonia a break some time to have a good plod round Plynlimon.

50   The Brecon Beacons

by Phil Cooper

The Brekky Beaks form the highest land in South Wales and you have to go as far north as Cader Idris before meeting anything higher. It always seems a shame to me that Pen y Fan did not quite reach the 3,000ft. level, for, had it done so, the Welsh 3,000's walk would have been an entirely different challenge. There is a lot of Wales between the Snowdonian giants and the milder mountains of the south.

But hill-walkers are thankful for the mountains of South Wales. Here is good walking country, much of it unfrequented even in July and August. The Brecon Beacons are indisputably champions for shape and scene, and give the closest approach to the sterner type of walking found in the more rugged mountain areas. The South Wales mountains stretch some thirty miles from the Black Mountain group to the west, and work eastwards over Fforest Fawr, then the Brecon Beacons to the Black Mountains on the Welsh border with Herefordshire. The back-packer could have a good trek across the complete length of these mountains. Keeping to the main ridges and crossing most main roads at the watersheds, he would need several days' food supply with him.

It is a popular walk, to visit only the three main peaks of the Brecons. These are Pen y Fan (2,907ft.), Corn Du (2,863ft.) and Cribin (2,608ft.). These three shapely sentinels comprise the best of the group, but it is well worthwhile to make a longer day and include the minor tops as well. In all, there are twelve summits over 2,000ft.

To complete a round trip, a start from the north or south is best. The three sentinels have their most appealing aspects from the north and this is probably the better side from which to start. A disadvantage is the tarmac trudge back along the lanes which border the fields between the Beacons and the town of Brecon. They are pleasant lanes, but often have high hedgerows which, like the trees in forest walks, cut out your view.

Y Gyrn, a fine summit, tiered on its northern side by a spectacular band of sandstone, is the first objective. Walk in from Brecon to Modrydd, from where a path heads up Pen Milan, a step on the north-west ridge of Corn Du. It's a minor diversion west of Y Gyrn. At this point, you are only a couple of miles from Fforest Fawr's northern outliers,

Craig Cerrig gleisiad and Fan Frynych. The former has a mild form of corrie on its north side. Below, the busy A470 winds its way between Brecon and Merthyr.

Passing Tommy Jones' Obelisk with Llyn-cwm-Llwch below, one puffs up the slopes of Corn Du; but, to include the top of Craig Gwaun-taf, it is best to veer right, crossing Bwlch Duwynt, then reaching Gwaun-taf. This long south ridge of the Brecons has its foot on Merthyr's door-step. Anyone starting their Beacons round from the south will make Gwaun-taf their first top. It is but a quick step from Corn Du, first of the real Beacons. The bulk of Pen y Fan rather blocks the view to the east, but to the west there is a good view across all the peaks of Fforest Fawr to Banneau Brycheiniog and the supporting ridges and summits of the Black Mountain. The low ridges above the South Wales valleys fill the southern prospect. The view north is limited only by the clarity of the atmosphere. The moors of Mynydd Eppynt, which lie round the 1,500ft. mark, are north across the Vale of Usk. Beyond them lie moors culminating in Drygarn Fawr and Gorllwyn, remote and little-known summits. Plynlimon you might just possibly see beyond that, shaped like a squashed and inverted 'W' by virtue of the two main summits, Pen Pumlumon Fawr and Pen Pumlumon-Arwystli. The rounded dome of

Walk   The Brecon Beacons.
Maps   O.S. 1:25,000 Leisure Map of Brecon Beacons National Park, Central Area; O.S. 1:50,000 Sheet 160. Start and finish at Brecon (ref. 044285).
Grading   An easy walk over undulating and mostly grassy hills but with fine north facing escarpments.
Time   7-8 hours.
Distance   25 miles.
Escape Routes   A road through the Gap (reached after 12 miles) leads down to Brecon.
Telephones   At Storey Arms 1½ miles west of Corn Du and at Pontbrengarreg 2½ miles north of the Gap.
Transport   Regular bus services to rail connections at Merthyr Tydfil and Abergavenny.
Accommodation   Hotels and Guest Houses in Brecon, Youth Hostels at Llwyn-y-Celyn 6 miles south of Brecon and at Ty'n-y-caeau 2 miles east of Brecon.
Guidebooks   *The Brecon Beacons National Park* (H.M.S.O.); *A Companion Guide to South Wales* by Peter Howell and Elizabeth Beazley (Collins).

Left: The grassy Bryn-teg (north) spur of Cribin, which provides an elegant route to the main Brecon ridge. *Photo: Tom Dodd*

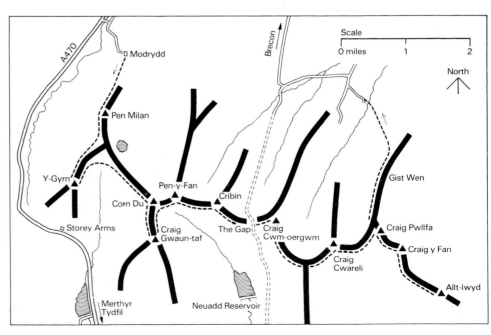

Above: Approaching Cribin at the start of the shorter, more conventional Brecon traverse. *Photo: Maurice and Marion Teal*

Near right: Near the top of Cribin's north spur. *Photo: Gordon Gadsby*

Top right: Walkers descend from Cribin, heading west towards Pen y Fan (right) and Corn Du (centre), the highest summits of the Brecon Beacons. *Photo: Maurice and Marion Teal*

The first four photographs, taken in sequence, illustrate the shorter Brecon walk. The longer walk described in the text traverses the range in the reverse direction.

Far right: A view to the east from near the summit of Cribin, looking across The Gap towards the seven summits that exceed 2,000ft. and combine to form the interesting extension to the Brecon walk. *Photo: Richard Pearce*

Radnor Forest may be identified in the north-north-east.

It is a short descent and short sharp ascent on to Pen y Fan, crowning Beacon and the highest point in Powys. The view out east is now opened, and it is the long ridges of the Black Mountains which fill the whole easterly arc. There are no jagged peaks here, merely huge gentle whale-back ridges with a handful of obvious summits. Waun Fach, at 2,660ft., is the highest, but the Sugar Loaf at the south end is the most shapely.

The third main mountain is Cribin, rather lower than its neighbours just west, but a good hill well worthy of the title 'Beacon'. Beyond Cribin, the whole range is cut in two by a pass known as 'The Gap'. There are six hundred or so feet of descent to make into The Gap, where shelter can usually be found on one side or the other for lunch. The track through this pass is an old Roman Road and would provide worthwhile entertainment on an off-day, or could be used as an access track to the main Beacons for anyone not visiting the eastern parts.

East of The Gap, the hills are moor-like and reminiscent of some Peak District moorlands in walking quality. There are seven summits in the eastern half, each one having its own contour ring over 2,000ft. Their names are taken from the broken crags just below the tops which, from west to east, are Craig Cwm-oergwum, Craig Cwareli, Craig Pwllfa and Craig y Fan. There are a couple of subsidiary tops. The views north down below the crags are especially good.

Beyond these crag-girt moorland tops is an eastern outlier, Allt-lwyd, which, like Y Gyrn back at the west end, does not break the 2,000ft. barrier by a large margin.

Allt-lwyd is many miles distant from Brecon and you must retrace your steps to Craig Pwllfa before descending the ridge of Gist Wen to the valley of Nant Menascin. Thence thread your way through the maze of lanes and tracks to base.

51   Wicklow Challenge: the Lug Walk Classic

by Simon Stewart

Walk   Wicklow Challenge: the Lug Walk classic.
Maps   O.S. 1:63,360 Sheets 120, 121, 129, 130;
O.S. 1:126,720 Sheet 16.
Start from Stone Cross (ref. 007203).
Finish at Seskin (ref. 907904).
Grading   A very long and tough walk over high mountainous terrain.
Time   12-14 hours.
Distance   33 miles.
Escape Routes   Roads cross the line of the walk at Sally Gap and Wicklow Gap.
Telephones   Brittas;   Kilbridge;   Ballyknockan; Laragh; Rathdangan.
Transport   Dublin — Brittas bus service to the start at Stone Cross. From the finish use the daily Dunlavin-Dublin or the Baltinglass-Dublin service.
Accommodation   Youth Hostels at Ballinclea and Aghavannagh. Bed and Breakfast at Glendalough or Dunlavin.
Guidebooks   *Dublin and the Wicklow Mountains* (Ramblers' Association); *Walking in Wicklow* by J.B. Malone (F.M.C.I.); *Mountaineering in Ireland* by C. W. Wall (F.M.C.I.); Irish Walk Guides, Vol. 5, *The East, Dublin — Wicklow* by David Herman, Gene Boydell, Michael Casey and Eithne Kennedy (Gill and Macmillan).

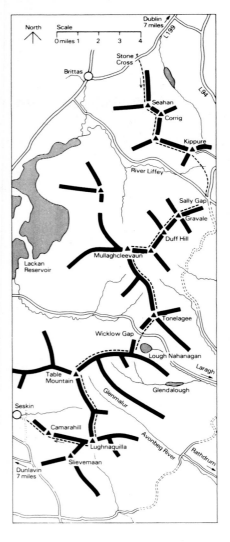

Wicklow has the largest and most continuous area of mountainous country in the whole of Ireland. Its remoteness and unspoilt quality have attracted walkers for generations, and several long and arduous traverses of the Wicklow Mountains have become classics. The Hart Walk, the Art O'Neill Walk, the Aughavannagh Walk and the Lughnaquilla Walk are perhaps the most popular of these. However, without a doubt the best walk, and that which receives the most attention, is the last, known universally in its abbreviated form as 'The Lug Walk'.

The Lug Walk takes a logical north-south route through the mountains, following an ill-defined ridge, often more a collection of humps, but traversing most of the major summits. A distance of some thirty-three miles, it provides a sizeable test of navigational skill and stamina across wild and rugged country. The average walking time for a fit party is twelve to fourteen hours, but it has been run in five hours, thirty-five minutes, by C. Rice in 1977.

Wicklow weather is entirely unpredictable and, since the walk does not drop below 1,500ft. from start to finish, you are advised to prepare for enveloping mists, continuous rain, and snow in the winter months. Route-finding on the rounded, indistinct ridges can be problem, and an ability to navigate with map and compass is essential. Contour lines on Irish maps are notorious for their inaccuracy and distance apart; the one-inch maps have a contour interval of 250ft. above the 1,000ft. level, and half-inch maps have 100ft. contours. Thus from the map the mountains appear quite rounded and featureless.

In the first part of the nineteenth century, when Ordnance Surveys were being carried out throughout the British Isles, the Wicklow mountain of Kippure was a principal sighting station. Sightings ('rays') from Kippure extended to the Cambrian Mountains, 102 miles distant across the Irish Sea. Take heart, fine clear days are not unknown in Wicklow.

The Lug Walk may be conveniently divided into three sections, split by the roads through the Sally Gap (L94) and the Wicklow Gap. For the walker proceeding from north to south, each section is progressively more difficult, in terms of boggy ground and route-finding. The terrain is sharply influenced by the weather

over the previous weeks.

Start the walk at Stone Cross, which is a five-foot high feature beside the L199 road between Rathfarnham and Brittas, about two miles beyond Bridget Burke's pub. At the time of writing there is a roughly painted sign in the field opposite the cross, proclaiming: 'Trespassers will be Persecuted'.

Head towards Ballymorefinn Hill, keeping the edge of the forest to your right. A fence and wide track are soon reached, taking you almost to the top of the first real summit of the walk, Seahan (2,131ft.), which is marked by a trig point. On a clear day it will be possible to see the ascending series of peaks leading to Mullaghcleevaun.

You will begin to appreciate the style of the walk, with its slow rises on well-rounded, heather-covered mountains. The route proceeds south-east over Corrig and Seefingan, the latter a rather confusing flat-topped mountain carrying a huge mound of stones. The unsightly TV mast on Kippure (2,475ft.) beckons, but your way is barred by black bog and eight-foot peat-hags. But having gained the summit there is easy going down to the Kippure road and the crossroads at Sally Gap, where ends the first stage of the Lug Walk.

The view east from Sally Gap gives the walker a bird's-eye view of the high boglands of Wicklow. The seemingly unending peat is riven in places by the small beginnings of three of the best known east coast rivers, the Liffey, the Dargle and the Cloghoge. So close are their sources that there is a battle between them. At present the Cloghoge has captured the headwaters of the Dargle, reversing the verdict of the O.S. maps.

Mullaghcleevaun is the next target, reached by way of an ascending series of smaller peaks. The first, Carrigvoher, is crowned by several granite erratics. An ill-defined track leads through the heavy heather on Gravale, and then a distressing loss of height is encountered, followed by a steep rise to the summit of Duff Hill.

On your journey to the next major peak, Mullaghcleevaun, you can avoid the subsidiary Mullaghcleevaun East by a traverse line on the north side. Descending to Barnacullian, you pass over a very wet and boggy area, but note that by keeping to the left hand edge of the mire you are soon able to

regain the rough heather.

Tonelagee (2,686ft.) is a fine mountain with a rock-strewn summit, where I have seen a herd of wild goats. Now descend, over good terrain, 1,000ft. to the Wicklow Gap and the successful completion of stage two.

Wicklow Gap is dominated by the Lough Nahanagan pumped water scheme, built by the Irish Electricity Board. The maze of paths, trenches, pipes and access roads can be very confusing in mist, but your next reference point should be Lough Firrib. This can be gained by following the reservoir road to its highest point and then locating a deep trench which leads to the lake.

Two routes are possible from Lough Firrib to Table Mountain: that over the summit of Conavalla, or that via the Three Lakes. If I tell the reader that the broad ridge approaching Convalla is nothing more than a lake of soft bog with a few islands of heather, I am sure he

will be able to make his own choice.

Beyond Table Mountain you pass the remnants of an old road called the Table Track, which was built in 1780 but destroyed in the upheavals eighteen years later. Easy going takes you over Camenabologne (2,495ft.) and Cannow, via a well-defined ridge.

Lughnaquilla, Wicklow's proud Munro at 3,039ft., is soon reached and you can take shelter behind its massive cairn. Although the Wicklow Mountains are for the most part composed of granite, the summit of Lughnaquilla is of weathered schist.

Set a bearing for Camarahill to avoid leaving by the wrong ridge, and then head south to the road at Seskin and a much earned pint at Fenton's Pub. Don't relax your vigilance until you are clear of Camarahill, for it was used as an artillery firing range and there have been several fatal accidents involving unexploded shells.

Above: Walkers stride purposefully across the boggy moors of the Wicklow mountains. In this view from near Kavanagh's Gap to the west of Table Mountain, Lughnaquilla is the highest of the distant summits, with Slievemaan and Ballineddan to the right. *Photo: Donal Enwright*

52   The Mourne Wall Walk

by Denis Rankin

Walk   The Mourne Wall Walk.
Maps   O.S. 1:63,360 Sheet 9 — South Down; O.S. 1:126,720 Sheet 9 — Mourne Mountains.
Start and finish at Dunnywater Bridge (ref. 354222).
Grading   A long but fairly simple mountain walk with no navigational problems.
Time   8-9 hours.
Distance   20 miles.
Escape Routes   Cols on the western section of the Mourne ridge provide easy ways down to the Hilltown — Kilkeel road. Hare's Gap provides escape N. to Slievenaman and S. to Silent Valley.
Telephones   S. end of Silent Valley; Slievenaman Youth Hostel two miles N.W. of Hare's Gap; Newcastle.
Transport   Regular bus service from Belfast to Newcastle. Dismount at Annalong and walk two miles to the start at Dunnywater Bridge.
Accommodation   Youth Hostels at Newcastle, Kinnahalla and Slievenaman. Hotels in Newcastle. I.M.C. Cottage The Bloat House in Annalong Valley; write to R.A.S. Merrick, Hon. Sec. I.M.C. 82 Marlborough Park North, Belfast BT9 6HL.
Guidebooks   *Hill Walks in the Mournes* by J. S. Doran (Mourne Observer Press, Newcastle). *Mountaineering in Ireland* by C. W. Wall (F.M.C.I.); Irish Walk Guides, Vol. 4, *The North East, Down — Antrim — Armagh — Derry — Tyrone — Fermanagh* by Richard Rogers (Gill and Macmillan).

Below: Looking along the Mourne Wall, from Slieve Meelbeg to Slieve Meelmore (left) and the craggy summit of Slieve Bearnagh.
Photomontage: Northern Ireland Tourist Board

'The mountains of Mourne sweep down to the sea', we are told by the haunting Irish song. This fine range of granite hills does indeed sweep down from the highest point, Slieve Donard at 2,796ft., to the seaboard of County Down in less than two miles.

The Mourne Wall Walk is a very unusual mountain walk, for almost no navigational skills are necessary. The walk follows the course of a dry granite wall which was built in order to relieve unemployment in the 1920s and which encloses the water catchment area of the now superseded Belfast and District Water Commissioners.

Now, a word of warning. Unless you are highly competitive or suffer from agoraphobia, avoid the Mourne mountains on the Sunday following the Spring Bank Holiday. On this particular day the Youth Hostel Association for Northern Ireland organizes the annual Mourne Wall Walk. Inaugurated in 1957, when only a handful of YHANI types took part, the event now attracts over 2,000 participants and is firmly established in the Ulster sporting calendar. Whilst nothing short of the highest possible praise is due to the small band of YHANI volunteers who have been reponsible for enticing so many people from many walks of life to get off their backsides, one cannot help but express reservations over such mass

participation in the hills, especially when many of those taking part are going into the hills for the very first time in their lives. If the Mourne Wall were to disappear overnight, the event would be restored to a true test of hill-craft ability!

The Hilltown-Kilkeel road bisects the Mourne Mountains into the Western Mournes, which are mostly grassy moorland hills, and the Eastern Mournes which are characterized by heather-clad granite domes, sometimes capped by granite tors, as on the summits of Slieve Binnian and Slieve Bearnagh. The backbone of connecting summits in the Eastern Mournes takes the form of the letter 'E' with its prongs projecting southwards from its spine, which runs from Slieve Meelmore in the north-west to Slieve Donard in the north-east. The 'E' encloses two valleys – the Silent Valley with its two reservoirs, and the Annalong River Valley – which form the water catchment area on whose watershed the Wall was built. The walk connects the summits lying on the outer extremity of the 'E', but leaves out the hills (Slieve Lamagan and Cove Mountain) which form the middle prong of the 'E'.

The Walk starts (and finishes) at the Dunnywater Bridge over the Annalong River, at the southern extremity of the easternmost

prong of the 'E', and follows the road westwards for one kilometre before striking up a stony lane which leads to a stile at the Mourne Wall proper. The ascent of Slieve Binnian (the southernmost extremity of the middle prong of the 'E') which follows is the longest, both in terms of distance and height, of any of the summits on the walk. At half-height a fine view is obtained into the Annalong Valley, which is circumvented by many fine rock-climbing crags. On approaching the summit tors, the best route, unless one wishes to sample the many short rock climbs that abound, is to make for a gap immediately above South Tor, from which a fine view is to be had of the Silent Valley below, the Western Mournes beyond and the Carlingford Hills in the distance.

All 2,000ft., tediously gained, must be lost immediately in the steepest descent of the walk. Although there is no scree, the terrain immediately below the summit is loose, and care is needed not to dislodge any rocks. At the bottom the rocky tor of Little Binnian is circumnavigated by a contouring up leftwards, before more grass and heather lead to a cottage and lane. The point marked on the map 'Moolieve' is not crossed, as the walk follows a route further south from the Wall proper, until the tarmac road is once again reached.

The road is followed westwards for two kilometres, past the hairpin bends at the entrance to the Silent Valley reservoir, to the point where the Wall meets the road at the end of a forest. This section is wet underfoot, but rapid progress is possible by walking on the

Below: Looking back to Slieve Bearnagh and Hare's Gap from the summit of Slieve Donard (2,976ft.), the highest peak of the Mourne group. *Photo: Walter Poucher*

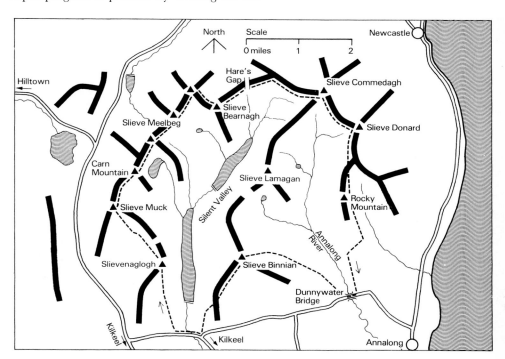

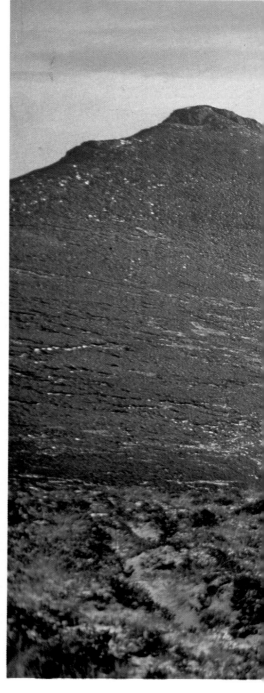

granite slabs on top of the Wall itself. Where the Wall turns to the west the walk continues north-west before embarking on the ascent of Slievenaglogh, which is heather-clad. The 2,000ft. contour is crossed for the second time before topping Slieve Muck which, being composed of shales, is grassy. Though the ascent of Slieve Muck is steep, thereafter this section provides the most level stretch of the whole walk, until the granite domes with their steep descents and re-ascents are again encountered on Slieve Lough Shannagh. On a misty day, care is needed at the tops of both Slieve Muck and Carn Mountain, because the

Wall proper takes sudden right-angled bends, though it is possible to continue straight on by following minor walls which join the Mourne Wall at these points.

The section from Slieve Lough Shannagh to the Hare's Gap, though short, constitutes the most strenuous section of the whole walk, and the 2,000ft. contour is crossed three times in traversing the summits of Slieve Mellbeg, Slieve Meelmore and Slieve Bearnagh. The scenery, as elsewhere on the walk, is wonderfully varied, with the forbidding nature of the inner Mournes contrasting with the extensive views over the numerous small

Above: A view across the Silent Valley from the ridge above Lough Shannagh towards the distant Slieve Binnian. Doan is the small hill on the left. *Photo: Denis Rankin*

farm holdings in the surrounding Mourne country.

A halt is traditionally called for at the Hare's Gap, as it is such an obvious landmark. Only one-third of the walk remains, though admittedly this includes the two highest summits of Slieve Commedagh and Slieve Donard. Though not to be underestimated, their greater bulk makes their ascents more drawn-out than the switch-backs which preceded them, enabling the fine views into and over the north-facing corries of Slieve Commedagh to be enjoyed. After the initial descent from Slieve Donard, progress over the gently descending terrain is eased by walking on the excellent granite slabs on top of the wall, which passes close to the summit of Rocky Mountain before turning left to gain the lane which leads back to the starting point.

The statistically minded hill walker may be interested to know that he has walked almost twenty miles and climbed 8,500ft., in traversing nine summits over 2,000ft. in height; a distance and height covered in under four hours in 1978.

53   The Maum Turks of Connemara

by Joss Lynam

Walk   The Maum Turks of Connemara.
Maps   O.S. 1:63,360 Sheets 84 and 94; O.S. 1:126,720 Sheet 10.
Start from the pass 2 miles south of Maum Bridge (ref. 223179).
Finish at Leenane Hotel (ref. 997542).
Grading   A long mountain traverse involving much ascent and descent. An annual walk (in May) is organised by the Mountaineering Club of University College, Galway.
Time   10-11 hours.
Distance   15 miles.
Escape Routes   Many of the cols or gaps provide easy ways down to lower ground on the east or west.
Telephones   Leenane; Maum Bridge; Maum Cross; Teernakill Bridge.
Transport   Daily bus service to Leenane from Westport and Galway. The Galway — Clifden service goes to Maum Bridge.
Accommodation   Hotels at Maum Bridge and Leenane. Bed and Breakfast available locally. Bunk house at Maum. Youth Hostel at Ballinahinch, Killary Harbour.
Guidebooks   *Mountaineering in Ireland* by C. W. Wall (F.M.C.I.); Irish Walk Guides, Vol. 2, *The West, Clare — Galway — Mayo* by Tony Whilde (Gill and Macmillan).

The 'Maum Turks Walk' starts from the road near Maum Cross and goes all the away along the ridge to Leenane. It took the great H.C. Hart fourteen hours and that, I thought for many years, made it a two-day walk for me. But in the summer of 1974, four friends, none of them superhuman, did it in twelve hours, and then the University Mountaineering Club in Galway announced an organized Maum Turks Walk for July 1975. As an alleged Connemara expert, I had to try it!

So Simon and I drove down on the Friday evening and camped with forty humans and several thousand midges, at Maum. In the morning the weather looked passable, so I dressed accordingly in shorts. We drove up to the pass between Maumwee and Leckavrea, checked in, and started up Leckavrea (2,012ft.). It is just a steep steady plod of 1,700ft. – not too bad at the start of the day. The checkpoint arrived in position only a couple of minutes before us! The cloud level was about 1,400ft. as we set off on a compass

course north-west, and we were glad to drop down below the cloud to the col. A really steep pull up into the cloud again on the other side brought us to Shannagirah (2,045ft.). Somewhere here two army lads and a dog passed us.

We navigated on, using the old one-inch map, and trying to recognize the little lakes marked on the Shannakeala plateau. In particular, a 'banana-shaped lake' aroused fierce argument. On Shannakeala (2,174ft.), we found the Army, but no checkpoint; well-disciplined, they went to look for it, while we shrugged our shoulders and hurried down out of the mist to Maumeem. There we met wind and rain, funnelled through the gap; huddled in a sheep-shelter eating some food, I bitterly regretted my bare knees and skimpy anorak.

The steep climb — 1,200ft. with half a dozen false tops — up to Derryvoreada (2,076ft.)

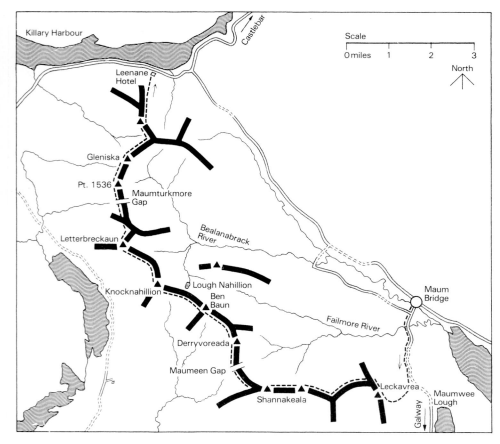

Above: The northern end of the Maum Turks from the road near Killary Harbour. *Photo: Sean Rothery*

warmed me a little, but then we had to follow the windswept ridge to Ben Baun. By good luck, we avoided the mistake of following the subsidiary ridge out to Slieve Naroy (2,015ft.). (Simon and I, going solo in even worse conditions in 1976, both made this mistake and had to descend to 1,000ft. in the unmarked coombe in the north to re-orientate ourselves.) NOTE WELL — from point 2,076, head 15° west of the bearing you take from the map.

Buffeted by the wind, we clambered along the rocky ridge, west from the south top and then north-east to Ben Baun itself at 2,307ft., the highest of the Maum Turks. No checkpoint, so we carried on and ten minutes later met the embarrassed checkpoint team on its way up. We continued down over steep ground with crags (keep right to avoid the worst) and came out of the mist at Lough Nahillion, where the Army stormed past again.

Some more food and then we tackled the steady climb up to Knocknahillion (1,993ft.), nearly 1,000ft. of ascent, but at least it was grassy. No checkpoint there, either, so we continued along the curving, humpy ridge to Letterbreckaun (2,193ft.). On a fine day you can avoid the humps on the west but this too tricky in the mist. Eventually we found Barbara near the summit with a tent and, wonderfully, a hot drink. (In 1976 I arrived there, exhausted, and had to rest for half an hour; I was ready to give up and settle for the 'short walk' — down to the Bealanabrack, but the news that no-one was ahead spurred me to action and I carried on. Minutes later Simon arrived and the news that I had gone on spurred him to continue too!).

239

Above: The central part of the Maum Turks range seen from Ben Corr in the Twelve Bens group. Lough Inagh is in the middle distance, with Letterbrechaun (left), Knocknahillion and Ben Baun (right) the main summits in the background. *Photo: Phil Cooper*

The navigation from Letterbreckaun to the Maumturkmore Gap is difficult; neither half-inch nor one-inch maps bring out the shape of the land, and it was not until 1977, when we actually saw the terrain, that we could understand our wanderings. In 1975, just when we felt we should be at the Gap ('Tober' meaning 'a well' on the map), the ground dropped away to a small col — was this it? No checkpoint but that meant nothing! We climbed out the other side and then the mist cleared momentarily revealing a deep valley in front of us — where *were* we? We trusted the compass and descended diagonally to the right across the slope. We climbed down beside a small crag, miracle, there was the pass and the checkpoint.

There is a very steep but mercifully short climb up to point 1,536. The weather, I think, had improved slightly; at least it had ceased to bother me, except as a hindrance to navigation. Soon after the top of point 1,536, we picked up the sheep fence that surrounds the Bealanabrack valley and, much as I may object in principle to fences on the hills, we welcomed this one thankfully and followed it to the pass between the Bealanabrack and Bunowen valleys.

The last long climb lay ahead, 1,000ft. to the top of point 1,806. We made it, I think, with one halt but my memories of this section are overlaid by those of 1976 when I was alone, deadly tired, cold, wet and eleven and a half

hours out, and of 1977 when in fine weather we laboured up the slope, watching over our shoulders a group from the Irish Ramblers Club, who had passed us and re-passed us all day, flood up the ridge behind us and then, when it seemed they must pass us again, suddenly sit down for a rest. (Of course the walk is non-competitive!)

In 1975, we saw a curiously regular smooth summit cairn on point 1,806, which turned out to be the checkpoint, Cecil, squatting under a hooded cape. Then we hurried down, down, down, while the shins and knees rebelled, to the finish in the bar of the Leenane Hotel. Several hot whiskies later, our minds digested the fact that out of the seventy starters, most had given up. In the end, eight finished, Niall Rice and one other in the magnificent time of five and three-quarter hours, ourselves in ten and a half, and the last man (who fell asleep on the way down from point 1,806) in thirteen hours.

It is a magnificent walk. 7,500ft. of ascent and 15 miles does not sound much, but the first ten miles are really hard going with lots of bare quartzite rock and scree. If there was a 1:25,000 map, British style, the navigation would be easy, but with a microscopic half-inch map, or a one-inch map with 250ft. contours above the 1,000ft. level, navigation in mist is hard! My 1976 solo in bad weather was one of the most demanding walks I have ever done, and I treasure the memory.

Macgillicuddy's Reeks

by Neil Mather

Macgillicuddy's Reeks are to natives of the larger island at once the most Irish of Ireland's mountains. The very name is evocative of mists and bogs, with perhaps a whiff of Celtic mystery thrown in. The traveller from Cork, if fortunate, has his first glimpse of the group from the Cork/Kerry boundary, some twelve miles east of Killarney, and sees a compact group with the two summits of Carrauntoohill and Beenkeragh dominating. Of rugged outline, they are carved out of the old red sandstone and, though disappointingly short of major crags, nevertheless present a spectacular backdrop, with a rise of more than 3,000ft. above the road from Killarney to Killorglin and the sea.

The south-westerly corner of Ireland has five ragged peninsulas, jutting into the Atlantic and containing some of the finest coast and mountain scenery in these islands. The largest of these promontories runs west-south-west from Killarney, between Kenmare River to the south and Dingle Bay to the north and, while the whole peninsula is mountainous, the Reeks are separate from and considerably higher than their neighbours. Like most other hills in south-west Ireland, the folding has resulted in the ridges running roughly east-west. To the east, the Reeks are cut off from their neighbours, Purple Mountain and Tomies Mountain, by the Gap of Dunloe, a deep glacial overflow channel, while the River Caragh, rising south of the ridge and bending north into Lough Caragh and thence to Dingle Bay, bounds them on the west.

The Reeks include eight summits of over 3,000ft., the highest of which, Carrauntoohill (3,414ft.), is the highest point in Ireland. As with all ridges on the western seaboard, the classic traverse is from east to west, so that the glorious seaward views are with the walker all the way. The best starting point is Kate Kearney's cottage in the Gap of Dunloe; this is a tourist centre and last-minute requirements such as maps, chocolate or Guinness can be purchased here.

The walk is best started by a diagonal ascent of the scrubby hillside to reach the broad peaty ridge which leads to the first top at 2,308ft. Continuing south-westwards for about a mile, the going becomes firmer and more heathery, until the first of the three-thousanders, Knockapeasta (3,062ft.), is reached. Here the

situation is transformed, with corries to north and south, each holding its tarn, while the ridge becomes narrower and rocky and beckons one to the next top – Lackagarrin (3,100ft.) — via the narrowest part of the ridge. You will rarely see anyone else on these hills, except during the annual Reeks Walk, organized by the Kerry Mountaineering Club, when scores of people take up the challenge to traverse the ridge from Kate Kearney's to Lough Acoose. This event usually coincides with a holiday weekend, when visiting climbers from Dublin and Cork join local ramblers, young and old, whose time for the traverse ranges from less than three hours to the whole day.

The ridge dips gently before rising in a series of rugged steps to Lackagarrin. It is necessary to use the hands for just a few easy, though exposed, moves where the rocks seem to overhang the northern corrie. Once over the summit the ridge continues narrow and rocky, though easily, downwards. One April day of wind and rain, when old wet snow covered the rocks, I was traversing this section with two Cork friends and stopped to take a photograph through a gap in the clouds. Willie and Steve carried on into the mist while I fumbled with the camera before hurrying to rejoin them. Stepping down to the left from the crest, I misjudged the drop and, landing out of

Walk   Macgillycuddy's Reeks.
Maps   O.S. 1:63,360 Killarney District (Tourist Map); O.S. 1:126,720 Sheet 20 or 21.
Start from Kate Kearney's Cottage (ref. 870878). Finish at Lough Acoose (ref. 758850).
Grading   A moderate walk along a switchback and at times rocky ridge.
Time   6-7 hours.
Distance   11 miles.
Escape Routes   North down Hag's Glen from the col S.E. of Carrauntoohill.
Telephones   Kate Kearney's Cottage; Climbers Inn S.W. of Lough Acoose.
Transport   Regular bus service from Killarney to Killorglin. Alight at Beaufort Bridge for Kate Kearney's Cottage (2½ miles).
Accommodation   Bunkhouse at the Climbers Inn 2½ miles S.W. of Lough Acoose; Youth Hostel 1 mile S. of Gap of Dunloe; Hotels at Killarney and Killorglin.
Guidebooks   *Mountaineering in Ireland* by C. W. Wall (F.M.C.I.); *The Mountains of Killarney* by J. C. Coleman (Dundalgan Press); Irish Walk Guides, Vol. 1, *The South West, Kerry — West Cork* Sean O Suilleabhain (Gill and Macmillan).

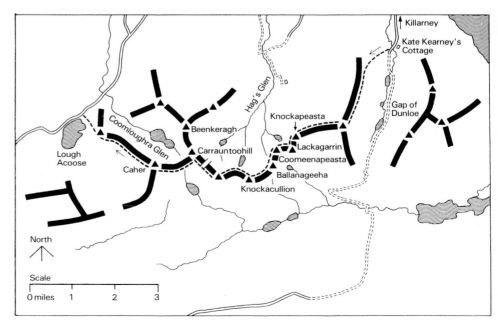

Top left: On the eastern Reeks ridge, looking towards Lackagarrin from Knockapeasta. *Photo: Joss Lynam*

Bottom left: Macgillicuddy's Reeks from the north. The classic Reeks Walk traverses the range from left to right. *Photo: Irish Tourist Board*

Near left: Looking east from Coomeenapeasta to Knockapeasta and Lackagarrin — the first section of the traverse. *Photo: John Allen*

Above: Carrauntoohill (3,414ft.), the highest peak in Ireland, seen from Knockbrinnea to the north. *Photo: Neil Mather*

balance, toppled over a ten-foot slab. Glancing off the snow-covered ledge below, I was spun outwards and over a small rock buttress for a further ten feet, to land on all fours in deep snow, completely unscathed. It was like an action replay: there was time to speculate on the steepness of the flank and the distance I was likely to fall. The only emotion I can recall is a tremendous feeling of elation at my good fortune in this escape from my own carelessness.

Beyond Coomeenapeasta (3,190ft.), the ridge becomes broader and grassier and one easily reaches the next two tops, Ballaghnageeha (3,160ft.) and Knockacullion (3,141ft.), before dropping to the only real pass on the ridge between Hag's Glen and Coomeenduff Glen. Carrauntoohill looms large from here and presents a rise of one thousand feet to its summit, which is graced by a shrine and a visitor's book. All the hills of Kerry are visible from here, including the bulk of Brandon, thirty miles to the north-west in the Dingle Peninsula, the most westerly Munro in Europe.

The ridge branches here and a northerly spur runs out to Beenkeragh (3,314ft.), via another fine rocky ridge with deep corries on either hand; the westerly continuation, also rocky, flanks the wall of Coomlaughra Glen to Caher (3,200ft.), the final summit. A direct though rough descent brings one, in a further three-quarters of an hour, to the road at the head of Lough Acoose.

The complete east to west traverse is the classic route, though it does entail the use of two cars, or some hitch-hiking to regain one's starting point; alternatively, by driving to the Hag's Glen, it is possible to traverse all the peaks in an extended horseshoe of that glen. From the farm at the road-end one can easily reach the ridge at the first three-thousander, Knockapeasta, thence westward to Caher, flanking Carrauntoohill to the south. The return is made over Carrauntoohill summit, Beenkeragh and Knockbrinnea (2,782ft.), before dropping down once more to the Hag's Glen.

My outstanding memory of the Reeks is of a March day of sun and calm, when the mountains were sheathed in firm snow above 2,000ft. My wife and I enjoyed superb conditions, which on Crib-goch, Striding Edge or Aonach Eagach would have produced queues of people, yet on the Reeks there was not another soul, not even a footprint to be seen during the whole day.

Top left: The upper part of Hag's Glen from the slopes of Knockapeasta. Carrauntoohill is the highest peak, flanked on the right by Beenkeragh and Knockbrinnea. A shorter alternative to the Reeks traverse is the Hag's Glen circuit, starting at Knockapeasta and ending on Knockbrinnea. *Photo: John Allen*

Bottom left: Beenkeragh from Carrauntoohill, with Dingle Bay and the peaks of the Dingle Peninsula in the distance. *Photo: John Allen*

Above: Another view from Carrauntoohill — looking west to Caher and the distant Meenteog group. The walker and his dog are heading off towards Beenkeragh. *Photo: John Allen*

55   The Beara Border Walk

by Willie Cunningham

Walk The Beara Border Walk.
Maps O.S. 1:63,360 Sheets 191 and 192; O.S. 1:126,720 Sheet 24.
Start from Lauragh (ref. 775580).
Finish at the tunnels of the Kenmare — Glengarriff road (ref. 901610).
Grading A long walk over rugged mountainous country. Route finding can be problematic.
Time 8-9 hours.
Distance 20 miles.
Escape Routes Descend E. from the Eskatarriff — Knocknagree col to reach Glanmore Glen. Main road is met at the Healy Pass.
Telephones Lauragh; Adrigole; Glengarriff; Bonane Post Office.
Transport Kenmare to Castletown bus service passes the start at Lauragh. For the finishing point use the Kenmare to Glengarriff service.
Accommodation Youth Hostels at Letterdunane 3 miles N. of the finish and at Glanmore Lake below the Healy Pass in the Caha mountains. Hotels at Glengarriff, Lauragh and Kenmare.
Guidebooks *Mountaineering in Ireland* by C. W. Wall (F.M.C.I.); A good general account of mountaineering in Ireland is *Climbing in the British Isles — Ireland* by H. C. Hart. Irish Walk Guides, Vol. 1, *The South West, Kerry — West Cork* Sean O Suilleabhain (Gill and Macmillan).

The Beara Peninsula, situated in the extreme south-west corner of Ireland, reaches out into the Atlantic between Kenmare Bay and Bantry Bay. The old red sandstone ranges of Slieve Miskish and Caha rise quickly from sea level to over 2,000ft. and almost cover the entire area. A narrow strip of arable land extends around the coast and sometimes penetrates into the long coombe valleys. The peninsula is surely a hill-walker's paradise, offering a complete range of routes to suit all groups and weather conditions. The terrain is generally rugged, and in poor visibility calls for precise navigation.

I propose a route which in my opinion offers the very best of the peninsula in a single day's walk. Starting at sea level, it ends at 1,000ft. at a point about thirty-five miles away by road. It follows, by and large, the border between County Cork and County Kerry, starting near Killmakilloge Harbour and ending near the tunnels on the main Kenmare to Glengarriff road (N71).

Any approach to Tooth Mountain from the north will do to start the walk. The most usual is from a point just west of Lauragh on the Glanmore road. This allows access on the eastern spur to point 1,183 (Cummeennahillan). The dense undergrowth soon relents as you bear west and reach the ridge which runs north from Knocknaveacal ('Hill of the

Teeth'). The Sassanach mappees of 1840 almost got the title of this aptly-named mountain correct ('Tooth Mountain'). We first meet the Cork/Kerry border (dotted line on map) at Coom Cloughane (1969). A bearing of 211° for two and a half miles brings us down first to the wide col west of the 'Pocket', then across the western shoulder of Eskatarriff ('Bulls' path') and finally down to the col at the head of spectacular Glenbeg. Our next objective is Hungry Hill, which at 2,251ft. is the highest peak in the peninsula. Navigate to reach the most northerly of the Glas Loughs ('green lakes') between Knocknagree and point 1,519. It is worthwhile to take the 'boundary' ridge before turning south to reach the summit.

I am reminded of a group of French walkers for whom this was really a 'hungry hill'. We left Glanmore Lake at nine o'clock with what proved to be a mixed-ability group on their first day in Ireland. They insisted on eating on the hour, and soon their pack-lunch was eaten. Nothing but food was mentioned on the climb up from Glas Lough to the summit, and it transpired that, for some unknown reason, they expected to find a restaurant on top! I must admit that I enjoyed my sandwiches very much amid all the foreign language!

If visibility is good you face the fine Kerry mountain ranges to the north, with Macgillicuddy's Reeks dominating, and Brandon on the north-east sky-line. South and west the Atlantic stretches endlessly beyond Sheep's head and Mizen. Bear Island, beneath us, shelters the fishing port of Castletown — Bear Haven. This is the country ruled by the O'Sullivans until their stronghold at Dunboy Castle (just visible) was overrun in 1602. Their epic 300-mile march to Leitrim in mid-winter was a grim and stirring affair. O'Sullivan remains the dominant surname on the peninsula. The area is steeped in folklore, as indeed are most remote areas. The place names conjure up some fantastic stores — part fact, part fiction, sometimes amusing and always interesting. I might add that Sean O'Suilleabhain in *Irish Walk Guides (South West)* has done a fine job in collecting some of these.

Leaving Hungry Hill we face the long trek east which, from this point, stays remarkably close to the Cork/Kerry border. From the summit the north-west ridge passes over Derry-

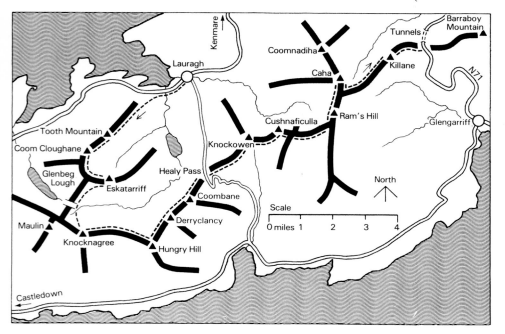

clancy and Coombane before dropping to the Healy Pass. This point is used as a stage end or start for other routes, but our route leads us to continue on the north-west ridge over Claddaghgarriff, and on to Knockowen. By now you have, no doubt, come to grips with the inadequacies of our maps for hill-walking purposes. It is important to realize, before starting on the next section, that the positions of all lakes and streams may not be accurately mapped and that contours are of an approximate nature. In poor visibility it is usually safer to navigate from peak to col to peak. In this particular area there are many stories of experienced walkers getting into difficulties — it

is a very desolate area. On the route between Knockowen and Cushnaficulla you will come across the large isolated boulders from which, presumably, the latter peak got its name ('Near the Teeth'). The county border marks the next section of our route — to Knockeirky through the wide col and north to Ram's Hill. From here a bearing (if necessary) will lead you to gain the well-defined ridge which runs from a peak south of Caha, and takes in several tops including Killane and Baurearagh before it swings eastward to our destination.

There are several places near the tunnels where a car may be parked safely, even overnight if desired.

Typical scenery on the Beara Peninsula a few miles east of the tunnels on the Kenmare to Glen Garriff road. The walkers are passing Lough Nagarriva on their way towards Barraboy Mountain in the background. *Photo: Bill Gregor*

Safety and Sanity in the Mountains

by Richard Gilbert

The Big Walks contains the very best of the long and challenging expeditions that are to be found in the British Isles. While I hope that the book will stimulate mountain lovers to activity, I must emphasize that none of the fifty-five expeditions should be undertaken lightly. The terrain covered by many of the walks is hostile and the weather in our hills can be severe in any month of the year, with the possibility of arctic conditions in winter.

Even on easy hills there will be risks, and you may find thrills and excitement when traversing narrow ridges or scrambling up steep rocks, but danger should not be an integral part of the expedition. You must keep the risks down to the minimum.

Many of the walks described involve mountaineering in its broadest sense. The walker needs a sound knowledge of route-finding using map and compass, safety procedures, rudimentary rope-work, and snow and ice craft. The more skills he can develop, the greater the number of expedition options there will be open to him.

The experienced mountaineer, with years of regular activity in the hills behind him, can assess and evaluate the countless variables that confront him on his walks. Decision-making becomes second nature.

Statistics show that it is the novice who runs the greatest risk of mishap in the hills. I do implore the young and inexperienced walker who is inspired by *The Big Walks* to proceed with the utmost caution when tackling these expeditions. Do not be too ambitious, and be prepared to turn back at once if conditions start to deteriorate.

In 1978 there were 276 accidents involving physical injury on the hills of Britain, 37 of them resulting in fatalities. But to see these figures in perspective we must appreciate that a great many climbers and walkers are active in the mountains. The largest estimates compiled by the Countryside Commission amount to 600,000 walkers and 60,000 rock climbers.

Although the number of accidents involving hill walkers has increased over the past ten years, the percentage of fatalities has decreased. There are still walkers who get lost in the mountains, who venture out unfit and ill-equipped and who make wrong decisions, but the majority are better trained and equipped and have a much greater awareness of particular hazards, such as hypothermia.

Without wishing to detract from the carefree pleasures of hill walking, I have listed below the essential safety factors to be borne in mind at all times. The novice should seek further advice on mountain safety, route-finding and first-aid from specialist books, experienced mountaineers or mountain training centres.

Equipment

The best way to turn a delightful walk over the hills into purgatory is to carry a heavy rucksack, but a minimum amount of gear must be taken. This should include a map and compass, an emergency bivi bag, a first-aid kit, a rope (if required by the walk), a whistle, a torch and spare battery, and food and emergency rations. Lack of food is very debilitating in the mountains and it is important to eat at regular intervals. Food should be appetizing to encourage you to eat. Chocolate and glucose tablets work wonders at the end of a long day. In winter an ice axe *must* be carried, and crampons are highly recommended.

Clothing

Remember that conditions can deteriorate rapidly as one gains height. A stiff breeze and driving rain in the valley can become a howling blizzard on the tops. Always carry waterproofs, a windproof anorak, gloves and a spare jersey. In winter, wear warm breeches, woollen socks and snow gaiters. Shorts are quite unsuitable.

Hypothermia

In the wet and cold climate of the British Isles, hypothermia is a major hazard. It is a condition resulting from chilling of the body surface with reduction in body heat. Wet clothing provides poor insulation from the cold and, in a strong wind, the rapid rate of evaporation quickly cools the body. Action must be taken to alleviate the condition or death can result. Signs of approaching hypothermia include severe, uncontrolled shivering, lack of co-ordination of the limbs, slow thinking, slurred speech and disturbed vision. Subsequent loss of consciousness is particularly serious as it indicates that the core temperature has fallen so low that the brain is starved of blood.

In exposed situations, high up in the mountains, it is not easy to treat hypothermia. If any member of the party shows signs of the condition, the following procedure should be adopted: provide energy-giving foods, check that adequate clothing is being worn, distribute any rucksack load amongst other members of the party, and proceed to lower ground with all possible speed. If the patient's condition doesn't improve, rest in a sheltered place, keep the patient warm by all means possible, and seek help.

The International Distress Call

To seek help give six blasts on a whistle, or six shouts or flashes of a torch, followed by a pause of a minute. Then repeat the signal. The answering signal is three blasts.

Seeking help

Don't wait for help to arrive, as there may not be any other people in the area to hear your signal. Send the fittest members of the party to the nearest telephone to dial 999. The police co-ordinate all mountain rescue services. It is essential that the following information be given to the police: time of accident; place of accident (a detailed description, together with the six-figure map reference); an indication of the type and extent of the injuries; the name of the patient. In mist or darkness it can be very difficult to locate an injured person, and the position should be marked by a cairn or a brightly coloured garment.

Route-Finding

The walker should be thoroughly acquainted with map and compass work, having a knowledge of magnetic variation and being familiar with the following procedures: interpretation of contour lines, setting a map, taking a bearing, walking on a bearing and drawing a resection.

River Crossings

Never underestimate a river crossing. After heavy rain a gentle stream can become a roaring torrent. If in doubt about the safety of a crossing, don't attempt it. Walk to the nearest bridge, or wait for the floods to subside. If a crossing is unavoidable, try first to find the shallowest stretch, face upstream so that the force of the water is not acting behind your knees, use an ice axe or stick to help maintain your balance, and keep your boots on. If you are using a safety rope, make your attempted crossing downstream from the anchor point.

The Weather

Obtain an up-to-date forecast before leaving for your walk. Acquire a basic knowledge of meteorology, so that you can predict an approaching storm. During electrical storms avoid mountain summits, rock ridges and pinnacles.

Snow and Ice Technique

On the hills of Britain, snow can fall on any day of the year. Small snow-fields last throughout the year in several gullies and north-facing corries in Scotland, the most renowned being on the north faces of Ben Nevis and Braeriach. Although I do not suggest that you arm yourself with ice axe and crampons in the summer months, even then snow and iced-up rocks can occasionally force a detour.

In winter you must be prepared for snow and ice anywhere in the mountains. Always carry an ice axe, and for expeditions over high tops it is usually advisable to take crampons as well. Walkers should be quite familiar with these items and prepared to use them as soon as snow and ice are encountered. Every year there are accidents, some of them fatal, involving hill walkers and climbers who slip on ice slopes because of faulty technique, and who fail to arrest the slip by swift use of a braking procedure. It is essential for novices to train thoroughly in these skills before embarking on a mountain walk in winter, and even experts are well advised to practise the techniques periodically. This is easily done on a low-level snow and ice slope, with an easy run-off and no obstacles. The various crampon, ice axe, braking and glissading techniques are described in numerous instructional books (e.g. *Climbing Ice* by Yvon Chouinard, Hodder and Stoughton; *Modern Snow and Ice Techniques* by Bill March, Cicerone Press). It is perfectly feasible to train oneself adequately in such techniques, but a short mountain-craft course at an Outdoor Centre during winter is a quick and efficient method of acquiring the full range of basic skills required. Whichever method you choose, a good basic training is one of the most important safety precautions you can take for winter expeditions.

Glissading in the correct place provides the means for fast descents on snowy mountains, but here again it is necessary to be fully proficient in the technique. It is best to adhere to certain basic rules. Do not glissade unless you can see the whole slope and an easy run-off at the bottom. Never lose control. If in doubt about the state of the snow and your ability to stop, do not make the glissade.

Fitness

Keep as fit as possible. A fit walker can quickly extricate himself from a potentially dangerous situation. On our comparatively low British hills it is usually possible to get down rapidly from high ground to the shelter of a valley. A notable exception is the Cairngorm plateau, where extra care must be taken.

Rock Climbing

Don't attempt an expedition which is going to involve any degree of rock climbing, unless you are thoroughly acquainted with belay techniques and the correct use of the rope, or unless there is an experienced rock climber in the party.

The Rescue Services

In Britain, the Mountain Rescue Committee is the organizing body for the various rescue services. Each area of mountain and moorland country has its own rescue team, which can be called out at any time. The teams are composed of local climbers who know the area thoroughly, and they hold regular training sessions to practise rescue techniques.

The Mountain Rescue Posts hold specialized rescue equipment, such as stretchers, radio sets and medical supplies. They also maintain boxes of rescue equipment at certain strategic sites in the mountains. If necessary, outside help can be called upon to provide additional facilities, such as helicopters or dogs trained for avalanche rescue.

The R.A.F. mountain rescue teams are highly mobile and they may turn out to reinforce the local services.

It is extremely irresponsible to cause the rescue services to be called out unnecessarily. For this reason, before departing you must leave word with the authorities or with friends regarding your destination and route. Make sure that you have left a note in the window of your unattended car and in your tent.

Mountain accidents are newsworthy. In order to avoid the attendant publicity you may find yourself tempted to evacuate an injured companion yourself. Unless the injuries are superficial and you are near a road, this practice is not usually to be recommended. The inexpert handling of an injured person can cause rapid deterioration in condition, and for spinal and head injuries it can prove fatal.

Never take the mountain rescue services for granted. It is foolhardy in the extreme to plan an overambitious day's walk, which could result in the rescue services being called out. Assistance must not be expected in the mountains. Most emergency bivouac shelters have now been removed, since they were thought to cause more accidents than they prevented. It is essential to make a constant assessment of the progress and strength of the party, in relation to time, weather conditions and distance yet to be walked. If necessary, the walk should be shortened in plenty of time to make a safe return.

→

Conclusion

This list of mountain safety points provides only a general guideline. The enormous number of variables and special conditions met in the mountains means that set rules cannot be made. Each situation requires to be judged and acted upon in an appropriate way.

Experience is paramount and this realization led recently to the abandonment of the Mountain Leadership Certificate and its replacement by log-book endorsement for successful candidates seeking approval of their mountain walking competence.

So much mountain safety advice is common sense that open-ended discussion amongst mountaineers can only help the general awareness of safety problems. In some situations it may well prove correct to ignore standard text-book procedure. Let us take an example.

A small party of fit but mainly inexperienced walkers is traversing the snow-covered plateau of Beinn a' Bhuird in winter. A member of the party staggers and complains of severe chest pains. The clouds come down, visibility is extremely poor, the snow is soft and exhausting. Help is far away. One cannot say that any plan of action is necessarily right or wrong in the circumstances. The choice is wide.

The party could attempt to carry the patient down to the valley, knowing that they will be benighted before a refuge is reached. Although weather conditions should be better in the valley, the delay in seeking outside assistance could be serious.

The patient could be pushed and cajoled into continuing to walk towards the nearest escape route. But he might collapse with a heart attack at any time.

The party leader and some helpers could stay with the patient, while two others go for help. Have these sufficient expertise to negotiate the cornices in the mist? Might not they, too, become exhausted? If they fail to reach a telephone, the other members of the party might die waiting for the rescue team.

The leader could go for help. But can the others cope on the high plateau without his guidance?

Finally, the entire party could rest awhile, hoping that the patient will recover. But by doing so they commit themselves to a bivouac, possibly in severe conditions.

With mountain accidents it is too easy to be wise after the event. In a Coroner's Court a mountain leader cannot win. If the party was light, insufficient safety equipment was being carried; if full gear was being carried, they were overweight and moving too slowly. If they bivouacked, they should have descended to the valley; if they pressed on, they should have bivouacked. Too many people in authority with little or no knowledge of the mountains are prepared to pass judgement.

The castigation, by authoritarian police chiefs, coroners, doctors and the like, of mountain lovers seeking peace in remote areas is particularly distressing. Often, police authorities urge people to stay away at just the time when the hills are in their most interesting and challenging condition — that is to say, heavily snowed-up.

A few years ago, a mountain walker was staying in a bothy in Glen Affric in mid-winter, having walked in from Cluanie where he had left precise information as to his whereabouts and itinerary. The weather had deteriorated, so he had sensibly modified his plan and was using the bothy as a base for short expeditions up nearby mountains. He was well equipped and fully supplied with food. Yet he was rescued. An anxious parent had phoned the hotel and, despite being in full possession of the facts provided in the walker's note, the police and mountain rescue services decided to start a search. Two rescuers soon found his equipment in the bothy, and at nightfall he returned from his day out. The rescuers had no food, so the walker fed them. The following morning a helicopter arrived and the rescuers urged the walker to return with them on the grounds that he was putting the rescue services to worry and expense. With his supplies now depleted, he reluctantly agreed. On his return he was roundly criticized by police, mountain rescue service and press for being foolhardy, when in fact he had displayed exemplary common sense, skill and judgement.

Over-zealous rescue services and paternalistic authorities triggering unwanted rescues now pose a serious factor for the hill walker to consider. The number of incidents is growing. The problem was amusingly described in Geoff Dutton's fictional lampoon, *A Good Clean Break**, but if one is the victim of an unwanted rescue it is usually not funny. It is therefore essential to take all reasonable steps to avoid this situation, leaving the rescue organizations to concentrate their energies on cases of genuine distress.

Solitary hill walking, even for experienced mountaineers, is condemned in many books. But one of the greatest joys for me, and for many of the contributors to this book, is solo walking. Very seldom do solo hill walkers get into difficulty. Providing you have the necessary fitness and expertise, solo walking is a perfectly feasible proposition, though obviously it involves a far greater level of commitment.

In our bid to minimize the possibility of accidents occurring in the hills we can learn from the study of certain notable incidents of recent years. The Cairngorm tragedy of 1971 is a typical example of the errors in judgement which may be made in a crisis situation. In particular it highlights the dilemma faced by the leader of a weak party at nightfall on an open snow slope in a blizzard.

Another accident took place in December, 1954, when five naval cadets were killed when they slid into upper Coire Leis whilst descending from the summit of Ben Nevis towards the Carn Mor arête. This notorious, convex slope becomes iced-up very early in the year, and it has claimed many lives. Following this accident, marker posts and a warning sign were erected. But there are many similar dangerous slopes on our hills, and they do not have warning notices. In winter you must be prepared to meet with steep ice at any time, and be equipped to tackle it with ice axe, crampons and rope.

But it must not be thought that all accidents occur in high mountain areas. At New Year, 1951, a party of five experienced mountaineers, including a woman, left Corrour Lodge at the east

*In *The Games Climbers Play*, Diadem, 1979.

end of Loch Ossian bound for Ben Alder Cottage on Loch Ericht, a distance of about seven miles. Having cooked a meal they set off at 8.30 p.m. on a dark but calm night, carrying full equipment and supplies, including sleeping bags and stoves. About 2½ miles up the glen, close to Lochan Allt Glaschoire, three of the party bivouacked for the night, while the other two pressed on towards the bealach under the south-west slopes of Ben Alder. Half an hour later they, too, bivouacked.

The next morning a full gale was blowing, and the snow was deep. At 9.15 a.m., all five walkers met again at the Lochan Allt Glaschoire bivouac site, where they left their rucksacks, which were by now frozen solid. Their nightmare struggle against the wind and hail in an attempt to return to Corrour Lodge ended in tragedy. The first man died after half an hour, and the remainder succumbed during the morning. The woman alone survived, reaching Corrour Lodge at 2.30 p.m.

The immediate cause of the tragedy was the exceptional force of the gale. Although such violent conditions are rare, they are always a possibility, particularly in Scotland. The victims perished in a glen at 1,600ft., belying the widely held view that all will automatically be well with walkers if they descend from the high tops to lower ground.

This incident also demonstrates the superior stamina and survival qualities of women — a factor that has been noted on other occasions, as for example in the Cairngorm tragedy when a woman was one of the only two survivors after two exposed bivouacs.

Another factor that should be taken into account in this respect is the great difference in staying power and endurance between adults and teenagers or children. I have introduced hundreds of children to the mountains, and I must give the following advice to adults who are proposing to lead young people on mountain walks. (i) Allow a large margin of error when calculating the overall time for the walk. (ii) Don't allow the party to split up, or let fit young walkers get out in front, as difficult ground could lie ahead round the corner. Appoint a back marker. (iii) Remember that youngsters are more prone to hypothermia than adults. In bad conditions watch for warning signs. (iv) Young people are forgetful. Before leaving, check each individual rucksack for waterproofs, extra clothing and lunch. (v) Establish a steady rhythm and don't allow too many rests. (vi) Be cautious in your choice of walk. Think of the children. Work out your personal ambitions when you are alone or with adults. (vii) Keep the party small and get to know your charges and their capabilities.

It can be a thankless task to take young people to the mountains. Group leaders get very little credit for the organization involved and the responsibility carried. They are in the firing line from all sides if things go wrong. If you are an experienced mountaineer and you should meet a harassed leader having some difficulties with a young party, an offer of help might well be appreciated. You could be averting a tragedy.

A fierce squall at Esk Hause. Photo: Tom Parker

The Country Code

1 Guard against all risks of fire
2 Fasten all gates
3 Keep dogs under proper control
4 Keep to paths across farm land
5 Avoid damaging fences, hedges and walls
6 Leave no litter
7 Safeguard water supplies
8 Protect wildlife, plants and trees
9 Go carefully on country roads
10 Respect the life of the countryside

The Country Code is not a list of restrictions placed on the walker. It should be seen as a recipe for freedom. We must not forget that free access to the hills depends on continuing co-operation of farmers and landowners. No charge is levied for access to the hills and the least we, as walkers, can do in return is to scrupulously observe the Country Code.

It is morally indefensible to leave paper, polythene bags, tin cans and bottles on hillsides or in ditches. Such rubbish can be a serious hazard to livestock and in some cases can be a fire risk. Moreover unless we keep the hills clear of rubbish we will destroy the very reason for their attractiveness.

Another important point is the need to protect dry stone walls and fences. These should never be climbed. A gate or stile can usually be located and some walls have specially constructed steps. Nothing enrages a farmer more than to have to repeatedly repair walls and fences after thoughtless damage caused by walkers. Harold Drasdo rightly emphasises this point in his chapter on the Rhinog Ridge, and our relationship with the farming community can be seriously undermined by such incidents.

Other Good Walks and Scrambles

The following walks are recommended as suitable ways of shortening the described routes or as shorter alternative routes.

Foinaven and Arkle	From the Foinaven summit of Ganu Mor, proceed to Creag Dionard and return down Strath Dionard to Gualin House. 5-6 hours
Suilven	Traverse Quinag from the A894 road summit on the east side of the mountain. 5 hours
The Fannichs	From the A835, one mile west of Loch Droma, walk the Fannich horseshoe of Beinn Liath Mhor, Sgurr Mor and Meall a Chrasgaidh. 5 hours
Dundonnell to Poolewe	Dundonnell House to Gruinard House via Achneige and Loch na Sheallag. 5 hours
Liathach	Traverse Beinn Alligin from Torridon House. 5-6 hours
The Five Sisters Ridge	Climb from the Glen Shiel road to the low bealach west of Saileag. Traverse the ridge to Sgurr Fhuaran and descend its steep west shoulder. 4 hours
Glen Affric/Mam Sodhail	From the summit of Mam Sodhail, descend over Sgurr na Lapaich to Affric Lodge. 7 hours
Ladhar Bheinn	Traverse Gleouraich and Spidean Mialach from Quoich Bridge to the Quoich dam. 5 hours
Rois Bheinn	From Lochailort climb An Stac by its north ridge and continue to Rois Bheinn. Descend via the west ridge to Roshven Farm. 5 hours
The Round of Coire Lagan	Climb Sgurr Dearg from Coire Lagan by the An Stac screes. Continue to Sgurr na Banachdich, and return to Glen Brittle by the Sgurr nan Gobhar ridge. This route involves very little scrambling. 5 hours
The Cuillin Hills of Rhum	From Bealach an Oir descend Glen Dibidil to the bothy and return to Kinloch by the coastal path. 6 hours
Creag Meagaidh	Walk to Lochan Coire Ardair and climb Creag Meagaidh from The Window. Descend the south-west ridge to Craigbeg. 5 hours
The Mamores	Ascend Sgurr a'Mhaim from Polldubh, traverse the Devil's Ridge to Sgor an Iubhair and descend An Garbhanach's north ridge to Steall. 5 hours
Ben Nevis/Lochaber Traverse	Descend Carn Mor Dearg to the Inverlochy Distillery. 6-7 hours
	Alternatively, from Torlundy, climb the north-west ridge of Aonach Mor and complete the second part of the walk — over the Grey Corries to Spean Bridge. 8-9 hours
Lochnagar	From the summit of Lochnagar cross the White Mounth and descend to the Dubh Loch. Return to the Spittal of Glen Muick by the path along the south shore of Loch Muick. 6 hours
Beinn a'Bhuird/Ben Avon	From the Sneck, return to Deeside by Gleann an t-Slugain. 9-10 hours
Cairngorm Four Thousanders	Walk to the north end of Loch Einich and ascend the western shoulder of Braeriach. Return over Sron na Lairig to the Lairig Ghru. 8 hours
Ben Alder Forest	From Corrour station traverse the hills of Beinn na Lap, Chno Dearg and Stob Coire Sgriodain descending to Tulloch station for the return train. 6 hours
The Ben Lawers Range	Cut the walk short at Beinn Ghlas and descend the easy southern slopes to Loch Tay. 6-7 hours
The Ben Lui Horseshoe	Walk up Coire Laoigh from Cononish and climb the south ridge of Ben Lui. Return over the Ciochan. 5 hours
The Crianlarich Hills	Traverse the peaks of Ben More and Stob Binnein returning down the Benmore Glen. 5 hours
Arran's Rocky Ridges	Climb Goat Fell from Corrie and descend the south ridge to Glen Rosa. No scrambling involved. 4 hours
Merrick/Rhinns of Kells	From the summit of Merrick descend the east ridge to Loch Enoch and return to Glen Trool alongside the Buchan Burn. 5 hours
The Southern Uplands	Walk the path on the north side of the Grey Mare's Tail to Loch Skeen. Return over the summit of White Coomb. 4 hours
The Cheviots	Climb Cheviot from Langleeford and descend the west shoulder to Hen Hole and the College Burn. 4-5 hours
The Ennerdale Horseshoe	Having traversed the Buttermere Fells to Scarth Gap, descend to Black Sail and walk back through the Ennerdale Forest. 6 hours
The Langdale Horseshoe	From New Dungeon Ghyll walk up to Stickle Tarn. Traverse Pavey Ark and the Langdale Pikes returning down Mickleden. 4-5 hours
Highest Pennines	Take the Pennine Way path from Dufton over Knock Fell and Great Dun Fell to Cross Fell. Return via Grumply Hill and Milburn. 7 hours
Wild Boar Fell/Howgills	The Kirkby Stephen to Rawthey Bridge section over Wild Boar Fell (4 hours), and the Rawthey Bridge to Sedbergh section over the Howgills (5 hours), make delightful shorter walks.
Lyke Wake Walk	Follow the western edge of the Cleveland Hills from Sutton Bank, over Black Hambleton, to Osmotherley. 4 hours
The Derwent Watershed	Follow the path on the east side of the River Derwent up on to Howden Edge. Walk round to Bleaklow Stones, and return down the Westend river valley. 6 hours
Marsden to Edale	From Edale take the Pennine Way track up Grinds Brook to Kinder plateau. Walk on to the Northern Edge and return via Kinder Downfall and Jacob's Ladder. 5-6 hours
Dartmoor North to South	The Dartmoor north to south walk can conveniently be split into two shorter sections, Bellever to Postbridge and Dartmeet to Bittaford. Both sections about 6 hours
The Snowdon Horseshoe	Climb the Pyg Track and descend the Watkin Track. 4 hours
Tryfan and the Bristly Ridge	Reach the summit of Tryfan via the Heather Terrace or Cwm Bochlywd. Descend the Gribin Ridge. A combination of these easier routes can shorten the walk to 3½ hours.
The Welsh Three Thousanders	The walk can be curtailed at either the Llanberis Pass or the Nant Ffrancon Pass. Foel Grach and Foel Fras can be left out in favour of a descent from Yr Elen into Cwm Llafar.
The Rhinogs Ridge	Various sections of the walk are possible making use of Cwm Bychan or Cwm Nantcol.
The Arans and Berwyns	Traverse the Aran range from north to south. Llanuwchllyn to Dinas Mawddwy. 5 hours
The Black Mountains	The stretch of the Offa's Dyke Walk betwen Hay-on-Wye and Glandwr provides a superb walk with few route-finding problems. 6 hours
The Brecon Beacons	The shorter version of the walk, from the north, ascending the Bryn-teg ridge to Cribin and thence over the Beacons and descending by Pen Milan is the classic Beacons traverse. Equally fine, but with more varied scenery, is the southerly circuit from Neuadd Reservoirs, ascending Cribin and descending by Craig Fan-ddu. Each walk takes 4-5 hours
The Mourne Wall Walk	This walk can be split into two sections divided by Hare's Gap and the Annalong Valley: Western section over Slieve Bearnagh (6 hours); eastern section over Slieve Donard (4 hours).
The Lug Walk Classic	Walk the highest and most impressive section of this walk, over Lughnaquilla, from the road summit at Wicklow Gap to Seskin. 5 hours
Macgillicuddy's Reeks	From Hag's Glen climb up to the Coomeenduff pass and traverse Carrauntoohill, Ireland's premier peak, returning over Beenkeragh. 4-5 hours
The Maum Turks	The walk can be shortened by descending from the ridge at several cols and returning to Maum Bridge.
The Beara Border Walk	Starting from Lauragh the walk may conveniently be ended at the Healy Pass when the most attractive section has been completed. 5 hours

Index

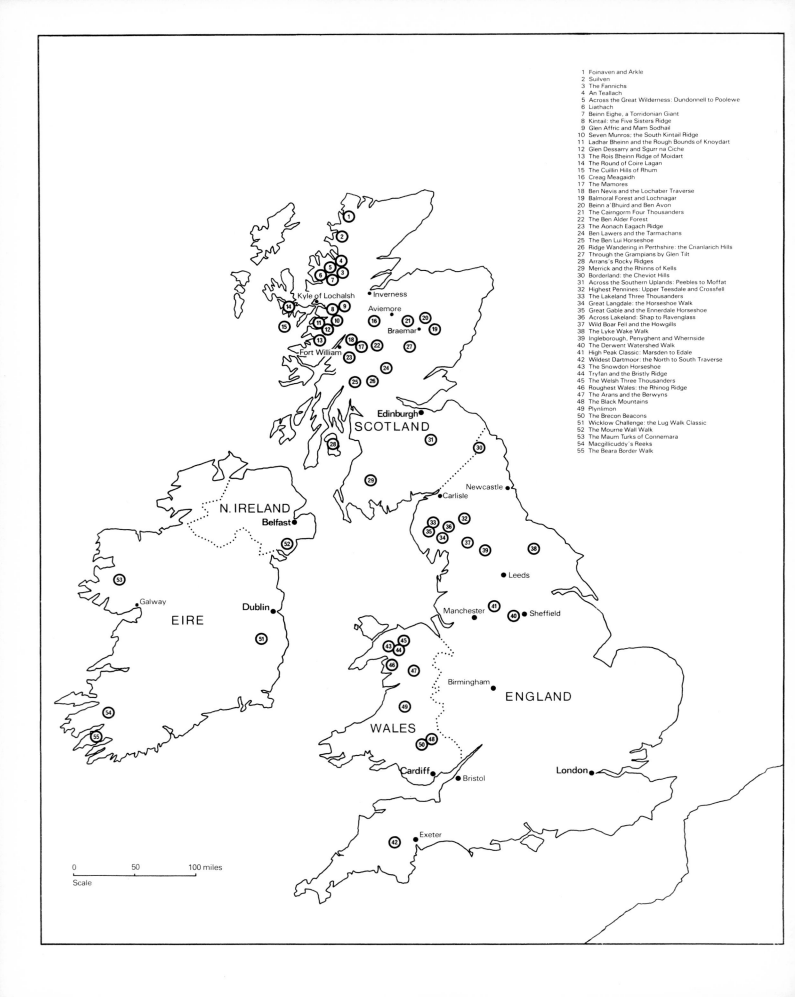

1 Foinaven and Arkle
2 Suilven
3 The Fannichs
4 An Teallach
5 Across the Great Wilderness: Dundonnell to Poolewe
6 Liathach
7 Beinn Eighe, a Torridonian Giant
8 Kintail: the Five Sisters Ridge
9 Glen Affric and Mam Sodhail
10 Seven Munros; the South Kintail Ridge
11 Ladhar Bheinn and the Rough Bounds of Knoydart
12 Glen Dessarry and Sgurr na Ciche
13 The Rois Bheinn Ridge of Moidart
14 The Round of Coire Lagan
15 The Cuillin Hills of Rhum
16 Creag Meagaidh
17 The Mamores
18 Ben Nevis and the Lochaber Traverse
19 Balmoral Forest and Lochnagar
20 Beinn a' Bhuird and Ben Avon
21 The Cairngorm Four Thousanders
22 The Ben Alder Forest
23 The Aonach Eagach Ridge
24 Ben Lawers and the Tarmachans
25 The Ben Lui Horseshoe
26 Ridge Wandering in Perthshire: the Crianlarich Hills
27 Through the Grampians by Glen Tilt
28 Arrans's Rocky Ridges
29 Merrick and the Rhinns of Kells
30 Borderland: the Cheviot Hills
31 Across the Southern Uplands: Peebles to Moffat
32 Highest Pennines: Upper Teesdale and Crossfell
33 The Lakeland Three Thousanders
34 Great Langdale: the Horseshoe Walk
35 Great Gable and the Ennerdale Horseshoe
36 Across Lakeland: Shap to Ravenglass
37 Wild Boar Fell and the Howgills
38 The Lyke Wake Walk
39 Ingleborough, Penyghent and Whernside
40 The Derwent Watershed Walk
41 High Peak Classic: Marsden to Edale
42 Wildest Dartmoor: the North to South Traverse
43 The Snowdon Horseshoe
44 Tryfan and the Bristly Ridge
45 The Welsh Three Thousanders
46 Roughest Wales: the Rhinog Ridge
47 The Arans and the Berwyns
48 The Black Mountains
49 Plynlimon
50 The Brecon Beacons
51 Wicklow Challenge: the Lug Walk Classic
52 The Mourne Wall Walk
53 The Maum Turks of Connemara
54 Macgillicuddy's Reeks
55 The Beara Border Walk